STUDIES IN PHARISAISM
AND THE GOSPELS

STUDIES IN PHARISAISM
AND THE GOSPELS

BY

I. ABRAHAMS, M.A.

READER IN TALMUDIC, UNIVERSITY OF CAMBRIDGE,
FORMERLY SENIOR TUTOR, JEWS' COLLEGE, LONDON

FIRST SERIES

Cambridge:
at the University Press
1917

CAMBRIDGE
UNIVERSITY PRESS

University Printing House, Cambridge CB2 8BS, United Kingdom

Published in the United States of America by Cambridge University Press, New York

Cambridge University Press is part of the University of Cambridge.

It furthers the University's mission by disseminating knowledge in the pursuit of education, learning and research at the highest international levels of excellence.

www.cambridge.org
Information on this title: www.cambridge.org/9781107417953

First published 1917
First paperback edition 2014

A catalogue record for this publication is available from the British Library

ISBN 978-1-107-41795-3 Paperback

PREFACE

IN 1909 Mr C. G. Montefiore published what may without exaggeration be termed an epoch-making Commentary on the Synoptic Gospels in two volumes. It was intended that I should have the honour of contributing a third volume, containing Additional Notes. This plan has not been fulfilled. The reason is simple. I had promised more than I could perform. The problems proved so many, so intricate, that I have found it beyond my capacity to deal with them all.

But if the original design could not be fully carried out, neither was it entirely abandoned. A saying of Rabbi Tarphon seemed appropriate to the situation. "It is not thy part to complete the work, yet art thou not altogether free to desist from it." On this principle, Notes were from time to time written and printed, until by the year 1912 the contents of the present book were in type. Most of the Notes were actually written between the years 1908–1911. I have recently gone through the proofs carefully, and have added some references to later literature, but substantially the Notes remain as they were written several years ago. The abandonment, for the present at least, of the hope to do much more has impelled me to publish what I have been able to do.

The circumstance that this volume was designed as an Appendix to Mr Montefiore's work accounts for the inclusion of subjects of unequal importance. Certain Notes, natural and necessary to a consecutive Commentary, would hardly have suggested themselves

for a series of independent Studies. Moreover, some of the
Chapters in the present book, though possibly they might pass as
exegetical comments, are quite inadequate as essays. It must be
remembered that it was purposed to supplement several of these
Notes by further Notes on other aspects of the same problems as
they presented themselves in the course of the Synoptic narratives.
The author is not without hope that he may be able before long
to issue a second series of Studies in which some of the omissions
are rectified. In point of fact several Studies on other matters
are practically written, and others definitely planned. Among the
subjects to be discussed in this second Series would be: certain
aspects of "Life under the Law," the "Yoke of the Commandments," "Ritual Purity," the "Traditions of the Elders," the "Last
Supper," "Rabbinic Conceptions of Sacrifice and Prayer," the
"Trial of Jesus," the "Am Ha-ares," the "Two Ways," the "Psychology and Liturgy of Confession," and above all the "Kingdom
of God," "Pharisaic Eschatology," and the "Jewish Apocalypses."

This being the case, I have deferred for a later occasion any
general appreciation of the Gospel teachings. Nor do I think it
necessary to justify at any length the intrusion of a Jewish student
into the discussion of the Synoptic problem. Mr Montefiore, as is
admitted on all hands, rendered a conspicuous service both to
Jewish and Christian scholars by his frank and masterly examination of the Gospels from a professedly Jewish stand-point.
Undoubtedly *a* (though not *the*) real Synoptic problem is: how to
hold the balance truly between the teaching of Jesus on the one
hand and of Pharisaic Judaism on the other. Obviously, then,
Jewish students have both the right and the duty to attempt a
contribution to this balanced judgment. Apart from the fact that
their studies in Pharisaic literature are inevitably more intimate,
there is another very important consideration. Pharisaism was
not a mere historical phase; it has remained a vital force, it has
gone on without a moment's break from the centuries before the
Christian era to the twentieth century of that era. It has been

put to the test of time and of life. It has survived throughout
an experience, such as no other religious system has undergone.
Hence the Jewish student is able to apply to current criticisms
of Pharisaism not merely literary tests, but also the touchstone
and possibly the corrective of actual experience.

There is perhaps room for yet another suggestion. Jewish
students of the Old Testament have gained much from the re-
searches made by Christian scholars, not merely philologically and
in the archaeological field, but also theologically. For the Jew
has so ingrained a belief in the organic union of ritual with religion,
is so convinced that the antithesis of letter and spirit is mistaken
psychologically, that he needed the analytical criticism to enable
him to appreciate historically the difference between the prophetic
and the priestly strata in the Hebrew Bible, between the abiding
principles and Messianic dreams of religion and those detailed
rules of ritual and maxims of conduct by which it is sought
to realize those principles and dreams in actual life. But it is
just because of this that the Jew may be able to return the
compliment, and help Christians to understand certain phases of
the Gospels. Many modern Christians seem torn between two
sides of the teaching of Jesus—his prophetic-apocalyptic visions of
the Kingdom and his prophetic-priestly concern in the moral and
even ritual life of his day, in which he wished to see the Law
maintained in so far as it could be applied under existing circumstances. The Christian scholar, impregnated with Paulinism,
sometimes appears to find these two aspects of the Gospel teachings
inconsistent. Hence we have the disturbing phenomenon of waves
in Christian thought, the humanists who regard Jesus as almost
exclusively a moralist, and the apocalyptists who treat him as
almost exclusively a visionary. The Jew sees nothing inconsistent
in these two aspects. The very causes which make Christian
commentaries useful for the Jew if he would understand the Old
Testament, may make Jewish commentaries helpful to the Christian
for understanding some aspects of the New Testament.

I am well aware of the many imperfections of the Studies here presented.   But I do claim that I have not written apologetically. Still less have I been moved by controversial aims.   Only on rare occasions have I directly challenged the picture of Pharisaism drawn in Germany by Prof. Schürer and in England by Canon Charles.   I have preferred to supplement their views by a positive presentation of another view.   In this sense only are these Studies apologetic and controversial.   At all events, though I acknowledge that I have fallen far below Mr Montefiore in the faculty of un-prejudiced judgment, I have never consciously suppressed defects in the Pharisaic position, nor have I asserted in behalf of it more than the facts, as known to me, have demanded.   I am confident that those who are best acquainted with the difficulties of the problems discussed will be the most lenient critics of my errors and misconceptions.

I. A.

December, 1916.

CONTENTS

It may be well to indicate the relation of the present Chapters to the Additional Notes referred to in Mr Montefiore's work. The correspondence is as follows:

Additional Notes in Mr Montefiore's work.	Chapters in the present volume.
1	xviii.
2	iii.
3	iv.
4	v.
6	i.
7	xiii.
8	xix., xx.
9	vii.
11	vii.
12	xvi.
13	xvii.
14	xii.
15	xiv.
16	xiv.
17	vi.
18	ix.
19	xv.
20	xiv.
21	xi.
22	viii.
23	xxi.
24	ii.
25	x.

I. THE FREEDOM OF THE SYNAGOGUE.

The Synagogue,—that most gracious product of Jewish legalism—cannot have been the invention of the Hellenistic diaspora (as is maintained, without adequate evidence, by M. Friedländer, Introd. to *Synagoge und Kirche*, 1908). If it was due to a diaspora at all, it must be attributed to the exile in Babylon. This is no modern guess, for we have the statement of Justin (Dialogue with Trypho 17) that Jews applied Malachi i. 11, 12 to the prayers of the Israelites *then* in dispersion. We may confidently assert (with W. Bacher, Hastings' *Dictionary of the Bible*, s.v.; G. A. Smith, *Jerusalem* I. 364) that the Synagogue was a Palestinian institution of the Persian period. It was an institution momentous for the history of religion. "Their (the Jews') genius for the organisation of public religion appears in the fact that the form of communal worship devised by them was adopted by Christianity and Islam, and in its general outline still exists in the Christian and Moslem worlds" (C. Toy, *Introduction to the History of Religions*, 1913, p. 546).

In the Greek diaspora the Synagogue undoubtedly became of special importance. But its connection with Palestinian models is clear. Philo's account of the services in the Greek synagogues points to the two features which distinguished the Palestinian system; the reading and interpretation of the Scriptures, and the recitation of passages to which the assembly responded by terms of liturgical assent (cf. *Cambridge Biblical Essays*, 1909, p. 190). These features are shown in Ezra and Chronicles, and in all the Palestinian records that have come down to us (as in Sirach). True, the Maccabean history makes no direct reference to the Synagogue, but the main interest in that history was Jerusalem and the Temple. None the less, the books of the Maccabees prove most clearly that the people were in possession of copies of the Scroll of the law from which they read publicly (1 Macc. i. 57, iii. 48), were in the habit of gathering

for prayer (iii. 44), and above all of singing hymns with such refrains
as "His mercy is good, and endureth for ever" (iv. 24).

That there is little allusion in the Books of the Maccabees to places
of worship is intelligible—though the silence is not absolute. It must
not be overlooked that (iii. 46) Mizpah is described not as an ancient
shrine or altar but as "a place of prayer" (τόπος προσευχῆς). But the
fact seems to be that the institution of the Synagogue was earlier than
the erection of places of worship. In the Temple itself, the reading
of the Law was conducted by Ezra in the open courts, which remained
the scene of the prayer-meetings to the end, as the Rabbinic sources
amply demonstrate (e.g. Mishnah Sukkah chs. iv—v; cf. Sirach l.
5—21; 1 Macc. iv. 55). So, too, with the first prayer-meetings in the
"provinces." The meetings were probably held in the open air; and
that this was the most primitive form is shown by the fact that the
assemblies on occasions of national stress, even in the last decades of
the existence of the temple, were held in the public thoroughfares
(Mishnah Taanith ii. 1). By the first century A.D. Synagogue
buildings were plentiful both in the capital and the provinces. They
probably came into being under the favourable rule of Simon. It
must always, however, be remembered that Synagogue buildings in
various parts of Palestine are possibly referred to in Psalm lxxiv. 8,
usually assigned to the early years of the Maccabean age.

This is not the place to discuss the whole question, but one supreme
fact must not be omitted. From first to last, there was an organic
relation between Temple and Synagogue (though Friedländer, loc. cit.,
denies this). That there were prayers in the Temple is of course
certain (Mishnah Tamid v; Philo on Monarchy vi). Isaiah's phrase
(lvi. 7) a "house of prayer" (LXX. οἶκος προσευχῆς) applied to the
Temple was fulfilled to the letter. It is probable that all the Greek
words used in the diaspora for the Synagogue (that word itself,
Proseuche and place of instruction,—the last occurs in the Hebrew
Sirach) were derived from Hebrew or Aramaic equivalents. Certain is
it that, in Palestine, no Greek terms were imported to describe the
Synagogue. The real model for Palestine and the diaspora was the
Temple. It was a true instinct, therefore, which identified the "smaller
sanctuary" of Ezekiel xi. 16 with the Synagogue (T. B. Megillah 29 b).
The very word Abodah used of the Temple service became an epithet
for the service of prayer (the "Abodah of the heart," Sifrê Deut. § 41).
The link between Temple and Synagogue was established in Palestine
by the system in accordance with which local delegacies accompanied

the priests during their course of service in Jerusalem, while at home there were simultaneously held public readings of the law (Mishnah Taanith iv. 2).

The evidence from the Greek sources points in the same direction. Agatharchides of Cnidos (second century B.C.) records how the Jews spend their Sabbath in rest, and "spread out their hands and *pray* (εὔχεσθαι) till the evening." The whole context of the passage (as cited in Josephus *Against Apion* I. 22) shows that Agatharchides was referring to Jerusalem. That, however, in Egypt the Synagogue imitated the Palestinian methods is clear from Philo. Even Philo's Egyptian Therapeutae have their analogue, and possibly exemplar, in the Palestinian Essenes. As regards Alexandria, Philo gives unmistakable proof of the dependence of the Synagogue on the Temple method. His account, though its force has not been adequately realized, entirely depends on the Palestinian model. He tells us how (II. 630) "the multitude listens in silence, except when it is customary to say words of good omen by way of assent to what is read." This can only refer to the recitation of passages (chiefly no doubt Psalms) by one while the rest answer by "Amen" and similar ancient liturgical responses, such as were used in the Temple. That this must refer to prayers and not to reading the law is certain, for Philo then *proceeds* to describe the Scriptural readings and the expositions. Very instructive as to the connection between the Synagogues of the diaspora and the Temple is Philo's further statement that the exposition of the Scriptures was delivered by *one of the priests who happened to be present* (τῶν ἱερῶν δέ τις ὁ παρὼν) or by one of the elders (ἢ τῶν γερόντων).

This picture of the activity of the priests in teaching the law is a remarkable testimony to the truth that though the Temple was essentially the home of the sacrificial ritual, its influence on life was far-reaching and beneficial. Had it been otherwise, Philo would not have eulogised the Temple and priesthood—as he does in many places. Perhaps nothing could more piquantly show how completely Jerusalem, its Temple and its services, contrived to harmonise sacrificial ritual with prayer and a manifold activity, than the quaint report given by one who lived in Jerusalem during the existence of the Temple and survived its fall. R. Joshua b. Ḥananya said: "When we rejoiced (during Tabernacles) at the Joy of the Water-drawing we saw no sleep with our eyes. How so? The first hour, the morning Tamid (sacrifice), and thence to the prayer; thence to the musaph (additional) offering, thence to the musaph prayer; thence to the House of Study, thence to the meal; thence to the afternoon prayer, thence to the evening Tamid; thence onwards to the joy of the water-drawing" (T. B. Sukkah 53 a).

The Synoptists draw a pleasing picture of the freedom of teaching permitted by the Synagogue. Jesus performed this function throughout Galilee. The Fourth Gospel and Acts confirm the Synoptic record as to the readiness of the "rulers of the Synagogue" to call upon any competent worshipper to interpret and expound the Scriptures that had been read. Such instruction was usual in the Synagogue long before the time of Jesus as Zunz has shown (*Die gottesdienstlichen Vorträge der Juden*, ch. xx.), and the evidence is admirably marshalled and supplemented by Schürer (*Geschichte des jüdischen Volkes* etc. II⁴. pp. 498 seq.). Philo (II. 458) describes how one would read from the book, while another, "one of the more experienced" (τῶν ἐμπειροτάτων), expounded. In Palestine, too, the only qualification was competence, just as for leading the services experience (cf. the רגיל of the Mishnah Taanith ii. 2) was a chief requisite. As the discourses grew in length the *locale* for the sermon seems to have been transferred from Synagogue to School, and the *time* sometimes changed from the morning to the afternoon or previous evening. We find later on both customs in force together (T.J. *Taanith*, i. § 2 etc.). But at the earlier period, when the discourse was brief, it must have been spoken in the Synagogue, and immediately after the lesson from the Prophets.

The only two occasions of which we have a definite account of teaching in the Synagogue are, curiously enough, treated by Schürer (II⁴. 533 n. 123) as exceptions. His reason for doing so is derived from a purely philological argument. In the two cases, Luke iv. 17 and Acts xiii. 15, it is specifically recorded that the address followed the reading from the Prophets. In the first instance Jesus speaks after reading a couple of verses from Isaiah; in the second, we are explicitly told that in the Synagogue of Antioch, after the reading of the Law and the Prophets, the rulers of the Synagogue sent to them [Paul and his company], saying, "Brethren, if ye have any word of exhortation for the people, say on." We may note in passing that whereas Jesus both reads the lesson and expounds it, Paul does not seem to have read the lesson. This indicates an interesting difference in practice, for which there is other evidence. Rapoport (*Erech Millin*, 168) concludes from various Rabbinical passages that in the second century the reader of the Prophetical lesson was, in general, one who was able also to preach.

It may be that this custom existed side by side with another method which encouraged the *children* to read the lessons in Synagogue (cf.

Blau, *Revue des Etudes juives*, LV. 218). The two customs can be reconciled by the supposition (based on *Soferim*, xii. 7, xiv. 2) that when a preacher was present, he read the Prophetical lesson, and in the absence of such a one the children read it, perhaps at greater length. For the Prophetical reading was by nature a sermon, and as the service concluded with a sermon, the Prophetical lesson concluded the service when no preacher was present. It is clear from the narrative in T.B. *Beza*, 15 b, that the homily of the Rabbi was the end of the service, and it follows that the homily was given after the reading from the Prophets. But Schürer holds that as a general rule the discourse followed on the Pentateuchal lesson, and that the Prophetical reading without explanation concluded the service. True it is that the Prophetical lesson was named *haftara* (הפטרה or אפטרה), a word corresponding to *demissio*, i.e. the people was dismissed with or after the reading from the Prophets. But this surely is quite compatible with a short discourse, and the dismissal of the people might still be described as following the Prophetical lesson. Moreover, it may well be that the term *haftara* refers to the conclusion not of the whole services but of the Scriptural readings, the Prophetical passage being the *complement* of the Pentateuchal section. This was the view of various medieval authorities as cited in Abudarham and other liturgists. (It is accepted by I. Elbogen in his treatise *Der jüdische Gottesdienst in seiner geschichtlichen Entwicklung*, Leipzig, 1913, p. 175).

The oldest Prophetical lessons were most probably introduced for festivals and the special four or five Sabbaths in order to reinforce and interpret the Pentateuchal lessons, and (in the view of some) to oppose the views of schismatics. The Pharisees, owing to the conflicting theories of the Sadducees, attached to the sections from the Law such readings from the other Scriptures (particularly the "Earlier Prophets" who offered historical statements) as supported the Pharisaic exposition of the festival laws. (Cf. Büchler, *J. E.*, VI. 136 a. The same writer there cites T.B. *Megilla*, 25 b, T.J. *Megilla*, iv. 75 c, *Tosefta*, iv. 34 as Talmudic evidence that the reading of the haftara on the Sabbath had already been instituted in the first century of the common era). According to Abudarham, the author of a famous fourteenth century commentary on the Synagogue liturgy, the Prophetic readings grew up in a time of persecution, and were a substitute for the Pentateuchal readings when these were interdicted. On the other hand, L. Venetianer has lately suggested (*Z. D. M. G.* vol. 63, p. 103) that there were no specific readings from the Prophets till the end of the second century, and that the Prophetical lectionaries were chosen polemically in reply to lectionaries and homilies in the early Christian Church. But it seems far more probable that the haftaras were chosen for other reasons: (*a*) to include some of the most beautiful parts of the Scriptures, (*b*) to reinforce the message of the Pentateuch, and (*c*) to establish firmly the conviction that the whole of the canonical Scriptures (which, when the haftaras were first appointed, did not yet include the hagiographa) were a *unity*. (Cf. Bacher, *Die Proömien der alten jüdischen Homilie*, 1913, Introduction.)

There does not seem to have been any interval between the two readings, in fact the reciter of the haftara previously read a few verses from the Pentateuchal lesson (T.B. *Megilla*, 23 a). The sermon often dealt with the substance of the Pentateuchal lesson, and the preacher frequently took his text from it. But it is initially unlikely that the sermon should precede the haftara, seeing that the latter was introduced to help the understanding of the Law. We are not, however, left to conjecture. For we possess a large number of discourses which were specifically composed round the haftara. Many of the homilies in the *Pesiqta Rabbathi* are of this class; they are of course not, as they now stand, so early as the first century, but they represent a custom so well established as to point to antiquity of origin. The famous fast-day discourse reported in the Mishnah Taanith ii. 1 is based on two texts from the prophets (Jonah iii. 10 and Joel ii. 13), —both of which passages were eminently suitable as the lesson for such an occasion. Of the forty-seven chapters in the Pesiqta (most of which are compounded of many discourses) in Friedmann's edition, more than twenty are based on haftaras; in the *Pesiqta of R. Cahana* there are eleven such chapters. That these discourses *followed* the reading from the Prophets is shown by the recurrence of such a phrase as: "As he has read as *haftara* in the Prophet" (מה שהשלים בנביא Friedmann, 1 b) when quoting the text expounded. (The verb שלם is equivalent in this context to אפטר, just as שלמתא is another word for הפטרה, and it must signify to *complete* the lesson rather than to *dismiss* the congregation.) Similar evidence that the discourse was preceded by the actual reading of the *haftara* is derivable from Friedmann's edition, pp. 29 a, 42 a (ממה שהשלים הנביא), 54 a, 142 b (ממה שכתב בעניין "As he has written in the passage read"), 149 b (ממה שקראו בעניין הנביא), 179 a (ממה שקרינן בעניין). Perhaps the most instructive passage of all is on 172 a. Here the discourse is on the Pentateuchal text Leviticus xxiii. 24 read on the New Year

festival: "In the seventh month, in the first day of the month, shall
be a solemn rest unto you, a memorial of blowing of trumpets." At
the end of the last Pisqa the homily runs: "Says the Holy One,
blessed be He, in this world, through the trumpet (shofar) I have had
compassion on you, and so in time to come I will be merciful to
you through the trumpet (shofar) and bring near your redemption.
Whence? From what we have read in the lesson of the Prophet
(מניין?) ממה שקראו בעניין בנביא): Blow ye the trumpet in Zion...for
the day of the Lord cometh (Joel ii. 1)." In this case it is quite clear
that the discourse on the Pentateuchal text *followed* the *haftara*.

I have been at some pains to show that the New Testament
accounts of the preaching in the Synagogues refer to the normal
and not to the exceptional, because these accounts are the most
precise we possess and it is important to know that we may rely
on them completely. What then can we exactly infer as to the extent
of freedom which the worshippers enjoyed not only with regard to
teaching but also with regard to the selection of passages on which
to speak? I do not find it possible to accept the view that the
homilist was allowed a *perfectly* free hand, that he might open the
Prophet or Prophets where he willed, read a verse or two and then
address the congregation. That the readings from the Law and the
Prophets were in the time of Jesus very short is fairly certain.
The rule that at least 21 verses were read from the Law and the
Prophets was, as Büchler shows (*J. Q. R.*, v. 464 seq.; vi. 14 seq., 45),
late. In the Massoretic divisions we find Sabbath lessons (Sedarim)
which contain seven, eight and nine verses, and there are many in-
dications that the oldest *haftara* often comprised very few verses.
This follows indeed from the very nature of the *haftara*. It originally
corresponded in substance with, and agreed often in its opening word with
the opening word of, the Pentateuchal lesson. But this correspondence
mostly only concerns a single verse or two, not long passages. Thus
the reading Isaiah lxi. 1—2 (Luke iv. 16) was possibly the whole of
the *haftara*. Later on, it became usual to round off the reading by
skipping until a suitable terminating verse was reached.

Let us try to define exactly what it is that Luke describes. Jesus
stood up to read. Then "there was delivered unto him a book of the
prophet Isaiah." The verb used for "delivered up" ($\epsilon\pi\epsilon\delta\delta\theta\eta$) might
be interpreted "was delivered unto him in addition." In that case
Jesus would have first read a verse of the Pentateuchal lesson (perhaps
Deut. xv. 7) and then proceeded with the *haftara*. But it is impossible

to press the Greek verb in this way. Yet it is at all events clear
that the *prophet* was not Jesus' choice; it was handed to him. Moreover, the wording in Luke makes it almost certain that just as the
book of Isaiah was not Jesus' own choice, so the passage from Isaiah
was not chosen by Jesus himself. "He opened the book and found
the place where it was written." The word "found" (εὗρεν) does not
mean he looked for it and chose it, but he "found" it ready. This is
implied by a change in the verbs which has I think been overlooked.
We are simply told that Jesus "opened" (ἀνοίξας) the book. Jesus
does not unroll it, as he would have done had he searched for a text.
(The reading ἀναπτύξας is rejected by W.H., Nestle etc.) Luke on
the other hand tells us that when he had finished the reading he
"rolled it up." The A.V. "he closed the book" does not give the
force of the Greek (πτύξας). Thus when he has finished Jesus rolls up
the scroll which he did not unroll, for it was given to him already
unrolled, so that he only opened it at the place already selected and
found the passage in Isaiah ready for him to read. In fact, while the
Pentateuch was read in an unbroken order, the *haftara* might be
derived from any part of the Prophets, provided always that one
condition was fulfilled: the passage was bound to resemble in subject-
matter the Torah portion just read. As Dr Büchler well puts it:
"This is clear from the origin of the institution itself; and moreover
the examples quoted by the Mishna, Boraitha and Tosefta, bear unmistakable testimony to the existence of this condition" (*J. Q. R.*,
VI. 12).

It has often been pointed out that Jesus sat down (Luke iv. 20) to
expound the Scriptures, and that this accords with Rabbinic custom.
There is no contradiction in Acts xiii. 16, where "Paul stood up."
Though Paul's exhortation follows Jewish lines in its structure, it is
not an explanation of the Law. For, though the address may be due
more to Luke's hand than to Paul's, it resembles the exhortations in
the Books of the Maccabees; and, at all events, so far from expounding
the Law, it is an ingenious eulogy of it up to a point, and thence an
argument against its sufficiency. The climax of Paul's whole speech is
reached in verse 39, and the opposition which followed, from those
who venerated the Law against one who proclaimed its insufficiency,
cannot be regarded as any breach in that freedom of the Synagogue
which he had previously enjoyed. On the other hand, Jesus expounded
the Scriptures, applying Isaiah lxi. 1, 2 to himself. He seems to have
combined lviii. 6 with lxi. 1. The right to "skip" while reading the

Prophets was well attested (Mishnah *Megilla* iv. 4). Being written on a Scroll, the two passages might easily be open together, and Jesus, in accordance with what at all events became a usual Rabbinic device, intended to use both texts as the key to his exposition. Such skipping to suitable passages may be noted in the Geniza fragments of haftaras in the triennial cycle.

If the view here taken of the incident in Luke be correct, then we have distinctly gained evidence that, at the opening of the public teaching of Jesus, the Synagogue lectionary was becoming fixed at all events in its main principles. That this was the case with the essential elements of the service is very probable. There is no reason whatever to doubt the tradition (T.B. *Berachoth*, 33 a) which ascribed the beginnings of the order of service to the "Men of the Great Synod," the successors of the three post-exilic prophets, Haggai, Zechariah, and Malachi. The doubts which Kuenen threw on the reality of this body—doubts which for a generation caused the "Great Synod" to be dismissed as a myth—are no longer generally shared, and Dr G. Adam Smith in his *Jerusalem* has fairly faced the absurd position in which we are placed if we deny, to a highly organised community such as Ezra left behind him, some central legislative and spiritual authorities in the Persian and Greek periods. The two functions were afterwards separated, and it may well be (Büchler *Das Synhedrium in Jerusalem*, 1902) that two distinct Synhedria, one with civil the other with religious jurisdiction, existed in the last period before the fall of the Temple. As regards the Synagogue service, it probably opened with an invocation to prayer, must have included the *Shema* (Deut. vi. 4—9, xi. 13—21; to which was added later Numbers xv. 37—41), a doxology and confession of faith, the eighteen benedictions in a primitive form, readings from Pentateuch and Prophets, and certain communal responses. With this Schürer (*loc. cit.*) is in substantial agreement. The actual contents of the liturgy long remained fluid; the fixation of the Synagogue prayers was the work of the post-Talmudic Gaonim of the seventh century onwards.

Attention should be paid to a remarkable difference of language with regard to prayer and study of the Law. Nothing better brings out the real character of Pharisaism. It relied on rule and based much confidence on the effect of good habits. But it left free the springs of emotion and the source of communion. While, then, Shammai urged (Aboth i. 15) " **Make thy** *Torah* **a fixed thing** " (עשה תורתך קבע), Simon—a disciple of Joḥanan b. Zakkai—proclaimed (*ib.* ii. 18) " Make not thy *prayer* a fixed thing " (אל תעש תפלתך קבע). Study was to be a habit, prayer a free emotion. The true tradition of Pharisaism from beginning to end of the first century is seen from Hillel, through Joḥanan, to his disciples—one of whom in answer to Joḥanan's problem : "Go forth and see which is the good way to which a man should cleave" said : "A good heart." And the master approved this solution as the right one (Aboth ii. 13). No fixation of a liturgy changed this attitude. Prayer might be, as time progressed, ordained to follow certain forms, but within those forms freedom prevailed, as it still prevails in the most conservative Jewish rituals.

With regard to reciting the Scriptures, the public reading of the Law for occasions was certainly instituted by Ezra, and continued by his successors in authority; the passages read were translated into the vernacular Aramaic (Targum). We know that the Palestinian custom, when finally organised, provided for a cycle of Sabbath lessons which completed a continuous reading of the Pentateuch once in every three years (T.B. *Megillah*, 29 b). As to the antiquity of the beginnings of this Triennial Cycle Dr Büchler's epoch-making Essays leave no doubt (*J. Q. R.*, v. 420, VI. 1). The strongest argument for this supposition is of a general character, but it is reinforced by many particular facts. Many events in the Pentateuch which are left undated in the original are dated with exactitude in the Rabbinic tradition. This is amply accounted for by the simple fact that these events are contained in the Sabbath lessons which fell normally to be read on certain dates, which Tannaitic tradition thereupon associated with those events. This argument enables us to work backwards and assume a somewhat early origin for the fixation of the readings on those particular dates.

It may here be of interest to interpolate one or two instances of the light thrown on passages in the N.T. by the Cycle of lessons. Dr King (*Journal of Theological Studies*, Jan. 1904) has ingeniously shown that the association (in the second chapter of the Acts) of the Gift of Tongues with Pentecost falls in admirably with the Triennial Cycle. The first year of the Cycle began on Nisan 1, and the opening verses of Genesis were then read. The eleventh chapter of Genesis was reached at the season of Pentecost. This chapter narrated the story of Babel, i.e. the Confusion of Tongues. The Gift of the Spirit is a "reversal of the curse of Babel." A second instance may be found in the Fourth Gospel. The discourse of Jesus

regarding the Manna must have occurred in the spring, although the
date "the Passover was near" (John vi. 4) is justly held to be a
suspicious reading.   But the note of time "there was much grass in
the place" (verse 10) is confirmed by the "green grass" of Mark vi. 39.
John particularly specifies that the five loaves were made of "barley"
(verses 9, 13).   The new barley would certainly not be available till a
few weeks after the Passover, and the poor would not have possessed
a store of the old barley so late as the spring.   Everything points,
then, to a date soon after the Passover.   Now in the second year of
the Triennial Cycle the lessons for the first weeks in Iyyar (end
of April or beginning of May) were taken from Exodus xvi., the
very chapter in which the miracle of the Manna is reported.   Of
course the dates of both Acts and the Fourth Gospel are uncertain.
But such coincidences as these (to which others could easily be added)
point to the use of good and old sources, and they at least confirm the
view that, in its initial stages, a Cycle of lessons may have been already
in vogue in the first century.

Some obscure arguments in the Gospels might lose their difficulty if
we were acquainted with the Scriptural readings with which they were
possibly associated.   Thus in the Sabbath incident (Matthew xii.),
the argument would be more logical if Numbers xxviii. 9—10 and
1 Sam. xxi. 1—10 had been recently read in the Synagogues.   "Have
ye not read what David did?" and "Have ye not read in the Law?"
(Matthew xii. 3, 5) would have a sharp sarcastic point in that case.
It may well be, again, that the Parable of the Prodigal Son was spoken
during the weeks when Genesis xxv. onwards formed the Sabbath
lessons.   There is distinct indication from Philo (see below Note on
Parables) that the idea conveyed in the Parable alluded to was connected with the story of Esau and Jacob.   Another instance is, yet
clearer.   The discourse in the Fourth Gospel (vii. 37, 8) belongs to
Tabernacles.   "As the scripture hath said, out of his belly shall flow
rivers of living waters.   But this spake he of the Spirit."   The reference
probably is to Zechariah xiv. 8 (now read in the Synagogues on the first
day of Tabernacles, possibly under the Triennial Cycle read later in the
festival week).   Zechariah indeed has: "living waters shall go out
from Jerusalem."   But as in Rabbinic tradition (T. B. Sanhedrin 37 a,
Ezekiel xxxviii. 8, Jubilees viii.) Jerusalem was situated in the *navel*
of the earth, John may be using *belly* as a synonym for Jerusalem.
Even more significant are the words that follow: "But this spake he
of the Spirit."   The Ceremony of the Water-drawing (already referred

to above), which occurred on Tabernacles, was interpreted to mean the draught of the Holy Spirit (Genesis Rabba, ch. 70). Some far-reaching suggestions as to the nature of the teaching of Jesus, as found in the Fourth Gospel, in relation to the ideas of the *Doreshe Reshumoth* (on whom see a later Note), may be found in G. Klein's *Der älteste christ-liche Katechismus und die jüdische Propaganda-Literatur* (Berlin 1909). See especially the section (pp. 49—61) entitled "Jesu Predigt nach Johannes." My own general impression, without asserting an early date for the Fourth Gospel, is that that Gospel enshrines a genuine tradition of an aspect of Jesus' teaching which has not found a place in the Synoptics.

There is no reason to suppose that the freedom of teaching in the Galilean Synagogues was ever denied to Jesus. So important and dramatic an incident as such a denial must have found a mention in the Synoptists. Yet they are agreed in their silence as to an event of that nature; of course John (xviii. 20) represents Jesus as through-out, and to the last, teaching in synagogue. The cessation of references to such teaching in Mark after the sixth chapter may be best explained on the supposition that Jesus voluntarily changed his method when he found that he no longer carried the Synagogue audiences with him. The turning point is clearly given by Mark in his account of the experience of Jesus at Nazareth. The prophet found no honour in his own country, and this loss of sympathy appears to have induced Jesus to abandon the Synagogue discourses in favour of more in-formal teaching in the villages and in the open air, reverting indeed to the older practice. Prof. Burkitt (*The Gospel History and its Transmission*, p. 68) holds that the final rupture occurred with the religious authorities in Galilee in consequence of the healing of the man with a withered hand in the Synagogue on a Sabbath (Mark iii. 1). The Pharisees are said thereupon to have taken counsel with the Herodians to accuse and destroy Jesus. This was the definite breach (iii. 6). Prof. Burkitt with brilliant skill works out a scheme which accounts for Jesus spending the eight months in territory in which the jurisdiction of Herod Antipas did not run. During the greater part of the year before the last Passover Jesus "lives a wandering life in exile from Galilee or in concealment, and his chief work is no longer that of Revivalist but of the *Pastor pastorum*" (*op. cit.*, p. 89). This theory makes it necessary to explain as excep-tional not only the later attempts to teach in the Nazareth Synagogue (where the failure is certainly not due to Pharisaic hostility), but also the subsequent teaching in the villages recorded in general terms (Mark vi. 6 "And he went round about the villages teaching"; cf. the parallels in Matthew and Luke) and the teaching of the crowd (Mark vi. 34). Moreover the language of Mark viii. 27 points to public teaching (outside Galilee), and (x. 1) where he enters the borders of Judæa "multitudes come together unto him again, and *as he was wont* he taught them again." That the death of John the Baptist greatly influenced Jesus in avoiding Galilee is highly probable; and there may have been some growing suspicion of him in the official circles of the Synagogues. But it cannot be said that there is any evidence at all that Jesus ever attempted to teach in any synagogue and was met with a refusal.

Still less is there any ground for holding that "the influence of the Sanhedrin everywhere haunted" Jesus and his disciples. Prof. G. A. Smith (*Jerusalem*, I. 416–7) strongly maintains that this was so, though Schweitzer, *Quest.* p. 362, is of another opinion. My own conviction is that most of the controversies between Jesus and the Pharisees occurred in Jerusalem and not in Galilee. If the tradition of the Galilean scene be authentic, the Pharisees were Priests who had been in Jerusalem and had returned to their Galilean homes after serving their regular course. The references to Pharisees or scribes who came from Jerusalem (Mark iii. 22, Matthew xv. 1) do not point to deputations from the capital. The language of Mark vii. 1 is the most explicit: "And there were gathered together unto him the Pharisees and certain of the scribes which had come from Jerusalem and had seen that some of his disciples ate their bread with defiled, that is unwashen hands." This looks very much as though the Pharisees were there in quite a normal manner; it is forcing the words, here and in the other passages cited, to represent them as "deputations" or as dogging the footsteps of Jesus. Herod Antipas may have had some such designs, but the Sanhedrin of Jerusalem had neither power nor motive to take action until the scene was transferred to the capital.

With regard to the *effect* of Jesus' discourses in the Synagogues, we are told that "he taught as one having authority" (Mk i. 22; Mt. vii. 29; Luke iv. 32). If the only version of this record were Luke's, the reference would obviously be to the authority with which the words of Jesus "came home to the consciences of his hearers" (Plummer). But the other two Synoptists agree in contrasting this "authority" with the manner of the Scribes. H. P. Chajes suggests that the real meaning is that Jesus taught in Parables (see Note on Parables below).

This would possibly have to be compared with Philo's remark that the teaching in the Alexandrian Synagogues was by way of allegory (διὰ συμβόλων II. 630). More acceptable is A. Wünsche's explanation of the claim that Jesus spoke ὡς ἐξουσίαν ἔχων (*Neue Beiträge zur Erläuterung der Evangelien*, Göttingen, 1878, p. 110). The phrase recalls the Rabbinic idiom of speaking "from the mouth of power" (מפי הגבורה), connoting the possession of direct divine inspiration. The Pharisaic teachers certainly laid no general claim to the dignity. But the remark "he taught as one having authority" is usually explained by referring to the Rabbinical method as unfolded in the Talmud—with all its scholastic adhesion to precedents, and its technical and complicated casuistry. But this reference is not quite relevant.

For the Talmudical method was the result of long development after the age of Jesus, and the question is: to what extent can we reasonably assert that the method was already prevalent before the destruction of the Temple and the failure of the Bar Cochba War of Independence (135 A.D.) drove the Rabbis into their characteristic scholasticism? There was, moreover, all along a *popular* exegesis besides the *scholastic*, a form of homily specially intended for the edification and instruction of the simple and unlearned; and it would thus be improper to contrast the simplicity and directness of Jesus with the sophistication and precedent citations of the Rabbis even if the latter features were earlier than we have evidence of. Hillel, the greatest of the predecessors of Jesus, taught almost without reference to precedent; he only once cites an earlier authority. Hillel's most characteristic utterances are as free as are those of Jesus from the bonds of scholastic tradition. He, too, exemplifies the prophetic independence of conventions. Naturally, the appeal to and reliance on precedents presupposes an accumulation of precedents to appeal to and rely on. Such a mass of previous rule and doctrine would only be built up gradually. (See T. J. Pesahim 39 a, where Hillel cites his teachers. In the Babylonian Talmud Pesah. 66 the citation, however, is omitted. Cf. Bacher *Tradition und Tradenten in den Schulen Palästinas und Babyloniens*, Leipzig, 1914, p. 55.) It was mainly the Amoraim of the third century onwards that made the appeal to precedent, and naturally as the precedents accumulated so appeal to them would increase, as in the modern English legal experience with regard to the citation of illustrative "cases." The earlier Jewish teaching certainly goes to the Scriptures, but so does Jesus; and this earlier teaching (like that of Jesus) uses the Scriptures as a general inspiration. It is only later (in the middle of the second century) that we find a strict technical reliance on chapter and verse, and in point of fact Jesus (in the Synoptists) appeals in this way to Scripture quite as much as does any of the earlier Rabbis. It was perhaps just his eclecticism, his independence of any particular school, that is implied by the contrast between Jesus' teaching and that of the Scribes.

The solution may be found in the supposition that Jesus taught at a transition period, when the formation of schools of exegesis was in process of development. Hillel's famous contemporary, Shammai, does seem to have been a stickler for precedent, and his school was certainly distinguished from that of Hillel by this very characteristic. If it be the truth, further, that Shammai (as Dr Büchler conjectures) was a Galilean, then it is possible that especially in Galilee there was growing up in the age of Jesus a school which taught with close reference to particular rules and views with which Jesus had little in common. The ordinary Galilean Jew would then feel that there was a difference between the conventional style of the local scribes and that of Jesus, who did not associate himself with any particular school. On some points, however, such as his view of divorce, Jesus (if the text of Matthew xix. 9 be authentic) appears to have been a Shammaite. It is by no means improbable (Bloch, *Memorial Volume*, ספר היובל Hebrew Section, pp. 21 seq.) that at the time of Jesus the views of Shammai were quite generally predominant, the school of Hillel only gaining supremacy in Jewish law and custom after the fall of the Temple. If that be so, Jesus, in departing from the Shammaite method, might well seem to be one who taught with authority and not as one of the Scribes. At a later period the question as to the school to which a scholar belonged would no doubt influence his admissibility as preacher in a particular place.

Jesus spoke without reference to any mediate authority. To the Scribes it became an ever more sacred duty to cite the original authority for any saying, if it were consciously derived from another teacher. Such reference was an obligation which attained even Messianic import. "He who says a word in the name of its author brings Redemption to the world" (Aboth—Chapter of R. Meir—vi., *Megilla* 15 a). Verify your quotations, is C. Taylor's comment (*Sayings of the Jewish Fathers*, 1897, Additional Note 54). The saving-power of literary and legal frankness goes deeper than that. Such punctiliousness assuredly cannot be attributed to the Scribes as aught but a virtue, which if it encouraged scholasticism, also encouraged honesty. It did more. It promoted the conception of a continuous tradition, which conception while it obscured the facts of history, and required constant criticism by those facts and also by appeal to ultimate principles as distinct from derived rules, nevertheless gave harmony to the scheme of doctrine.

The view that Jesus was an original eclectic, that like Horace— though in a far from Horatian sense—he was " nullius addictus jurare in verba magistri," is confirmed by the difficulty of " placing " Jesus with regard to the schools of his age. The fact is not to be minimised that we are imperfectly acquainted with those schools ; we have only the sure knowledge (which is derivable from Philo and Josephus) that an amazing variety of religious grouping was in progress in the first century. But even as far as we know these schools Jesus seems to belong to none of them. It is undeniable that certain features of his teaching are Essenic. But he did not share the Essenic devotion to ceremonial ablutions. Further, he was an Apocalyptic, but he was also a powerful advocate of the Prophetic Judaism. Then, again, it is plausible to explain much of the gospel attack on the Scribes as due to contempt of the Sadducean priesthood. But R. Leszynsky (*Die Sadducäer*, Berlin 1912, ch. III.) finds it possible to claim Jesus as a Sadducee !

It is sometimes thought that the teaching with authority is shown by Jesus' frequent phrase " but I say unto you " (J. Weiss on Mk i. 21). But this use of the phrase needs interpretation. The most interesting passage in which it occurs is Mt. v. 43—4 : " Ye have heard that it was said, Thou shalt love thy neighbour and hate thine enemy, but I say unto you, Love your enemies." Now it is obvious that nowhere in the O.T. are men told to hate their enemies. But in the exegetical terminology of R. Ishmael (end of first century) there is a constantly recurring phrase which runs thus : " The text reads so and so. I *hear* from it so and so : *but* other texts prove that this is not its true meaning " (שומע אני...תלמוד לומר). If this as Schechter (*Studies in Judaism*) suggests (though Bacher *Die älteste Terminologie der jüdischen Schriftauslegung*, I. 190 dissents on inadequate grounds), underlies the passage just cited from Matthew, then Jesus' phrase : "Ye have *heard*... but I say unto you" would be parallel to the Rabbinic idiom. It removes the main difficulty in regard to the hating of one's enemy, for Jesus would not be referring to any text enjoining hatred, but to a possible narrowing of the meaning of the text enjoining love. In that case, Jesus' "but I say unto you" differs from the usual Rabbinical formula in that it introduces a personal element, but as with them,

Jesus' exegesis really leads up to the citation and interpretation of another text (in this case : ' "Ye shall be perfect as your heavenly father is perfect " ') which takes a wider sweep and illumines the particular matter under discussion. This is in full conformity with the Rabbinic method. They, too, derived the ideal of man's character from the character of God. "Be ye holy for I the Lord am holy" (Leviticus xix. 2, of which the turn in Matthew is a reminiscence) was with the Rabbis the ground text of the idea of the *Imitation of God*. It was with them the highest motive for lovingkindness and charity. (Sifrâ on Levit. xix. 2).

II. THE GREATEST COMMANDMENT.

The combination of the commandments to love God and to love
one's neighbour is "highly striking and suggestive." Commentators
rightly see that the Scribe's question as to the Greatest Commandment
was not captious, but (as Gould puts it) the Pharisee thought: "Here
is possibly an opportunity to get an answer to our standing question,
about the first commandment." For practical purposes of ethical
monition, the enunciation both of Love God and Love thy fellow man
is necessary. But on a profounder analysis the second is included in
the first, as is shown in the Midrash. Man being made in the image of
God, any misprision of man by man implies disregard of Him in
whose image man is made (*Genesis Rabbah* xxiv. last words). It therefore is not at all unlikely that such combinations as we find in the
Synoptics were a common-place of Pharisaic teaching. It is true that
Wellhausen—oblivious of the occurrence of the combination in the
Testament of the Twelve Patriarchs (Isaachar v. 2, vii. 5, Dan v. 3)—
holds that "the combination of commandments was first effected in this
way by Jesus." That excellent student of Rabbinics, Dr C. Taylor, was
not so certain on this point. It will perhaps be interesting to cite
what he says on the subject in one of his earlier works (*The Gospel
in the Law*, 1869, p. 276):—

It might seem that our Lord's teaching was novel in respect of its exhibiting the
twofold Law of Love as the sum of Old Testament morality. Thus, in Matt. xxii. 40,
Christ is represented as answering to the lawyer's question: 'Thou shalt love the
Lord thy God with all thy heart, and with all thy soul, and with all thy mind.
This is the first and great commandment. And the second is like unto it, Thou
shalt love thy neighbour as thyself. *On these two commandments hang all the law
and the prophets.*' But the addition in St Mark's account (xii. 32): 'Master, Thou
hast said the truth,' might imply that the answer to that oft-mooted question was
no new one, but rather that which was *recognised* as true. In another passage—
introductory to the Parable of the Good Samaritan—'a certain Lawyer' gives the
two commandments, *To love God*, and, *To love one's neighbour*, as a summary of the
law. He is asked: 'What is written in the law? how readest thou?' And he

answers: 'Thou shalt love the Lord thy God with all thy heart, and with all thy soul, and with all thy strength, and with all thy mind; and thy neighbour as thyself' (Luke x. 26, 27). But the fact that St Paul grounds this equivalence on reason solely, goes far to prove that he did not regard the mere statement of it as a characteristic novelty in the Christian scheme. 'Love,' writes the Apostle, 'worketh no ill to his neighbour: *therefore* love is the fulfilling of the law' (Rom. xiii. 10). In John xiii. 34 the words, 'A *new* commandment I give unto you, That ye love one another,' might seem to imply that the law of mutual love was put forward as new. But the words following explain wherein lay the novelty: '*As I have loved you,* etc.'

It is not clear why a "lawyer" (νομικός) is introduced in Matthew; Luke's frequent use of the word is more intelligible. But it seems probable that the word had become acclimatised in Hebrew—though there is only one instance recorded of it. Jose b. Ḥalafta (second century) was so famed as a profound and ready exponent of the Law that it was said of him "his information as to the Law is ever with him" (נמוקו עמו), where several authorities see the Greek νομική (sc. ἐπιστήμη). Cf. Levy and Krauss s.v.; Bacher *Agada der Tannaiten* ii. 155. Jastrow s.v. takes another view. In support of the identification, it may be pointed out that Νομικός had become a proper name in the first century. Joesdros, son of Nomikos, was one of the four orators who were sent to attack Josephus (2 *War*, xxi. 7). For the suggestion that the νομικός of the Synoptics was a Sadducean lawyer, see J. Mann in *J.Q.R.* Jan. 1916, p. 419. Possibly the use of the term should be sought in another direction. In the primitive account of the incident, the questioner may have been, not a born Jew, but a Gentile νομικός inclined to become, or who had recently become, a proselyte to Judaism. As will be shown, at the end of this note, such summaries of the Law were naturally made in the literature of propaganda or catechism.

Aqiba attached, as every Jew did, the highest importance to the text in Deut. vi. 4, and he died with it on his lips (T.B. *Berachoth* 61 b). He further saw in martyrdom the fulfilment of the law bidding Israel love God with all his soul or life. The various terms of this law are differently rendered in the LXX, Deut. vi. 5 and 2 Kings xxiii. 25, and this fact goes far to explain the dissimilar versions of the Deuteronomic text in the three Synoptics. Chajes aptly suggests (*Markus-Studien* p. 67) that the LXX in Deut. was influenced by Rabbinic exegesis. It there uses διανοίας for καρδίας, and it elsewhere employs the former word in rendering yeṣer (Gen. viii. 21 כי יצר לב האדם רע, ὅτι ἔγκειται ἡ διάνοια τοῦ, 1 Chr. xxix. 18 ליצר מחשבות לבב, ἐν διανοίᾳ καρδίας, Gen. vi. 5 וכל יצר מחשבות לבו, καὶ πᾶς τις διανοεῖται ἐν τῇ καρδίᾳ αὐτοῦ). Now the Rabbinic interpretation of Deut. vi. 5 also introduced the yeṣer (בכל לבבך) : "With all thy heart," i.e. with thy two yeṣers, בשני יצריך, Sifre on Deut. vi. 5, ed. Friedmann 73 a). Similarly though in 2 Kings xxiii. 25 the LXX renders מאדו by ἰσχύς in Deut. vi. 5 it uses the term δύναμις, a word which, as the LXX of Ezek. xvii. 18, 27 shows, may correspond to the sense *substance* (הון), which was precisely the Rabbinic interpretation of מאדך in Deut. vi. 5 (Sifre, *loc. cit.*; *Ber.* 61 b).

A well-known passage of the Sifra (on Leviticus xix. 18, ed. Weiss, p. 89 a) runs thus : "*Thou shalt love thy neighbour as thyself* : R. Aqiba said, This is the greatest general principle in the Law (זה כלל גדול בתורה). Ben Azzai said : *This is the book of the generations of man* (Genesis v. 1) is a greater principle than that (כלל גדול מזה)." There is no difference between these Tannaim on the question itself : love of one's fellow-man is fundamental, but while Aqiba derives the conclusion from Leviticus xix. 18, Ben Azzai points back to the story of the creation, to *the book of the generations of man*, as the basis of the solidarity of the human race, and the obligation that accrues to every man to love his fellow. Aqiba himself elsewhere traces the same duty to another phrase in the Genesis story (Mishnah, *Aboth* iii. 14, in Taylor iii. 21) : "Beloved is man in that he was created in the image of God" (Genesis ix. 6, cf. the quotation from *Genesis Rabbah* above). As Taylor remarks on this last passage in the Mishnah (*Sayings of the Jewish Fathers*, ed. 2, p. 56) : "Man is beloved by God in whose image or likeness he was created; and he should be beloved by his fellow-men as a consequence of this love towards God himself." The text cited (Genesis ix. 6) runs in full : "Whoso sheddeth man's blood, by man shall his blood be shed : for in the image of God made he man." As R. Aqiba comments (*Genesis Rabba* xxxiv.) : "If one sheds blood it is accounted to him as though he diminished the likeness." The same idea is also attributed (*Aboth d. R. Nathan*, xxxix. ed. Schechter, p. 118) to one of Aqiba's most noted disciples—Meir—while another of his disciples—Nehemiah—(*op. cit.* xxxi. p. מו), on the basis of Genesis v. 1, declares "A single human life is equal to the whole work of creation," אדם אחד שקול כנגד כל מעשה בראשית (with Aqiba's saying in *Aboth* iii. 14, especially the latter part of the Mishnah, cf. 1 Ep. John iii. 1).

These citations, it will be observed, are from Jewish authorities of the end of the first or the beginning of the second century. But, as is well known, the idea that forbearance to one's fellow-man is the basis of the Mosaic law goes back to Hillel (T.B. *Sabbath* 31 a ; *Aboth de R. Nathan* ii. 26). The mere formulation of the "Golden Rule" in the negative version is far older than Hillel. So far as Jewish sages are concerned it may ultimately rest on such phrases as Psalm xv. 3, where the man who sojourns in the Lord's tent is he that doeth no evil to his neighbour (לא עשה לרעהו רעה). The actual maxim of Hillel is found in Tobit iv. 15 (ὃ μισεῖς μηδενὶ ποιήσῃς). This version points to the conclusion that when Hillel used the word לחברך (דעלך סני לחברך לא תעבד, "What-to-thyself is-hateful to-thy-fellow thou shalt not do"), he meant by it *fellow man*. In the Aramaic text of Tobit (Neubauer, Oxford, 1878, p. 8) the reading is ודסאני לך לחורני לא תעביד (the Hebrew text, *ibid.* p. 24, runs ואשר תשנא לנפשך לא תעשה לאחרים). Hillel elsewhere (*Aboth* i. 12) uses the widest possible term : he speaks of love for one's fellow-creatures (אוהב את הבריות). As is well known, the negative form of the Golden Rule not only preceded Jesus it survived him. It underlies Romans xiii. 10. St Paul's remark runs : ἀγαπήσεις τὸν πλησίον σου ὡς σεαυτόν. ἡ ἀγάπη τῷ πλησίον κακὸν οὐκ ἐργάζεται—thus the Apostle explains or rather justifies Leviticus xix. 18 by the negative form of the Golden Rule (practically as in Ps. xv. 3). Curiously enough this is paralleled by the Targum Jer. on Leviticus xix. 18 (ed. Ginsburger, p. 206), for the Targum actually inserts the negative Rule as an explanation of "thou shalt love thy neighbour as thyself" (לא תהוון נקמין ולא נטרין דבבו לבני עמך ותרחמיה לחברך דמן אנת סני לך לא תעביד ליה אנא יי) Philo (ap. Eusebius, P. viii. 7), too, has the negative Rule, though his phraseology (ἃ τις παθεῖν ἐχθαίρει, μὴ ποιεῖν αὐτόν) is not verbally derived either from Tobit or from the source employed in the Didache (πάντα δὲ ὅσα ἐὰν θελήσῃς μὴ γίνεσθαί σοι, καὶ σὺ ἄλλῳ μὴ ποίει). But Philo's source can easily be suggested. It is not Jewish at all. Isocrates (*Nicocles* 39 c) has the maxim : ἃ πάσχοντες ὑφ᾽ ἑτέρων ὀργίζεσθε, ταῦτα τοῖς ἄλλοις μὴ ποιεῖτε. Moreover, a similar saying is quoted from the Confucian Analects (Legge, *Chinese Classics* I. Bk. xv. 23). Jacob Bernays, on the other hand, holds that Isocrates had no thought of a general moral application of the principle, and believes that Philo was drawing on a Jewish source (*Gesammelte Abhandlungen*, Berlin, 1885, Vol. I. ch. xx.). Bernays cites Gibbon's quotation of Isocrates in his account of the Calvin-Servetus episode (*Decline and Fall*, ch. liv. n. 36).

Here it may be pointed out that the contrasts drawn between the negative and positive forms of the Golden Rule are not well founded. One cannot share the opinion of some Jewish scholars (such as

Hamburger) that there is *no* difference between the negative and positive formulations. But Bischoff (*Jesus und die Rabbinen*, p. 93) is equally wrong in asserting that Hillel's maxim differs from that of Jesus just as "Neminem laede" differs from "Omnes juva," or as Clough puts it in his fine satirical version of the Decalogue: "Thou shalt not kill, but needst not strive officiously to keep alive." Augustine (*Confessions* I. xviii.) saw no objection to paraphrase the positive of Matthew vii. 11 into the negative *id se alteri facere quod nolit pati*. For the Old Testament commands in "thou shalt love thy neighbour as thyself" (Leviticus xix. 18) and "ye shall love the stranger" (Deut. x. 19) are positive enough, and Hillel himself elsewhere (*Aboth* i. 12), as already cited, uses a quite positive (and general) phrase when he accounts as one of the marks of the peace-loving disciples of Aaron "love for fellow creatures." It would be absurd to maintain that Philo, who also, as has been seen uses the negative form, teaches a negative morality. Similarly with Tobit. The negative rule occurs in a chapter full of positive rules of benevolence: Give alms of thy substance; Love thy brethren; Give of thy bread to the hungry, and of thy garments to them that are naked; bless the Lord thy God always—and so forth. Why should Hillel not have satisfied himself with citing the text of Leviticus xix. 18? One suggestion is given below. But a profounder answer may lie in the thought that the negative form' is the more fundamental of the two, though the positive form is the fuller expression of practical morality. Hillel was asked to summarise the Torah, and he used that form of the Golden Rule from which the Golden Rule itself is a deduction. The axiomatic truth on which the moral life of *society* is based is the right of the unimpeded use of the individual's powers, the peaceful enjoyment of the fruit of his labours, in short, the claim of each to be free from his fellow-man's injury. When we remember how great is our power of evil, how relatively small our power for good, how in Sir Thomas Browne's words, "we are beholden to every man we meet that he doth not kill us," how "the evil that men do lives after them, the good is oft interred with their bones," it is at least a tenable theory that the negative Rule goes deeper into the heart of the problem. "Do as you would be done by" is less fundamental than Hillel's maxim, just as it is less full than the Levitical law of neighbourly love, for love is greater than doing (cf. the writer's remarks in *Aspects of Judaism*, ch. VI). This criticism does not dispute, however, that the Gospel form is a splendid working principle which has wrought incalculable good to humanity. The persistence, however, of the negative after the pronouncement of the positive form, itself argues that the former is more basic.

But neither Tobit nor Philo, nor any other sources cited, do more than formulate the Golden Rule. Hillel not only formulates it, he describes it as the essence of the Torah, *Sabb.* 31 a : זו היא כל התורה כולה ("this is the whole law") and in the *Aboth d. R. Nathan, loc. cit.*: הוא כללה של תורה מה דאת סני לנרמך לחברך לא תעבד ("This is the principle, substance, of the law : what thou hatest for thyself do not to thy fellow"). This is on the same line with the famous saying of R. Simlai (third century), but it goes beyond it. Simlai said (T.B. *Makkoth* 23 b—24 a) : "Six hundred and thirteen precepts were imparted to Moses, three hundred and sixty-five negative (in correspondence with the days of the solar year) and two hundred and forty-eight positive (in correspondence with the number of a man's limbs). David came and established them (lit. *made them stand, based them,* העמידן) as eleven, as it is written (Ps. xv.) : Lord, who shall sojourn in thy tent, who shall dwell in thy holy mountain? (i) He that walketh uprightly and (ii) worketh righteousness and (iii) speaketh the truth in his heart. (iv) He that backbiteth not with his tongue, (v) nor doeth evil to his neighbour, (vi) nor taketh up a reproach against another; (vii) in whose eyes a reprobate is despised, (viii) but who honoureth them that fear the Lord. (ix) He that sweareth to his own hurt, and changeth not; (x) he that putteth not out his money to usury, (xi) nor taketh a bribe against the innocent. He that doeth these things shall never be moved. Thus David reduced the Law to *eleven* principles. Then Isaiah came and established them as *six* (xxxiii. 15) : (i) He that walketh in righteousness and (ii) speaketh uprightly; (iii) he that despiseth the gain of deceits, (iv) that shaketh his hands from holding of bribes, (v) that stoppeth his ears from hearing of blood, and (vi) shutteth his eyes from looking upon evil. Then came Micah and established them as *three* (Micah vi. 8) : What doth the Lord require of thee but (i) to do justice, (ii) to love mercy, and (iii) to walk humbly with thy God? Once more Isaiah established them as *two* (Is. lvi. 1) : Thus saith the Lord : (i) Keep ye judgement, and (ii) do righteousness. Then came Amos and established them as *one* (Amos v. 4) : Thus saith the Lord, Seek ye me and ye shall live, or (as R. Naḥman b. Isaac preferred) : Habakkuk came and made the whole Law stand on one fundamental idea (Habakkuk ii. 4) : The righteous man liveth by his faith."

Such attempts to find a basic principle for the whole of the Law

can thus be traced clearly from Hillel through Aqiba to the days
of Simlai. Simlai, it will be observed, quotes the prophets as the
authors of attempts in this direction, and it is interesting to note
(cf. Güdemann, *Nächstenliebe*, Vienna, 1890, p. 23) that while Hillel
contents himself with concluding "this is the whole Law," Jesus
(Matthew xxii. 40) adds the words "and the prophets." Naturally
there was no intention in the Pharisaic authorities who thus reduced
the Law to a few general rules, to deny the obligation to fulfil the rest
of the law. Hillel's reply to the would-be proselyte, who asked to be
taught the Law while he stood on one foot, runs : "That which
thou hatest (to be done to thyself) do not to thy fellow; this is the
whole law; the rest is commentary; go and learn it." Yet, the
person so addressed might omit to go and learn it. Hence in Jewish
theology an objection was raised to such summaries just because they
would tend to throw stress on part of the Torah to the relative
detriment of the rest. This feeling has always lain at the back of the
reluctance to formulate a Jewish creed; even the famous attempt of
Maimonides failed to effect that end. Could the legalistic spirit of an
earlier period permit a thoroughgoing distinction between important
and unimportant laws? When Aqiba and Ben Azzai spoke of
neighbourly love as the greatest fundamental law (כלל נדול) they meant
such a general or basic command from which all the other commands
could be deduced. Thus (as Güdemann rightly argues, *op. cit.* p. 21),
the Tannaitic Hebrew (כלל נדול) does not correspond to the Synoptic
Greek (μεγάλη ἐντολή). The Rabbi was not discriminating between the
importance or unimportance of laws so much as between their
fundamental or derivative character. This is probably what Jesus was
asked to do or what he did; the Greek obscures the exact sense both
of question and answer. That a Hebrew original underlies the Greek
is probable from the use of the positive : ποία ἐντολὴ μεγάλη ἐν τῷ
νόμῳ? It is more natural in Hebrew (cf. Güdemann, *op. cit.* p. 23) to
find the positive thus used as superlative (Aqiba's כלל נדול בתורה = the
greatest fundamental law in the Torah). But the passage from the one
idea to the other is easy. Easy, but not inevitable, whether by the
logic of thought or the ethics of conduct. For Pharisaism created just
that type of character to which *do these and leave not the others undone*
(Matthew xxiii. 23) admirably applies—a type which against all logic
effected a harmony between legislative punctiliousness as to detailed
rules and the prophetic appeal to great principles. The same second
century Rabbi (Ben Azzai) who said (*Aboth*, iv. 5) "Hasten to a light

precept" also maintained that the text relating the common origin of all the human kind was the fundamental text of the Torah (*Sifra* ed. Weiss, p. 89 a) and that the love of God was to be shown even unto death (*Sifre*, Deut. § 32). The Hebrew prophets, however, did discriminate between the moral importance of various sides of the religious and social life, and there may have been those who in Jesus' day desired such a discrimination, and welcomed its reiteration by Jesus.

In a sense, estimations of the varying importance attaching to precepts must have been in vogue at the beginning of the Christian era. If Matthew v. 19—20 be admitted as genuine, Jesus differentiated the precepts in this way ("one of the least of these commandments"), while exhorting obedience to all precepts alike. Philo in the context already quoted (Eusebius *P. E.* viii. 7) very distinctly occupies the same position (Gifford's translation, p. 389).

But look at other precepts besides these. Separate not parents from children, not even if they are captives; nor wife from husband, even if thou art their master by lawful purchase. These, doubtless, are very grave and important commandments; but there are others of a trifling and ordinary character. Rifle not the bird's nest under thy roof: reject not the supplication of animals which flee as it were sometimes for protection: abstain from any harm that may be even less than these. You may say that these are matters of no importance; but at all events the law which governs them is important, and is the cause of very careful observance; the warnings also are important, and the imprecations of utter destruction, and God's oversight of such matters, and his presence as an avenger in every place.

Some aspects of this problem—especially with regard to the lawfulness and even obligation to sacrifice some precept in the interests of fulfilling others—will be discussed later in the Note on the Sabbath. Here it must be enough to point out the continuity of the theory, that while the precepts could be divided between 'light' and 'heavy,' obedience to all was equally binding. While, however, Philo bases this general obligation on the punishment for disobedience, the Pharisaic tradition rested on the reward for obedience, and placed that reward in the life after this (much as in Matthew v. 19). When we reach the latter part of the second century, we find R. Jehuda Ha-nasi definitely teaching: "Be heedful of a light precept as of a grave one, for thou knowest not the grant of reward for each precept" (Aboth, ii. 1). But the very terms of the caution that one commandment is light (קלה) while another is heavy (חמורה), admit the differentiation. Rabbi Jehuda, it will be noted, asserts that *all* the commandments must be equally observed, because the reward for each is unknown.

This last clause is to be explained by the parable which is to be found in Debarim Rabba, ch. vi. and in parallel Midrashim (on the text, Deut. xxii. 7).

A King hired some labourers and sent them into his Pardes (garden, estate). At eve, he inquired as to the work of each. He summoned one. " Under which tree didst thou labour? "—" Under this."—" It is a pepper plant, the wage is a gold piece." He summoned another. " Under which tree didst thou labour? "—" Under this."—" It is a white-flowered tree (almond), the wage is half a gold piece." He summoned a third. " Under which tree didst thou labour? "—" Under this."— " It is an olive tree, the wage is two hundred zuzim." They said : " Shouldst thou not have informed us which tree would earn the greatest reward, that we might work under it? " The King answered : "Had I so informed you, how would my whole Pardes have been worked?" Thus the Holy One did not reveal the reward except of two commandments, one the weightiest of the weighty—honour of parents (Exod. xx. 12), the other the lightest of the light—letting the mother-bird go (Deut. xxii. 7) [note the parallel here with Philo], in both of which is assigned the reward, length of days.

Underlying the parable (as indeed is to some extent implied by the form of the Parable in the Tanḥuma) must have been a more primitive one in which all the labourers receive the same reward (cf. Matt. xx. 10), in accordance with the famous saying (end of T.B. Menaḥoth), that not the amount of service but its motive is the decisive quality. So, too, with regard to the very two precepts alluded to in the Parable, we have the view of R. Jacob (middle of the second century) as given in the Talmud (Qiddushin, 39 b).

R. Jacob held that the reward for the performance of the precepts is not in this world. For he taught : Whenever, side by side with a Precept written in the Torah, the reward is stated, the future life (resurrection) is concerned. Of the honour to father and mother it is written (Deut. v. 16) " that thy days may be prolonged and that it may be well with thee." Of the letting go of the mother-bird it is written " that it may be well with thee, and that thou mayest prolong thy days " (Deut. xxii. 7). Behold, a father bade his son, Ascend the tower (birah) and bring me some young birds. The son ascended, let the mother go, and took the young. In the act of descending, he fell and died. How was it well with him, and where his length of days? But the meaning is, that it may be well with thee in the world which is all good, and that thy days may be prolonged in a world whose duration is eternal.

Gradation of precepts was, nevertheless, admitted. Certain of them were described as *essential, corpora legis* (גופי תורה, Aboth end of ch. iii., Ḥagigah i. 8, see Dictionaries, s.v. גוף), others as less essential. This difference perhaps concerned rather the question as to the ease or difficulty of arriving at the Scriptural basis. Certain of these essentials related to the ritual laws committed to the (Aaronite?) Am-haareṣ (T.B. Sabbath, 32). Other views of gradation concerned the moral laws : thus in one famous enumeration (1) the most important rewardable performances were honouring parents, the exercise of loving-kindness, effecting reconciliation between man and his fellow, and the study of the Torah ; and (2) the most serious punishable offences were idolatry, incest, bloodshedding, and slander ; for the former there was reward, for the latter punishment, in this world and in the next (*Aboth de R. Nathan*, i. ch. xl., ed. Schechter, p. 120). Again, the seven " Noachide " precepts were regarded as the fundamental demands of ethics (on these see *Jewish Encyclopedia*, vol. vii. p. 648). Further, the obligation of the priest to disregard the laws of ritual purity when engaging in the burial of the dead for whose obsequies no one else was available (מת מצוה, on which see J. Mann, *loc. cit.*) ; the discussions as to the relative worth of studying the Torah and of performing the commandments ; the evaluation of the import of *fear of sin* and *wisdom* ; the supersession of the honour of parents ·by the higher law of reverencing God when the parents urged actions opposed to that reverence ; the metaphorical contrast of *root* and *branch*, meet us throughout the first and second centuries (cf. several citations in Mishnah Aboth, and Sifra on Leviticus xix.). This range of ideas reaches its culmination in the decision made by the famous assembly at Lydda after the Hadrianic persecutions of 135. What were the limits of conformity to the Roman demands? Rather than commit idolatry, murder, or incest a Jew must die ! (T.B. Sanhedrin, 74 a).

We may suppose, however, that just as there were scruples in later ages (Ḥagigah 11 b), so not everyone in the age of Jesus was willing to admit these gradations. As Güdemann writes : " If it be asked how it came about that a Scribe should need to ask the question of Jesus, it may be rejoined that the endeavour to bring Judaism within one or a few formulas would certainly not have been agreeable to the supporters of the Zealot party. They might perceive in such an endeavour a connivance towards what we should nowadays term the liberal position, and it is undeniable that every generalisation easily renders the particulars volatile. The ignorant, the Am-haareṣ, might, if he heard speak of a few fundamental rules, readily persuade himself that these alone—as Hillel and similarly after him Jesus expressed themselves—comprised the ' whole Law ' ; while the demand of Hillel to regard ' the rest ' as ' commentary ' and to ' learn it ' would be altogether ignored." The questioner of Jesus desired an opinion as to whether Jesus did or did not share this fear of reducing the Law to fundamental rules. At the same time, Jesus may well have been attaching himself to Hillel's example, while at the same time implying a moral discrimination between law and law. Yet this last point is not certain. In the Palestinian Talmud (*Berachoth* i. 8 [5]), R. Levi, a pupil of Aqiba, cites the Shema (Deut. vi. 4 *seq.*) as fundamental because the Decalogue is included within it (מפני שעשרת הדברות כלולות בהם; on the connection between the Shema and the Decalogue see Taylor, *Sayings of the Jewish Fathers*, Excursus IV.). It is noticeable (cf. Güdemann, *op. cit.* p. 22) that in Mark (xii. 29) the answer of Jesus begins with the Shema, Deut. vi. 4 (שמע ישראל), though in Matthew the verse is wrongly omitted. It does not seem that in any extant Rabbinic text, outside the *Testaments of the Twelve Patriarchs*, the Shema and the love of one's neighbour are associated, though there is mention of a passage in which this combination was effected by Ben Zoma and Ben Nanas with the strange addition that greater than any of these texts was Numb. xxviii. 4, possibly because of the atoning function of the daily sacrifices, or because of the association of God, Exod. xxv. 9 etc., with the Sanctuary, the divine dwelling place on earth (Introd. to the *En Jacob*; see Güdemann, *loc. cit.*, Theodor, *Genesis Rabba*, p. 237). In the Nash Papyrus the Decalogue is followed by the Shema; the two passages indeed stand close together (the Decalogue in Deut. v. 6—18, the Shema in vi. 4—9). The Didache (ch. i.) associates the combination as found in the Synoptics also with the negative form of the Golden Rule: "There are two ways, one of life and one of death, and there is much difference between the two ways. Now the way of life is this: First, thou shalt love God that made thee; secondly thy neighbour as thyself; and all things whatsoever thou wouldest should not happen to thee, neither do thou to another." The Decalogue follows. The Jewish provenance of this passage is indisputable. Taylor (*Teaching of the Twelve Apostles*) suggests that the negative rule grew out of the Decalogue, with its many *do nots*. What is the general principle of the things not to do to one's neighbour? Answer: "What-to-thyself is-hateful" (the דעלך סני of Hillel). Hence its description by Hillel as the sum total of the Law. One further point only calls for remark here. It is quite natural that simplifications or systematisations of the Law would be most required for proselytising propaganda. It would be necessary to present Judaism in as concise a form as possible for such purposes. Hence it is not surprising on the one hand that it is to a would-be proselyte that Hillel's summary as well as a similar citation of the principle by Aqiba

(*Aboth de R. Nathan*, ed. Schechter, p. 53) is addressed and on the other that we find it in the *Didache* and in connection with the doctrine of the two ways. Nor is it without significance that Philo's citation of the negative rule occurs in a passage in which he is selecting just those elements of the Jewish Law which were worthy of commendation and acceptance by the Greek world. (Cf. on these and several other matters the interesting work of G. Klein, *Der Aelteste Christliche Katechismus und die Jüdische Propaganda-Literatur*, Berlin, 1909, p. 85, and K. Kohler in *Judaica*, Berlin, 1912, pp. 469 seq. The latter points to the old Jewish Didaskalia, in his view enshrining the ethics of the Essenes.)

III. JOHN THE BAPTIST.

The Rabbinic literature contains no reference to John the Baptist. There is, however, an interesting passage on the subject in Josephus (*Antiquities*, XVIII., v. § 2). Some doubt has been thrown on the authenticity of this passage, but the suspicion has no firm basis.

Josephus gives a favourable account of John and his work. This is *à priori* what we should expect, for John has decidedly Essenic leanings and the Essenes were favourites with the Jewish historian. John, says Josephus, was "a good man who exhorted the Jews to exercise virtue (ἀρετή), both as to justice (δικαιοσύνη) towards one another and piety (εὐσέβεια) towards God, and to come to baptism (βαπτισμῷ συνιέναι). For baptism (τὴν βάπτισιν) would be acceptable to God thus (οὕτω), if they used it, not for the pardon of certain sins, but for the purification of the body, provided that the soul had been thoroughly purified beforehand by righteousness" (μὴ ἐπὶ τινῶν ἁμαρτάδων παραιτήσει χρωμένων, ἀλλ᾽ ἐφ᾽ ἁγνείᾳ τοῦ σώματος, ἅτε δὴ καὶ τῆς ψυχῆς δικαιοσύνῃ προεκκεκαθαρμένης). People, continues Josephus, flocked to him in crowds, were stirred by his addresses, and seemed willing to follow him in all things. Herod Antipas, fearing a popular rising, seized John, sent him in chains to Machaerus, and had him put to death there. When Herod's army suffered a reverse, the people attributed the king's misfortune to God's displeasure at the ill-treatment of John.

Both the recent editors of Josephus (Niese and Naber) admit this passage without question. There is a natural reluctance on the part of cautious scholars to pronounce unreservedly in its favour, mainly because of the fact that elsewhere the text of Josephus has been tampered with in a similar context. Thus Schürer (I³. 438), after presenting a forcible though incomplete argument in favour of the passage, adds: "Since, however, Josephus in other places was certainly subjected to interpolation by a Christian hand, one must not here place too absolute a reliance on the authenticity of the text." On the Jewish side, though his leanings are in favour of the authenticity, S. Krauss (*Das Leben Jesu nach jüdischen Quellen*, Berlin, 1902, p. 257) remarks: "The question as to the genuineness of the John-passage has not yet been decisively settled; the passage is anyhow open to suspicion." But, on the whole, the authenticity of the reference is accepted by scholars, Jewish and Christian. Thus to cite only two instances, H. St J. Thackeray (*Dictionary of the Bible*, Extra Volume, p. 471) passes judgment in these words: "There is no reason why it should not be accepted as genuine"; and K. Kohler (*Jewish Encyclopedia* VII. p. 218) does not even mention the controversy, but uses the passage without any question. The passage in Josephus referring to John the Baptist rests, of course, on a different footing to the "testimony to Christ" (Josephus, *Antiq.* XVIII. iii. § 3). The authenticity of the latter has been recently maintained with much plausibility by Profs. F. C. Burkitt (*Theologisch Tijdschrift*, 1913, xlvii. pp. 135–144), A. Harnack (*Internationale Monatsschrift*, June, 1913, pp. 1038–1067), and W. E. Barnes (*Companion to Biblical Studies*, 1916, p. 34). But it remains very difficult to accept Josephus' "testimony to Christ" as genuine, at all events as it stands; the reference to John the Baptist may well be so.

It seems to me that a Christian interpolator must have brought that passage into closer accord with the Gospels. I do not refer merely to such differences as the motive assigned for putting John to death. Josephus assigns fear of political unrest; the Gospels, the personal animosity of Herodias. But, as Schürer is careful to point out, these motives are not absolutely incompatible. Much more significant is the silence of Josephus as to any connection between John and Jesus. This, of itself, is almost enough to authenticate the passage. Gerlach has called attention to this fact in his book *Die Weissagungen des Alten Testaments in den Schriften des Flavius Josephus* (Berlin, 1863, p. 113) and Origen had long ago done the same thing. Origen (*c. Celsum* I. xlviii.) says: "The Jews do not associate John with Jesus." Gerlach misuses this statement, for Origen is not making an independent assertion, but (as the context shows, cf. *op. cit.* xlvii.) is basing his generalisation on the passage in Josephus. Origen, by the way, who cites this passage, has no knowledge of the supposed "testimony to Christ" (see, however, Burkitt, as already cited); the two passages stand, as said above, on quite different footings. That Jews other than Josephus may have taken a favourable view

of John's work is indicated also by several passages in the Gospels.
Luke, it is true, asserts (vii. 30) that the Pharisees and the lawyers
(scribes) rejected John, and refused to accept his baptism.   But
this is in opposition to the statement of Matthew (iii. 7): "[John]
saw many of the Pharisees and Sadducees coming to his baptism,"
and Mark (i. 5) implies no Jewish opposition to his call to baptism.
Moreover, all three Synoptics (Mark ii. 18; Matthew ix. 14; Luke
v. 33) represent the disciples of John as associated with the
Pharisees in fasting.   Thus just as Josephus assures us that the
Pharisees were not opponents of the Essenes (as they were of the
Sadducees) so there was no violent division between John and the
Pharisees; the assumption that the Jews rejected John belongs to
the later conception (whether originating with John himself or not)
that John was the forerunner of Jesus.   That John's own disciples
did not accept this conception is thus asserted by Prof. Adeney
(*The Century Bible*, St Luke, p. 185): "These [the disciples of John]
then hold together and keep up their customs after their master has
been removed from them, and in spite of the appearance of the new
Prophet, thus declining to follow John's own teaching in pointing on
to Christ. We meet such later at Ephesus (see Acts xviii. 25, xix. 3)."
Cf. also the remarks of Prof. Lake, *The Earliest Epistles of St Paul*,
1911, pp. 108, etc.

Still more important is another point to which Gerlach called
attention, and to which Naber has more recently again referred.
There is a real difference between the nature of John's baptism as
described by Josephus and the Gospels.   Mark (i. 4) introduces John
as proclaiming a "baptism of repentance for remission of sins" ($\beta \acute{a}\pi\tau\iota\sigma\mu a$
$\mu\epsilon\tau a\nu o\acute{\iota}a\varsigma$ $\epsilon\grave{\iota}\varsigma$ $\check{a}\phi\epsilon\sigma\iota\nu$ $\acute{a}\mu a\rho\tau\iota\hat{\omega}\nu$).   But in Josephus this significance of baptism is specifically dissociated from John. Not only is this deliberate,
it is clearly controversial. As Naber argues (*Mnemosyne* XIII. 281), it
is scarcely credible that Josephus was ignorant of the Christian baptism
which *was* "for the remission of sins." Naber suggests, then, that in
the passage in which Josephus refers to Jesus, the historian cited the
Christian baptism with expressions of disapproval, and as this was
displeasing to Christian readers, the passage was altered. On the
other hand the John passage was left standing, and the controversial
$\mu\grave{\eta}$ $\grave{\epsilon}\pi\grave{\iota}$ $\tau\iota\nu\hat{\omega}\nu$ $\acute{a}\mu a\rho\tau\acute{a}\delta\omega\nu$ $\pi a\rho a\iota\tau\acute{\eta}\sigma\epsilon\iota$ $\chi\rho\omega\mu\acute{\epsilon}\nu\omega\nu$ remained.   If this be so,
it may well be that Josephus really has preserved for us the exact
nature of John's baptism. But before saying a word on that, it is
necessary to turn to a question of language.

In his first editions Graetz accepted Josephus' account of John as authentic. But in his later editions of the *Geschichte der Juden* he strongly contends that the passage is spurious. He urges that Josephus would not have described John as the "Baptist" (τοῦ ἐπι-καλουμένου βαπτιστοῦ) without further explanation. Graetz does not see that it is possible to regard these three words as an interpolation in a passage otherwise authentic. But it is not necessary to make this supposition. For it is quite in Josephus' manner to use designa-tions for which he offers no explanation (cf. e.g. the term "Essene"). And the meaning of "Baptist" is fully explained in the following sentence, Josephus using the nouns βάπτισις and βαπτισμός to describe John's activity. The terminology of Josephus, I would urge, makes it quite unlikely that the passage is an interpolation. For, it will be noted (a) Josephus does not use βάπτισμα which is the usual N.T. form; (b) he does use the form βάπτισις which is unknown to the N.T.; (c) he uses βαπτισμός in a way quite unlike the use of the word when it does occur in Mark (vii. 4) or even in Hebrews (ix. 10). It is in fact Josephus alone who applies the word βαπτισμός to John's baptism. Except then that Josephus used the epithet βαπτιστής (which may be interpolated) his terminology is quite independent of N.T. usage. It is true that Josephus uses the common LXX. word λούω when describing the lustrations of the Essenes, but the verb βαπτίζω was quite familiar to Jewish writers. It is rare in LXX. but is curiously enough found precisely where bathing in the Jordan is referred to, in the significant passage 2 Kings v. 14: "Then went he down and dipped himself (ἐβαπτίσατο) seven times in Jordan[1]." Significant, too, is the fact that Aquila, who translated under Aqiba's influence, uses βαπτίζω where the LXX. uses βάπτω (Job ix. 31; Psalm lviii. 3). In the latter place the verb is also used by Symmachus, who further introduces it into Jer. (xxxviii. 22). To Josephus himself the verb was so familiar that he even makes a metaphorical use of it. In describing the masses of people "flocking into the city" he says ἐβάπτισαν τὴν πόλιν.

Another point on which a few words are necessary is John's relation

---

[1] Cheyne, *Encycl. Biblica* col. 2499, represents John the Baptist "who was no formalist" as using the Jordan in spite of the Rabbinic opinion that "the waters of the Jordan were not pure enough for sacred uses." But the Jordan water was only held insufficiently clean for one specific purpose: the ceremony of the Red Heifer (Parah viii. 9). No Rabbi ever dreamed of pronouncing the Jordan unfit for the rite of baptism.

to the Essenes. That Josephus means to identify him with that sect
is clear. For the very words he uses of John are the terms of entry
to the Essenic confraternity. In *Wars* II. viii. § 7 Josephus reports:
"If he then appears to be worthy, they then [after long probation]
admit him into their society. And before he is allowed to touch
their common food, he is obliged to take tremendous oaths, in the first
place that he will exercise piety towards God, and next that he will
observe justice towards men " (πρῶτον μὲν εὐσεβήσειν τὸ θεῖον, ἔπειτα τὰ
πρὸς ἀνθρώπους δίκαια διαφυλάξειν). The other terms used of John by
Josephus (ἀρετή, ἁγνεία) are also used by him of the Essenes. The
Gospels attribute to John Essenic characteristics. The account of
John in Mark i. is more than merely illustrated by what Josephus
says in his Life § ii.: "When I was informed that a certain Bannos
lived in the desert, who used no other clothing than grew on trees, and
had no other food than what grew of its own accord, and bathed
himself in cold water frequently, both by day and by night, in order
to preserve purity (πρὸς ἁγνείαν), I became a follower of his." John's
asceticism is not identical with this, but it belongs to the same order.
It is quite untenable to attempt, as many are now tending to do,
to dissociate John altogether from Essenism. Graetz seems right in
holding that John made a wider appeal than the Essenes did by re-
laxing some of the Essenian stringency: their communism, their
residence in separate colonies, their rigid asceticism. John, like another
Elijah, takes up the prophetic rôle. He calls to the Jews to repent,
in expectation of the Messianic judgment perhaps. Pharisaic eschatology, in one of its tendencies, which rising in the first century became
dominant in the third, connects the Messianic age with repentance.
There is, however, this difference. The formula of John (or Jesus)
was: Repent *for* the Kingdom is at hand. The Pharisaic formula
was: Repent *and* the Kingdom is at hand. Pharisaic eschatology did
not, however, ally this formula to the baptismal rite. John associates
his prophetic call with baptism, partly no doubt in relation to the metaphorical use of the rite in many parts of the O.T., but partly also
in direct relation to the Essenic practices. He treats baptism as a
bodily purification corresponding to an inward change, not as a means
of remitting sins. Cheyne, who takes a different view as to the
Essenic connection of John, expresses the truth, I think, when he
writes as follows (*Encyclopaedia Biblica*, col. 2499): "He led them
[his followers] to the Jordan, there to give them as representatives of
a regenerate people the final purification which attested the reality of

their inward change." Then he adds in a note: "No other exegesis
seems reasonable; Josephus, as we have seen, sanctions it. The true
baptism is spiritual (Psalm li. 7 [9]). But it needs an outward symbol,
and Johanan [John], remembering Ezekiel xxxvi. 25, and having
prophetic authority, called those who would know themselves to be
purified to baptism. It is no doubt true that baptism was regularly
required of Gentile proselytes, but Johanan's baptism had no connection with ceremonial uncleanness." It is interesting to note the
use made in Pharisaic circles of this same text in Ezekiel. "Said
R. Aqiba [end of first and beginning of second century A.D.]: Happy
are ye, O Israel! Before whom do you cleanse yourselves? Who
cleanseth you? Your Father who is in Heaven! As it is written,
And I will sprinkle clean water upon you and ye shall be clean."

On the question of Baptism in general see next Note. On John's
references to the Pharisees see note on Pharisees. John we are told
in a difficult passage (Matt. xi. 13; Luke xvi. 16) was the end of the
Law and the Prophets. He certainly was faithful to the Law and a
worthy upholder of the olden Prophetic spirit. But except in the
sense that, in the Christian view, he was the last to prophesy the
Kingdom in the spirit of the Law and the Prophets, John was the end
of neither. When John died the 'Law' was only in the first stages
of its Rabbinical development. And from that day to this there have
never been lacking in the Jewish fold men who, in accord with the
Prophetic spirit, have made a direct appeal to the hearts of their
brethren on behalf of repentance and inward virtue.

IV. PHARISAIC BAPTISM.

Unnecessary doubt has been thrown on the prevalence of baptism as an initiatory rite in the reception of proselytes during Temple times. Schürer, while exaggerating the number of ablutions prescribed by Pharisaic Judaism, rightly insists (III². 131) that both *à priori*, and from the implications of the Mishnah (*Pesaḥim*, viii. 8), proselytes must have been baptised in the time of Jesus. The heathen was in a state of uncleanness and must, at least as emphatically as the Jew in a similar state, have undergone the ritual of bathing. Only in a state of ritual cleanness could the new-comer be received "under the Wings of the Divine Presence"—a common Rabbinic phrase for prose- lytism (e.g. T.B. *Yebamoth*, 46 b) directly derived from the beautiful terms of Boaz' greeting to Ruth, the ideal type of all sincere proselytes: "The Lord recompense thy work, and a full reward be given thee of the Lord God of Israel, under whose wings thou art come to trust." So, too, Jesus, after his baptism, sees the spirit of God descending as a dove. The symbolism of the Holy Spirit by a dove is a notion found in Rabbinic books (see below note on "the Dove and the Voice"). But I think it is more fully explained when it is brought into con- nection with the figure that the proselyte comes under the Wings of the Divine Presence. Thus the fact that, in the Gospels, baptism precedes the metaphorical reference to the bird, strengthens the argument in favour of the early prevalence of the baptism of proselytes.

Yet it can hardly be said that the evidence so far adduced *proves* the case. Schürer (*loc. cit.*) and Edersheim (II. Appendix XII.) think that the Mishnah (cited above) does establish the point. But Dr Plummer, while conceding that "the fact is not really doubtful," asserts that "direct evidence is not forthcoming" (Hastings, *Dictionary of the Bible*, I. 239). The Mishnah cited (to which *Eduyoth*, v. 2 is parallel) de- scribes a difference of view between the schools of Hillel and Shammai. If a man has "been made a proselyte" on the fourteenth of Nisan and has then been baptised, (must he wait seven days before he is regarded as "clean" or) may he eat the Paschal lamb the same evening? (The suggestion of Bengel, *Ueber das Alter der jud. Proselyten-taufe*, p. 90, that the bath was not a proselyte-bath is groundless.) This Mishnah certainly implies that the baptism of proselytes occurred while the Paschal lamb was still being offered, i.e. during Temple times. But the passage does not quite prove this, for it is just possible that the discussion is merely scholastic. On turning, however, as neither Schürer nor Edersheim has done, to the Jerusalem Talmud and the Tosefta, it becomes certain that we are dealing with historical fact and not with dialectics. (See T.J. *Pesaḥim*, viii. last lines; Tosefta, *Pesaḥim*, vii. 13, ed. Zuckermandel, p. 167.) "Rabbi Eleazar ben Jacob says: Soldiers were Guards of the Gates in Jerusalem; they were baptised and ate their Paschal lambs in the evening." Here we have an actual record of the conversion of Roman soldiers to Judaism on the day before the Passover (an altogether probable occasion for such a step), and of their reception by means of baptism. This Eleazar ben Jacob the Elder is one of the most trustworthy reporters of Temple events and rites, which he knew from personal experience. (Cf. Bacher, *Die Agada der Tannaiten*, 1^2. p. 63.) "The Mishnah of R. Eleazar is a small measure, but it contains fine flour" (T.B. *Yebamoth*, 49 b) was the traditional estimate of the value of this Rabbi's traditions. The exact date of this incident cannot be fixed. Graetz places it in the year 67 A.D. If that be so, then we are still without direct evidence that proselytes were baptised half a century earlier. But the probability is greatly increased by this historical record.

It is noteworthy that, according to Bacher's reading of this account, baptism without previous circumcision seems sufficient to qualify the heathen proselyte to eat the Paschal lamb. This is directly opposed to the Law (Exodus xii. 48). Later on there was indeed found an advocate for the view that baptism was sufficient (without circumcision) to constitute a proselyte (T.B. *Yebamoth*, 46 a). But it seems more reasonable to suppose that R. Eleazar ben Jacob takes it for granted that the Roman soldiers were circumcised before baptism. In the corresponding Mishnah, and in the whole context in the Tosefta, this is certainly presupposed. The predominant and almost universal view was that in Temple times three rites accompanied the reception of proselytes: circumcision, baptism, and sacrifice (T.B. *Kerithoth*, 81 a). After the fall of the Temple the first two of these three rites were necessary (*ibid.* 9 b). In the case of women, when sacrifices could not any longer be brought, the sole initiatory rite was baptism. It may be that as women were of old, as now, the more numerous proselytes, baptism came to be thought by outside observers as the only rite in all cases. Thus Arrian, in the second century, names baptism as the one sufficing ceremony which completely turns a heathen into a Jew (*Dissert. Epictet.* II. 9).

The baptism by John resembles the baptism of proselytes in several points, among others in the fact that both forms of baptism are *administered*, not performed by the subject himself. At all events, the proselyte's bath needed witnessing.

In Mark i. 9 the repentant are baptized ὑπὸ 'Ιωάννου. But in Luke iii. 7, where the ordinary text (and Westcott and Hort) has βαπτισθῆναι ὑπ' αὐτοῦ, the Western text has βαπτισθῆναι ἐνώπιον αὐτοῦ (probably as Prof. Burkitt has suggested to me = קדמוהי). In the Pharisaic baptism of proselytes, at all events, the presence of others was entirely due to the necessity of witnessing (*Yebamoth*, 47 a). Sometimes a causative form, sometimes the *kal* form, of the verb *ṭabal* is used in the Rabbinic texts; but in the case of male proselytes there seems to have been no act on the part of the witnesses. In the case of women, the witnesses (three *dayanim*) stood outside, and other women "caused her to sit down" (i.e. supported her) in the bath up to her neck. The male proselyte stood, with the water up to his waist (*Yebamoth*, 46–48; *Gerim*, ch. i.). In all cases, the bathing was most probably by total immersion (for the evidence see the writer's article in the *Journal of Theological Studies*, XII. 609, with the interesting contributions by the Rev. C. F. Rogers in the same periodical, XII. 437, XIII. 411). Total immersion is clearly implied by the Zadokite Fragment (edited by Schechter, 1910, ch. xii.). If that fragment be a genuine document of the second century B.C., its evidence for the total immersion of the priests is of great weight. In the Talmud the bath in such a case had to be at least of the dimensions 1 × 1 × 3 cubits, sufficient for total immersion (שכל נופו עולה בהם, *Erubin*, 46). The bathing of the *niddah* (menstrual woman) was by total immersion, and we have the definite statement of a baraitha (*Yebamoth*, 47 b) that the rules for the bathing of proselytes (male and female) were the same as for the *niddah*. In only one case of baptism did the bystander participate actively. On entering Jewish service, a heathen slave was baptised. If he claimed that such baptism was for complete proselytism (לשם נירות) he became free. But in order to make it clear that the baptism was not for this purpose, the owner

of the slave was required to seize hold of him while in the water
(לתקפו במים‎), as a clear indication that the baptism was not a complete
proselytism (*Yebamoth*, 46 a). Obviously in cases of proselytes the
baptism would be the perfectly free, unfettered and unaided act of
the proselyte himself.

But there is, it is often said, this difference between Johannine
and Pharisaic baptism : the former was a moral, the latter a physical
purification. Josephus, it has been shown, hardly regarded this contrast as essential. Nor, in the case of the proselyte-bath, can it be
doubted that the two ideas are welded together. In the older Rabbinical literature we do not, it is true, find any specific reference to
a baptism of repentance. The phrase first meets us in the Middle
Ages. A thirteenth century authority for the first time distinctly
speaks of the man who bathes for penitence' sake (טובל לשם תשובה‎),
and of bathing in general, as an essential of repentance (שכל השבים‎
חייבים בטבילה‎). See *Shibbole Halleket*, § 93 (ed. Venice, fol. 41 a).
Apparently this rule that "all penitents are baptised" is traced to a
passage in the *Aboth de R. Nathan* (see the *Tanya*, § 72 ; ed. Venice,
p. 102 b). But though the passage in the *Aboth* (ch. viii.) does not
easily bear this implication (the text as we have it is certainly corrupt),
we can carry the evidence five hundred years further back than the
thirteenth century. In the Palestinian Midrash *Pirke de R. Eleazar*,
compiled about 830, Adam's repentance after expulsion from Eden
consists of bathing, fasting and confession (*op. cit.* ch. xx.). Older
still is the passage in the Apocryphal (and not obviously Christian)
Life of Adam and Eve, which represents the repentant Adam as
standing for forty days in the Jordan (Kautzsch, *Pseudepigraphen
zum Alten Testament*, p. 512 ; Charles, *Apocrypha and Pseudepigrapha
of the Old Testament*, Oxford, 1913, p. 134).

Earlier still is (probably) the famous passage in the fourth Sibylline
Oracle (iv. 165 seq.) which, even in its present form, must belong to
the first Christian century (c. 80 A.D.). In iii. 592 there is a reference
to the morning lustrations (cf. the *morning bathers* of T.B. *Berachoth*,
22 a. On this and other allied points see S. Krauss, *Talmudische
Archäologie*, Leipzig, 1910–1912, I. pp. 211, 217, 229, 669; II. p. 100;
III. p. 360). But in iv. 165 there is a direct association of repentance
with bathing. I quote Terry's rendering with some emendations :

> Ah! miserable mortals, change these things,
> Nor lead the mighty God to wrath extreme;
> But giving up your swords and pointed knives,

And homicides and wanton violence,
Wash your whole body in perennial streams,
And lifting up your hands to heaven seek pardon
For former deeds and expiate with praise
Bitter impiety; and God will give
Repentance; he will not destroy; and wrath
Will he again restrain, if in your hearts
Ye all will practise precious godliness.

This, it will be noted, is an appeal to the heathen world. It falls well within the range of the Jewish Hellenistic literature, and there is no necessity for assuming a Christian authorship.

Water was a *symbol* of repentance still earlier. The Targum to 1 Samuel vii. 6 (cf. Midrash, *Samuel* and *Yalkut*, ad loc., and T.J. *Taanith*, ii. § 7) explains the action of Israel at Mizpah in that sense. The text does indeed associate in a remarkable way a water-rite (of which nothing else is known), fasting, and confession as elements in repentance: "And they gathered together to Mizpah, and drew water and poured it out before the Lord, and fasted on that day, and said there, We have sinned against the Lord." Ascetic rites (such as fasting) were ancient accompaniments of the confession of sin, as in the ritual of the day of Atonement; and the association of asceticism with cold bathing is at least as old in Judaism as the Essenes. In the *Didache* fasting precedes baptism (vii. 4), but it is not clear how early the Synagogue introduced the now wide-spread custom of bathing on the Eve of the Day of Atonement in connection with the confession of sins. Talmudic is the rule "A man is bound to purify himself at the festivals" (T.B. *Rosh Hashana*, 16 b), no doubt with reference to ceremonial uncleanness. But Leviticus (xvi. 30) lays it down: "From all your sins before the Lord ye shall be clean" on the Day of Atonement, and the same word (טהור) which here means spiritually clean also signifies physically and ritually clean. "Wash you, make you clean, put away the evil of your doings" (Isaiah i. 16) is one characteristic text of many in which the prophets make play with the metaphor. The Sibylline call to actual baptism of the sinning Greek world is obviously based on this very passage. Another passage, to which great importance was justly attached in Rabbinical thought, is Ezekiel xxxvi. 25—27: "I will sprinkle pure water upon you, and ye shall be clean; from all your filthiness and from all your idols will I cleanse you. A new heart also will I give you, and a new spirit will I put within you; and I will take away the stony heart out of your flesh, and I will give you an heart of flesh. And

I will put my spirit within you, and cause you to walk in my
statutes, and ye shall keep my judgments and do them." Here we
have, together, all the main ideas of Pharisaic baptism; and it is
noteworthy that this passage from Ezekiel is extensively used in
Rabbinic homilies.

Such passages as these attest the early association between physical
and moral purification, such as meets us in the Johannine baptism.
And the ideas are close. Whoever invented the epigram "Cleanliness
is next to Godliness," it is a fair summary of Pharisaic conceptions on
the subject under discussion. Throughout the *Psalms of Solomon* "to
be clean" is identical with "to be forgiven." In Rabbinic Hebrew,
as in Biblical, the same word means physically and spiritually clean.
To "repent" is to "be purified." (Cf. the הבא ליטהר of T.B. *Yoma*,
38 b, and the phrase "before whom do you cleanse yourselves?" i.e.
repent of your sins, of the previous Note.) Sin is, conversely, uncleanness. There is no need to quote Biblical instances of the use.
In Rabbinic Hebrew the very strong word (סרח) which literally means
"to be putrid" is a common term for "to sin." A very remarkable
figure of speech is attributed to Hillel. He bathed his body to keep
clean that which was made in the image of God (*Levit. Rabba*, xxxv.).
The connection between sin and atonement by bathing is brought out
in the Midrash on Ps. li. 4 on the text, "Wash me thoroughly from
mine iniquity." The Midrash comments: "Hence, whoever commits a
transgression is as though he was defiled by contact with a dead body,"
and he needs sprinkling with hyssop. Here the reference is clearly to
moral not to ritual transgression. In 2 Kings v. 14 we are told of
Naaman that after his leprosy was healed "his flesh came again like
the flesh of a little child"; and so the proselyte on his baptism
"became like a little child" (T.B. *Yebamoth*, 22 a, 48 b). On the
text "Be thou a blessing" (Gen. xii. 2) the Midrash (playing on
the similar words ברכה "blessing" and בריכה "pool") comments:
"As yonder pool purifies the unclean, so thou bringest near the far
off and purifiest them to their Father in Heaven" (*Genesis Rabba*,
xxxix. § 11). And those thus brought near are created anew. "He
who makes a proselyte is as though he created him" (*ibid.* § 14)—
thus conversion is a re-birth. In this sense the lustrations of Exodus
xix. 10 were regarded as physical accompaniments of the approaching
revelation on Sinai, when all the world was made anew. Man's repentance is the cause, too, of the creation of the new heavens and the
new earth of Isaiah lxvi. (*Yalkut*, Isaiah, § 372). There are shades

of difference in this idea of renewal, especially as concerns the nature of man. John's baptism seems to have this point in common with the Pharisaic baptism of proselytes—it was a baptism once for all. For the proselyte had, in the Pharisaic view, adopted Judaism completely; and, like one born physically a Jew, he could not thereafter evade the responsibilities of the religion which he had freely accepted, just as he shared its hopes. Benedictions usually *preceded* the performance of precepts. Not so with the ṭebilah, baptism, of the proselyte. It was only as he ascended from the bath that he said: "Blessed art thou who hast sanctified us by thy commandment and commanded us concerning ṭebilah" (T.B. Pesaḥim 6 b). It may well be, as Bousset states (*Die Religion des Judenthums im neutestamentliche Zeitalter* ed. 2, 1906, p. 230) that there was nothing sacramental in Pharisaic baptism. But, like the performance of the whole Law, it was a consecration.

Pharisaic baptism, then, agreed with what seems to have been the primitive Christian view that it was once for all, though in the case of a revert, and of a slave seeking freedom, ṭebilah would be again necessary. Ṭebilah, however, did not ensure sinlessness, or the abrogation of the power to sin. That consummation was reserved for the Messianic age. If, however, Christian baptism was the introduction to the Kingdom, then no doubt baptism would carry with it the hope of sinlessness. (On the problem of sin after Christian baptism, and the apparent reversion to the Jewish theory of repentance, see Prof. K. Lake, *The Stewardship of Faith*, London, 1915, p. 181). John seems to imply also that the consequent change of mind ($\mu\epsilon\tau\acute{a}\nu\text{o}\iota a$) was also "once for all." In the Rabbinic theology such a permanent amelioration of the human character was not possible, at least in the earthly life. Men might move the stone from the mouth of the well, but it had to be replaced, and the "evil inclination" (*Yeṣer hara*) returned to where it had been and needed expulsion again and again (*Genesis Rabba*, lxx. § 8). God will in the end destroy the evil Yeṣer, but in human life the struggle is incessant and the Yeṣer leads to sin daily (T.B. *Qiddushin*, 30 b). "In this world," says God to Israel, "ye become clean and again unclean; but in the time to come I will purify you that ye never again become unclean" (Midrash, *Tanḥuma*, Meṣora, §§ 17—18). Contrariwise (as perhaps John's baptism intends), repentance brings the Messiah near (T.B. *Yoma*, 86 a, b. Cf. Montefiore, *Jewish Quarterly Review*, xvi. p. 236 and references there given). The renewal of man's nature by repentance, unlike the re-birth by conversion, is continuous and constant. It is a regular process, not a catastrophe. Israel is compared to the Angelic hosts. "As they are renewed day by day, and return, after they have praised God, to the fire from which they issued, so too the Israelites, if their evil passions ensnare them in sin, and they repent, are forgiven by God year by year and granted a new heart with which to fear him" (Midrash, *Rabba*, Shemoth xv. § 6; *Echa* on v. 5).

In Ezekiel's phrase, God sprinkles pure water on Israel and puts His spirit within him. By the middle of the second century the "last of the Essenes," Phineas ben Jair, treats "purification" as what Dr Schechter well calls "one of the higher rungs of the ladder leading to the attainment of the holy spirit" (*Studies in Judaism* II. p. 110). But the connection between water and the Holy Spirit can be traced much closer than this. In the Hebrew Bible the word "to pour out" (שָׁפַךְ), properly applicable only to liquids, is applied to the Divine Spirit. "In those days I will pour out my spirit on all flesh" (Joel iii. 1 [ii. 28]; cf. Ezekiel xxxix. 29). In Rabbinic Hebrew the word which means "to draw" liquids (שָׁאַב) is often used of drawing the holy spirit. In Isaiah xii. 3 we have the beautiful image: "With joy shall ye draw water from the wells of salvation." With all of this compare *Genesis Rabba*, lxx. § 8 (on Genesis xxix. 2 seq.). "*Behold there was a well in the field*: that is Zion; *lo there were three flocks of sheep*: these are the three pilgrim feasts; *from out of that well they drew water*: from thence they drew the holy spirit." Similarly the "Place of the Water-drawing," referred to above in Note I., is explained as the place whence "they drew the holy spirit" (T.J. *Sukkah*, v. § 1).

There is no ground then for the emphatic statement of Dr S. Krauss (*Jewish Encyclopedia*, II. 499) that "The only conception of Baptism at variance with Jewish ideas is displayed in the declaration of John that the one who would come after him would not baptise with water but with the Holy Ghost." The idea must have seemed quite natural to Jewish ears, as is evident from the parallels quoted above. It must be understood that some of these parallels (especially the last, which is not older than the third century) are cited not as giving the origin of the phrase in the Gospels, but as illustrating it. Such illustrations may be used irrespective of their date in order to discriminate from specifically un-Jewish ideas, those ideas which are found in the New Testament, and are found again in Jewish circles later on. It is important to know the ideas that recur. And, of course, the parallels may often be older than the first citation in which they are now to be found. On the other hand, some borrowing from the Gospels must not be dismissed as impossible or unlikely. An idea once set in circulation would become general property, and if it fitted in with other Jewish ideas might find a ready hospitality. It is well to make this plain, though I do not for a moment think that in baptism we have a case in point. The Rabbis have no hesitation in saying that prayer replaced sacrifice, but they never hint at the thought that baptism replaced the proselyte's sacrifice, as some writers suggest. My main contention is that the recurrence or non-recurrence of New Testament ideas and expressions is the surest test we have of their essential Jewishness or non-Jewishness. The test is not perfect, for parallels are occasionally missing to very Judaic ideas, and on the other hand alien ideas did occasionally creep into the theology of Judaism inadvertently. Often again, the usages and ideas of the New Testament stand *between* Old Testament usages and later Rabbinic; in such cases they are valuable links in the chain. This is emphatically the case with the New Testament references to Synagogue customs.

A good instance is also the metaphor of baptism with fire which, though absent from Mark, occurs in both Matthew and Luke. Fire in the Old Testament is not only capable of being "poured out" like water, but its capacity in this respect becomes the basis of a second derived metaphor: "He hath poured out his fury like fire" (Lamentations ii. 4). Fire is the natural element for purging, and is frequently used in the Old Testament in the two senses of punishing and refining. In the phrase "baptism by fire" we have thus two Old Testament ideas combined; fire is poured out, and it is used as a purifying and punitive agent. Some see in the baptism by fire an allusion to illumination. The light of day was removed by Adam's sin and restored on his repentance (*Genesis Rabba*, xi. ; T.B. *Aboda Zara*, 8 a). The illuminative power of repentance is already found in Philo (Cohn and Wendland, § 179): "From the deepest darkness the repentant behold the most brilliant light." In the Testament of Gad (v. 7, ed. Charles, p. 154) we read: "For true repentance after a godly sort driveth away the darkness and enlighteneth the eyes." The same illuminating function is (on the basis of Psalm xix. 8) often ascribed, of course, to the Law, which further (with reference to Deut. xxxiii. 2) is also typified by fire. But the context in which baptism by fire occurs in the Gospels precludes all thought of fire as an illuminant. In the Sibylline passage quoted above, the gracious promise of pardon after true repentance on immersion in water has a harsher sequel. If there be no repentance with baptism, there shall be destruction by fire. For the Oracle continues (iv. 70):

> But if, ill-disposed, ye obey me not,
> But with a fondness for strange lack of sense
> Receive all these things with an evil ear,
> There shall be over all the world a fire
> And greatest omen with sword and with trump
> At sunrise; the whole world shall hear the roar
> And mighty sound. And he shall burn all earth,
> And destroy the whole race of men, and all
> The cities and the rivers and the sea;
> All things he'll burn, and it shall be black dust.

Fiery baptism is a purging process, and in Luke (iii. 17) is associated with the winnowing fan ("but the chaff he will burn"). The context is equally clear in Matthew (iii. 12). This is a frequent Old Testament usage. The idea is carried out most fully in a saying of Abbahu (end of third century). Schöttgen has already cited this parallel from T.B. *Sanhedrin*, 39 a. Abbahu explains that when God buried Moses, he bathed himself in fire, as it is written: "For behold the Lord will come with fire" (Isaiah lxvi. 15). Abbahu goes on to say, "By fire is the essential baptism," and he quotes: "All that abideth not the fire ye shall make to go through the water" (Num. xxxi. 23). Thus baptism by fire is the divine analogue to man's baptism by water. Man could not bear the more searching test.

One other phrase needs annotation: baptising in or into the name of Christ. It is a difficult expression, but so are all the Rabbinic metaphors in which the word "name" occurs. (Cf. my article on "Name of God" in Hastings, *Dictionary of Religion and Ethics*, vol. IX.) Part of the significance of the Gospel expression is seen from the corresponding late Hebrew (Gerim i. 7): "Whoever is not a proselyte to (or in) the name of heaven (לשם שמים) is no proselyte." (Cf. for the phrase, *Koheleth Rabbah* on Eccles. vii. 8 end.) In this context the meaning is that the true proselyte is baptised for God's sake, and for no personal motive. It is a pure, unselfish act of submission to the true God. But in the Talmud (e.g. T.B. *Yebamoth*, 45 b, 47 b last lines) there is another phrase, which throws light on this. Slaves, on rising to the rank of freemen, were re-baptised, and this slave baptism was termed a baptism to or in the name of freedom (לשם שחרור or לשם בן חורין). A fine contrast and complement of baptism *in the name of freedom* is the proselyte's baptism *in the name of heaven*, or in its Gospel form—baptism in the name of Christ.   The Christian phrase, it is strongly contended by many, has a magical connotation.   But if so, (and it is hardly the case unless magical be interpreted as equivalent to mystical), it was an acquired rather than a primitive connotation.   The explanation suggested comes near that which regards baptism *into the name* as a Roman legal term, implying that the newcomer is admitted on the roll of the patron's clients or dependents.   Never, surely, was a legal term more transfigured, both in Church and Synagogue.

V. THE DOVE AND THE VOICE.

From two opposite sides the Rabbinic parallels to the Dove have been minimised, by Dr Edersheim and Dr Abbott. The former, in order to expose the "mythical theory," insists with "warmth of language" that the whole circumstances connected with the baptism of Jesus "had no basis in existing Jewish belief." The latter, in pursuance of his view that the "Dove" arose from a textual misunderstanding, argues equally that there was no extant Jewish symbolism which could justify the figure.

But the doubt would have been scarcely possible had the two ideas, the Dove and the Heavenly Voice, been treated together. It must not be overlooked that in several passages the Heavenly Voice (Heb. *Bath-Qol*, Daughter of the Voice) is represented as piping or chirping like a bird. The notes of a bird coming from aloft often unseen would naturally enough lend themselves to mystic symbolism in connection with the communication of a divine message. There are two clear instances of this use of the verb "chirp" with regard to the *Bath-Qol* in the Midrash Qoheleth Rabbah. In one (on Eccles. vii. 9) we read: "I heard the Daughter of the Voice chirping (מצפצפת) and saying: Return O backsliding children (Jer. iii. 14)." Even clearer is the second passage on Eccles. xii. 7, though the text explained is verse 4 of the same chapter: "*And one shall rise up at the voice of a bird.* Said R. Levi, For 18 years a Daughter of the Voice was making announcement and chirping (מצפצפת) concerning Nebuchadnezzar." (It is possible that in the Jerusalem Talmud, *Sabbath* vi. 9, we have another instance, and that we should correct מפוצצת, which is the reading of the text there, to מצפפת). The evidence goes further. For while in these passages the Heavenly voice is likened to the soft muttering of a bird, in one place the *Bath-Qol* is actually compared to a *dove*. This occurs in the Babylonian Talmud, *Berachoth* fol. 3 a): "I heard a *Bath-Qol moaning as a dove* and saying: Woe to the children through whose iniquities I laid waste My Temple."

It is this association of the bird and the heavenly voice that may underlie the Gospel narrative of the baptism, and at once illustrate and

authenticate the symbolism of the Synoptists. There is no need to enter
here at length into the question of the *Bath-Qol*, for Dr Abbott (*From
Letter to Spirit*, Book II. and Appendix IV.) has admirably collected the
materials. It is surely supercritical to question the antiquity of the
Bath-Qol in face of the evidence of Josephus (*Antiquities*, XIII. x. 3)
and of the Rabbinic tradition concerning Hillel: "There came forth
a *Bath-Qol* and said: There is among you a certain man worthy of the
Holy Spirit, but the generation is not worthy thereof" (Jer. *Soṭa* ix. 12,
otherwise 13). Dr Abbott aptly compares Mark i. 7. The whole
passage in Mark fits in with the belief that in the absence of the direct
inspiration of prophets by the Holy Spirit (after the death of Haggai,
Zechariah and Malachi), the *Bath-Qol* took its place (*loc. cit.*). The
Synoptists, like the Rabbis, never report a direct message from God.

In the Rabbinic literature the dove is for the most part an emblem
of Israel, its gentleness, fidelity, its persecution, its submission
(H. J. Holtzmann, *Die Synoptiker*, ed. 3, p. 44, has collected some useful
materials on the symbolism of the Dove in other literatures). Here is
a characteristic Rabbinic passage (Midrash Tanḥuma, p. Teṣave: cf. ed.
Buber, *Exod.* p. 96), "Israel is compared to a dove (Canticles i.). As
the dove knows her mate and never forsakes him, so Israel, once
recognising the Holy One as God, never proves faithless to him. All
other birds, when they are about to be slaughtered, wince, but the dove
holds out its neck to the slayer. So there is no people so willing as
Israel to lay down its life for God. Just as the dove (after the flood)
brought light to the world, so God said unto Israel, who are likened
to the dove, Take olive oil and light my lamp before me." It has been
suggested (R. Eisler in the *Quest*, July 1912) that the Jews expected
the Messiah to be a second Noah, and that he would inaugurate the
era by a punishment and a purification by a new flood. If the evidence
were sufficient to support this view (Eisler quotes Zech. xiv. 2, Joel
iii. [iv.] 18, and Ezekiel xlvii. 1) we might see a Messianic reminiscence
of Noah's dove. Elsewhere other points of comparison are made
(*Berachoth* 53b, etc.). As "the wings of a dove covered with silver
and her feathers with yellow gold" (Ps. lxviii. 13) are the bird's means
of escape from danger, so is Israel saved by the Law, the pure words
of the Lord which are "as silver tried in a furnace of earth, purified
seven times" (Ps. xii. 7). But, as Wünsche well remarks (*Neue Beiträge*,
p. 501) the very comparison of suffering Israel to a dove may have
influenced the growth of the metaphor as applied to the Messiah, whose
function it was to save Israel. The "Spirit of God" of the Cosmogony

in Genesis is thus sometimes (as we shall see later) compared to a dove, sometimes to the spirit of the Messiah, who will not come until Israel deserves the boon by Repentance (Genesis Rabba, ch. ii., ed. Theodor, p. 17; *Yalquṭ* on Gen. i. 2). The identity is carried farther. In the Bible God is said to have borne Israel on Eagle's wings, to protect Israel as a parent bird protects its nest (Deut. xxxii. 11); more generally (Isaiah xxxi. 5): "as birds flying so will the Lord of hosts protect Jerusalem." Nay more, just as the Divine Presence goes into exile with Israel, so God himself is, with Israel, compared to a troubled bird (though not a dove), driven from its nest (the Temple) while the wicked prevail on earth (Midrash on Ps. lxxxix., *Yalquṭ* § 833). It is quite in keeping with this whole range of ideas to find the Targum (Canticles ii. 12, etc.) interpreting as the "voice of the Holy Spirit of Salvation" the text, the "voice of the turtle-dove is heard in our land." (Cf. alfo *Sifre* on Deut. § 314, with reference to Canticles ii. 8.)

Now it is obviously near at hand to find the main source of the comparison of the Holy Spirit to a bird in Genesis i. 2, "And the Spirit of God brooded (as a bird) upon the face of the waters." We are happily not called upon to discuss the origin of the idea in Genesis itself and its relation to the "world-egg." The Jewish commentators (even on Jeremiah xxiii. 9) recognise no other meaning for the verb used in Genesis (רחף), except brooding or moving as a bird. It is well here to cite Rashi's note on the Genesis passage: "The Spirit of God was moving: the Throne of Glory was standing in the air and moving on the face of the waters by the Spirit of the Mouth of the Holy One blessed be he, and by his Word like a dove that broods on the nest, in French *acoveter*." This idea is derived by the commentator partly from the Midrash Cōnēn (Jellinek, *Bet Hamidrash*, ii. 24: "And the holy spirit and the holy Presence was moving and breathing on the water"), but chiefly from the famous incident concerning Ben Zoma, a younger contemporary of the Apostles. I have cited Rashi's adoption of it to prove that some moderns have misread the Talmud when they regard the Rabbis as deprecating Ben Zoma's idea. If anyone understood the spirit of the Talmud it was Rashi, and the fact that he (like other Jewish commentators) adopts the simile of the dove is of itself enough to show that Ben Zoma's simile was not considered objectionable. Moreover, the passage relating to Ben Zoma is too frequently reproduced in the Rabbinical sources for it to have been held in the disrepute which has strangely been assigned to it by those who would like to expunge this very clear parallel to the dove of the Synoptists, for it is obvious that we have not only a comparison to the dove, but also to its appearance "on the face of the waters," which fits in so well with the baptismal scene at the Jordan, the dove descending as "Jesus, when he was baptised, went up straightway from the water." Even without the Ben Zoma analogue one could hardly doubt that the Synoptists must have had Genesis i. 2 in mind.

The Ben Zoma incident is reported in the Talmud (Ḥagiga 15 a) as follows : "Rabbi Joshua the son of Ḥananiah was standing on an ascent in the Temple Mount, and Ben Zoma saw him but did not stand before him. He said to him : Whence comest thou and whither go thy thoughts, Ben Zoma? He replied, I was considering the space between the upper waters and the lower waters, and there is only between them a mere three fingers' breadth, as it is said, and the Spirit of God was brooding on the face of the waters like a dove which broods over her young but does not touch them. Rabbi Joshua said to his disciples, Ben Zoma is still outside; for, 'and the Spirit of God was hovering'—when was this? On the first day. But the separation was on the second day." There are several variants of the passage, but this on the whole seems to me the most original in the important reference to the dove. (Bacher, *Agada der Tanaiten*, ed. 2, Vol. I., p. 423, holds the Tosefta Ḥagiga ii. 5 and Jer. Talm. Ḥagiga reading more original because the allusion to the Temple is an anachronism.) Some of the variants either suppress the dove or replace it by an eagle, citing Deut. xxxii. 11 (where the same verb רחף is used of an eagle). Such a harmonisation shows the hand of an editor, and the dove would not have been introduced later. Dr Schechter (*Studies in Judaism*, II. p. 113) is convinced that the *dove* is the original reading. Now the theory that by the phrase "Ben Zoma is still outside" it was implied in this "fragment of a Jewish Gnosis" (as L. Löw, *Lebensalter*, p. 58 suggests) that he had not yet returned to the orthodox path is quite untenable. Other passages show that the meaning is : Ben Zoma is still out of his senses. He had pried too closely into the problems of creation, and had fallen into such perplexity that he confused the work of the first with that of the second day. At all events, the figure of the dove is not asserted to have originated with Ben Zoma, there is nothing in the passage to imply that it was regarded as an innovation, or that Ben Zoma's idea was unorthodox or heretical. Of course it is quite true, as Dr Abbott urges, that the Rabbinic figure does not imply that the Holy Spirit appeared visibly as a dove, but that the motion and action of the Spirit were comparable to the motion of a dove over her young.

VI. LEAVEN.

The term leaven (שְׂאֹר = Gk. ζύμη) is used in N.T. as a symbol of "corruption." Something of the same idea is found in a well-known Rabbinic passage to be discussed later. As to the O.T. conception of leaven, an excellent account is given by A. R. S. Kennedy in *Encyclopaedia Biblica*, col. 2754, "In the view of all antiquity, Semitic and non-Semitic, panary fermentation represented a process of corruption and putrefaction in the mass of the dough." Plutarch (*Quaest. Rom.* 109) has the same idea. Philo, on the other hand, has the idea with a somewhat different *nuance*. To him, leaven symbolises the puffing-up of vain self-conceit (Frag. on Exod. xxiii. 18), or the vice of insolence (on Levit. ii. 11, *de offer*. vi., Mangey II. 255). It is probable, too, that the Roman satirist Persius (I. 24) also implies by *fermentum* "vanity" rather than "corruption."

Later Jewish moralists (cf. Zohar on Gen. xlvii. 31) have made extensive use of the leaven metaphor (especially with reference to the prohibition of leavened bread חמץ on Passover). As, however, "leavened" bread was in itself more palatable as an article of food than unleavened, the metaphorical use of "leaven" sometimes expresses an improving process. Kennedy (*loc. cit.*) puts it rather differently: "In the N.T. leaven supplies two sets of figures, one taken from the mode, the other from the result, of the process of fermentation. Thus Jesus likened the silent but effective growth of the 'Kingdom' in the mass of humanity to the hidden but pervasive action of leaven in the midst of the dough" (Mt. xiii. 33). It is probable, however, that the parable also takes account of the result; the leavened mass of humanity, through intrusion of the leaven, attains a superior moral condition, just as the leavened bread is a more perfect food than unleavened. Paul applies the process in the opposite sense. Just as "evil company doth corrupt good manners" (1 Cor. xv. 33), so "a little leaven leaveneth the whole lump" (1 Cor. v. 6; Gal. v. 9). The latter idea is Rabbinic (Succah 56 b) both on this side (*Woe to the wicked, woe to his neighbour*

4—2

אוי לרשע אוי לשכינו) and on the reverse side, for the righteous extends
virtue and its consequences to his neighbour (*Happy the righteous,
happy his neighbour* טוב לצדיק טוב לשכינו). But the Rabbinic idea does
not associate itself with leaven, but with the plague-spot, which appearing in one house, compels the demolition of the next house (Mishna,
Negaim xii. 6; Sifra on Levit. xiv. 40; Weiss 73 b). A very close
parallel to Paul's proverb (μικρὰ ζύμη ὅλον τὸ φύραμα ζυμοῖ) is found in
Hebrew (כאשר השאור המועט מחמיץ עסה גדולה), but this occurs in a
fifteenth century book (Abraham Shalom b. Isaac's *neve shalom* xi. 2),
and is possibly a reminiscence of 1 Cor. But the sentence is not very
recondite, and may be independent of Paul. The permanence of the
effect of leaven in the mass is found in Yalquṭ Ruth § 601, where the
leaven is said to cling to proselytes up to 24 generations.

Most notable of all metaphorical applications of leaven is its
association with man's evil tendencies or inclinations (יצר הרע). The
chief references in Rabbinic thought are two, both of which are
alluded to in the passage about to be quoted from Weber. The latter
(in his *Jüdische Theologie*) identified the evil inclination with the *body*.
On p. 221 (ed. 2 p. 229) he writes:

That the body is impure, not merely as perishable, but because it is the *seat
of the evil impulse*, we see from what is said in Num. Rabba xiii. (Wünsche p. 312):
God knew before he created man that the desire of his heart would be evil from his
youth (Gen. viii. 21). "Woe to the dough of which the baker must himself testify
that it is bad." This Jewish proverb can be applied to the Jewish doctrine of man.
Then the dough is the body, which God (the baker) worked and shaped, and the
impurity of the body is grounded in the fact that it is the seat of the *yeṣer haraʻ*,
which is in the body that which the leaven is in the dough (שאור שבעיסה), a
fermenting, impelling force (Berachoth 17 a).

But, as Prof. F. C. Porter rightly comments, Weber's view is not
well founded. This is Prof. Porter's criticism ("The Yeçer Hara," in
Yale Biblical and Semitic Studies, p. 104).

Here the identification of the dough with the body, in distinction from the soul,
is mistaken. The dualistic psychology is supplied by Weber, not suggested by the
source. God's judgment upon man in Gen. viii. 21 is likened to a baker's condemnation of his own dough. The proverb is also found in Gen. Rabba xxxiv.
(Wünsche, p. 152) as a saying of R. Hiyya the Great (Bacher, *Agada der Tannaiten*
II. 530). The comparison of the evil impulse with leaven is an entirely different
saying, which should not be connected with the other. But in this case also the
dough is man, human nature, not the body. It is the prayer of R. Alexander
(Berach. 17 a): "It is revealed and known before thee that our will is to do thy will.
And what hinders? The leaven that is in the dough and servitude to the Kingdoms.
May it be thy will to deliver us from their hand."

Matthew (xvi. 12) interprets the "leaven of the Pharisees" to mean "teaching of the Pharisees," an interpretation which Allen (p. 175) rightly rejects. Luke (xii. 1) interprets it of "hypocrisy." Mark (viii. 14–21) gives no explanation, but reads "beware of the leaven of the Pharisees and the leaven of Herod." It will be seen that this reading strangely agrees with the words of R. Alexander's prayer: "the leaven that is in the dough (= the leaven of the Pharisees) and servitude to the Kingdoms (= the leaven of Herod)." Two things impede man: the evil *yeṣer* and the interference of alien rule. Both these preventives to man's advance will vanish with the coming of the Kingdom. With the advent of the Messiah the evil *yeṣer* will be finally slain (see refs. in Schechter, *Aspects of Rabbinic Theology*, p. 290); and in the second place with the Kingdom of heaven Israel triumphs over Rome (Pesiqta K. 50 a; Pesiqta R. 75 a).

There is a striking saying attributed to R. Joshua b. Levi, who belongs to the first half of the third century. It is obvious that the parable of the leaven requires a favourable application of the symbol. R. Joshua carries this application to the extent of likening leaven to peace. "Great is peace, in that peace is to the earth as leaven to dough; for had not God set peace in the earth the sword and the wild-beast would have depopulated it" (Pereq ha-Shalom, beginning; Bacher, *Agada der Palästinensischen Amoräer* 1. 136). The exact force of R. Joshua's comparison is not clear. He bases his idea on Leviticus xxvi. 6: and it is possible that he had in mind the thought found in the Sifra on that text (ed. Weiss, p. 111 a). "I will give peace in the land" and (in the usual translation) "I will make evil beasts to cease." So R. Judah interprets. But according to R. Simeon the meaning is that God will not destroy evil beasts, but will render them innocuous; for "the divine power is better seen when there are in existence evils which do not injure" (comparing Isaiah xi. 6—8). In this sense, peace would be not inert, but an active agency; a ferment of the good against the evil. The idea of stirring, agitating (רגז and כעס), is not only applied to the evil *yeṣer*. It is also used of the good *yeṣer*. "Let a man stir up his good *yeṣer* against his bad" (T. B. Berachoth, 5 a); "rouse thy [good] *yeṣer* and thou wilt not sin" (Ruth Rabbah, towards end). Peace is thus the leaven, stirring up the good *yeṣer*, to strive against hostile forces. If Peace is to have her victories, she must fight for them.

VII. PUBLICANS AND SINNERS.

The Roman taxes and custom duties and their mode of collection
are admirably described by Schürer (I. § 17) and Herzfeld (*Handels-
geschichte der Juden des Alterthums*, § 47). The taxes proper were in
Roman times collected by state officials, but the customs were farmed
out to *publicani*. In maritime places these were particularly onerous,
and Herzfeld ingeniously cites the proverbial maxim ('Aboda Zara, 10 *b*)
"Woe to the ship which sails without paying its dues" in illustration
of Matthew ix. 9, 10. That the demands of the *publicani* and their
underlings were often excessive is natural enough, and—especially
when the officials were native Jews (*cp*. Büchler, *Sepphoris*, pp. 13,
40, etc.)—the class was consequently the object of popular resentment.
It is not the case (as Schürer assumes) that the Jewish authorities
connived at frauds on the regular revenue. At all events the trick
permitted in the Mishnah (Nedarim, iii. 4) was interpreted by the
Talmud (Nedarim, 28 *a*) as having reference not to the authorised taxes
but to the arbitrary demands of unscrupulous extorters or inventors of
dues. "The law of the Government is law"—on which see Note VIII—
is used on the Talmudic folio just quoted as making it impossible
that the Mishnah (which permits one to evade "murderers, robbers,
confiscators and tax-gatherers" by falsely declaring the property
coveted to be sacerdotal or royal property) can refer to lawful taxes.

We have already seen that the tax-gatherers are associated with
robbers and murderers (*cp*. also Baba Qama, 113 *a*). Hence they were
regarded as unfit to act as judges or to be admitted as witnesses
(Sanhedrin, 25 *b*). An early baraitha made a tax-gatherer ineligible as
ḥaber ; in the older period the disqualification did not cease with the
abandonment of the occupation, afterwards this particular severity was
mitigated (Bechoroth, 31 *a*). It is clear from the last quotation that
the publican might sometimes be a man of learning. Yet this condemnation was not universal. Baya (or Mayan) the tax-gatherer (or

his son), who was charitable to the poor, was publicly mourned and honoured at his death (Sanhedrin, 44 *b*; J. Ḥagiga, ii. 2). So, concerning the father of Zeʿira (Sanhedrin, 25 *b*) a favourable report is made. There is also a (late) story of Aqiba (or in another version Joḥanan b. Zakkai), telling how the Rabbi with eagerness reclaimed the son of an oppressive tax-gatherer, teaching him the Law, and bringing peace to the father's soul (Kallah, ed. Coronel, 4 *b*. For other references see *Jewish Encyclopedia*, vol. i. p. 310).

The association in the Gospels of the two expressions Publicans and Sinners is parallel to the combination of "publicans and robbers" in the Rabbinic literature. The "sinners" were thus not those who neglected the rules of ritual piety, but were persons of immoral life, men of proved dishonesty or followers of suspected and degrading occupations. The Rabbis would have been chary of intercourse with such men at all times, but especially at meals. For the meal was not regarded simply as a satisfaction of physical needs. It was a service as well, consecrated by benedictions; it was also a feast of reason. The keynote of this is struck in the saying of R. Simeon (Aboth, iii. 3): "Three who have eaten at one table and have not said over it words of Torah, are as if they had eaten sacrifices of the dead (idols), for it is said : All tables are full of vomit and filthiness without *place* (*Maqom*)." This last word is taken in its secondary sense to mean the Omnipresent, God. "But," continues R. Simeon, "three who have eaten at one table, and have said over it words of Torah, are as if they had eaten of the table of God (*Maqom*), blessed be he, for it is said : This is the table that is before the Lord" (Ezekiel xli. 22). This conception is exemplified also in the table-discourses of Jesus to his disciples, and lies, to some extent, at the bottom of institution of the Eucharistic meal. In Jewish life this idea that the table is an altar gained a firm hold and led to a whole system of learned readings, devotions, and most remarkably, of hymns during meals, the Passover home-rites being but a conspicuous example of a daily Jewish usage. Just, then, as later on Christians would not share the Eucharistic meal with notorious evil-livers, so the Jewish Rabbi at various periods would (with less consistent rigidity) have objected to partake of any meal with men of low morals. So, also, Jesus' disciples are exhorted (Matthew xviii. 17) to treat certain offenders as "the Gentile and the Publican" with whom common meals would be impossible. The Essenes held a similar view as to the exclusion from their table of those who did not share the Essenic principles.

When, then, we find that the "pure-minded in Jerusalem would not sit down to a meal unless they knew who their table-companions were to be" (Sanhedrin, 23 *a*), the motive was neither pride nor exclusiveness, but a desire that the meal should not degenerate into mere eating and drinking. They would wish to be assured of the presence of fit comrades for learned and edifying discourse. They would not readily accept invitations to banquets at all, "the student who is always found at other people's tables profanes the name of God" (Yoma, 86 *b*, *Aboth de R. Nathan*, i. xxvi.). The Rabbis were convivial, but not gluttons; and many of them would never eat outside their own homes except at a "meal of duty," i.e. a semi-religious function, such as a marriage festivity. Instructive is the incident recorded as having occurred in Jerusalem c. 65 A.D. At the feast held on the circumcision of Elishah b. Abuyah, among those present were Eleazar b. Hyrqanos and Joshua b. Ḥananyah. While the other guests were partaking of meat and wine, these two sat "stringing together," like pearls on a cord, the words of the Scriptures. (Qoh. R. on viii. 8; see Bacher, *Prooemien* etc., p. 9.) To such men, a meal was not a mere occasion for eating and drinking. The reluctance to eat with the 'Am ha-areṣ was of a different origin; fears as to neglected tithes etc. arose (cf. Büchler, *Der Galiläisch Am-haareṣ* 162, 208). Similarly, with regard to joining the heathen at table, fear of mixed marriage came to the fore (cf. A. Wiener, *Die jüdischen Speisegesetze*, Breslau 1895, pp. 430 seq.; W. Elmslie on 'Abodah Zarah v. 5, with references there given). It is clear from the context that such joint meals did take place. But with all this there went a unique sense of obligation to the poor and the miserable. Isaiah (lviii. 7) had spoken of the duty "to bring the poor that are cast out to thy house," and from the middle of the second century B.C. it was laid down as a duty to entertain at meals "the children of the poor" (Aboth, i. 5), to which category were later added "those who were distressed in soul" (*Aboth de R. Nathan*, II. xiv.). It is not at all the case that a Pharisee would have declined to receive even "sinners" *at his own table*. But he might have refused an invitation to join them at *their* table, where the ritual and atmosphere could hardly fail to be uncongenial.

Probably the Pharisees exaggerated the force of evil example (cf. Hermas Mand. x. i. 4 against φιλίαις ἐθνικαῖς). We frequently find in the second and third centuries regulations due to a sensitive repugnance to placing oneself in a position of suspicion. (This is the meaning of some passages quoted by Dr Büchler in his essay on

"The Political and Social Leaders of the Jewish Community of Sepphoris," ch. iii. § 5.) On the other hand especial eulogy was expressed of those who defied suspicion and remained untainted in an environment of temptation (Pesachim, 113 a). But for the most part the Pharisees entertained an exaggerated fear both of the danger of actual moral lapse, and even more of the loss of repute from suspicion of such lapse, likely to be incurred by association with dishonest men or unchaste women. It was, however, a defensible theory of conduct, and one which most educationalists of the present day accept. We sometimes find Rabbis prepared to defy suspicion and temptation when engaged in what we now call rescue work, but such cases are rare. Moreover, as the women who were the unchaste associates of unchaste men were chiefly foreigners, the Rabbis felt no strong impulse towards putting their heads in the lions' dens.

But, to return to my main point, it is unnecessary to cite the Rabbinic passages in which men are warned of the personal dangers of associating with men or women of low morals. Some passages have already been quoted in Note VI. (Cf. also C. Taylor's Note on Aboth i. 8 [7].) Another common saying was that though the evil yeṣer of idolatry had been slain, the evil yeṣer of unchastity was very much alive (Yoma, 69 b; ʿAboda Zara, 17 b). There was much lack of courage, but less taint of self-righteousness, in the efforts of the moralist to preserve men from temptation and contagion. Luke's Pharisee who thanked God that he was not as the Publican (Luke xviii. 11) must have been an exceptional case, one of the weeds of ritualism, not one of its ordinary or natural fruits. "A familiar saying in the mouth of the Rabbis of Jabneh," says the Talmud (Berachoth, 17 a), "was this : I (who study the Law) am a creature (of God), and my fellow man is a creature (of God). My work is in the city, his in the field ; I rise early to my work, he rises early to his. Just as he cannot excel in my work, so I cannot excel in his. Perhaps thou wilt say : I do much and he does little (for the Torah). But we have learned (Menaḥot, 110 a), He who offers much and he who offers little are equal, provided that each directs his heart to Heaven." The penitent publican's prayer "God be merciful to me a sinner," as well as his gesture ("he smote upon his breast") are essentially Pharisaic ; it is interesting to see Luke introducing this last ritualistic touch in an attack on ritualism. The Pharisee placed the repentant sinner on a higher pedestal than the out-and-out saint (Berachoth, 34b). This was expressed in another way by saying that God honours the

repentant.   Again, "Broken vessels are a disgrace for a man to use,
but God loves the broken heart" (Midrash, Levit. Rabba, vii. 2 ; Mid.
Tehillim on xviii. 2).   A penitent publican, like any other repentant
sinner (cf. the fine passage on the harlot in Philo, *On Monarchy* ii. 8),
would find a ready welcome to the arms of the Rabbi.   True it was
held difficult for a publican to repent (Baba Qama, 94 *b*), but by
repent is meant in the context *to make restitution.*   The victims of the
publican's oppression were not easily identifiable, and it was not in
the sinner's power to undo the wrong which he had inflicted.   Besides,
the community must not connive at such plundering by manifesting
over-readiness to take back payment from ill-gotten gains.   The Rabbis
would have scornfully rejected the cynical principle *pecunia non olet.*
But though the community might decline the proferred restitution,
God would accept ; man might justly reject, yet the sinner must do
restitution (anonymously) for God's sake.   On the basis of this same
passage (Baba Qama, 94—95) Maimonides thus accurately sums up the
position : "If the robber wished to repent, and the thing actually
stolen being no longer in existence, offered to repay the value of the
stolen thing, it is an ordinance of the sages that they must not accept
the money, but they *help him and pardon him,* so as to make near
unto the penitent the right way ; yet if one received the money from
him he would not forfeit the approval of the sages" (Hilchoth גזילה,
i. 13).   And even though the Scripture says the opposite (Proverbs
xxi. 27 : "The sacrifice of the wicked is an abomination"), the gift-
offerings of sinners were accepted in the Temple in order to encourage
them to repent (Hullin, 5 *a* ; Pesikta R., 192 *a*).

There was in the Pharisaism of all ages a real anxiety to make the
return of the sinner easy.   It was inclined to leave the initiative to
the sinner, except that it always maintained *God's* readiness to take
the first step.   Jesus in his attitude towards sin and sinners was more
inclined to take the initiative.   Yet, until the modern epoch of a new
humanism, society has worked by reprobation rather than attraction,
and the practical methods of Western communities in dealing with
criminals have been as harsh as the methods of any other system.
And Rabbis did often act in the same spirit as Jesus.   In the first
place if a genuine Pharisee ever thanked God that he was not as the
publican, he would only have done so in the spirit of the famous
utterance : "There, but for the grace of God, goes John Baxter."
Thus a first century Rabbi (Nehunya ben Haqana) utters a prayer in
which he contrasts the happier lot of the speaker—who frequents the

house of study—and the less happy lot of someone else—who frequents theatre and circus (Berachoth, 28 a).   This prayer is simply a grateful recognition for good fortune; it in no sense implies (except quite indirectly) that the speaker prides himself on being a better man.   His lines have been cast in happier places.   Such prayers and such an attitude are moreover an encouragement to right living.   They aim at showing that virtue has its abundant reward in a sense of duty done and in the confident hope of future bliss.   And here arises the real difficulty.   Praying *for* sinners (i.e. for other people), fussy efforts at rescuing outcasts (i.e., again, other people) may come very close indeed to "pharisaic" self-righteousness.   These psychological problems are so complex that they transcend the grasp of most theologians, and the latter are driven to look at the problems incompletely and therefore erroneously.   One might put it generally by asserting that the Rabbis attacked vice from the preventive side; they aimed at keeping men and women honest and chaste.   Jesus approached it from the curative side; he aimed at saving the dishonest and the unchaste.

The Rabbis thought that God loves the prayers of the righteous; they held that *all* the divine sympathy was not expended on the petitions of the sinner.   But the association of the sinner with the righteous—in prayer and fasting—was necessary to make religion a real thing (Kerithoth, 6 b).   And as regards actual, practical intrusion into the life of the sinner, there is much in the Rabbinic literature urging men to seek the active reclamation of the erring.   "He who does not pray for his neighbour or bring him to penitence himself will suffer" (Midrash Jonah).   As Maimonides puts it (on the basis of several Talmudic passages, Ber. 12 b etc.): "Whoever has it in his power to prevent others from sinning, yet leaves them in their stumbling, has no forgiveness" (Teshuba, iv. 2; Deoth vi.).   So far does this counsel go, that the Israelite is required to press his reproof and his efforts at reclamation on the sinner though the latter revile and even strike his monitor (Erachin, 16 b).   Thoroughly in accord with Rabbinic teaching (Sifra on Leviticus xix. 17) is the Targum rendering of that same text: "Thou shalt rebuke thy neighbour and not receive punishment for his sin" which your active reproof might have prevented.   *His* sin becomes *your* sin.   The parable of Moses and the stray sheep which he seeks in the desert and bears in his bosom (Midrash, Shemoth Rabba, ch. ii.) points the same moral.   This idea is already found in the Psalter, "I have gone astray like a lost sheep; *seek* thy servant" (Ps. cxix. 176).   So, Ps. xxxiv. 14, "Seek peace and pursue it," was held by the Rabbis

to compel men to go about the world as peace-makers. Perhaps the
most apt citation in this connection (the subject is further discussed
in the note on Forgiveness) is the manner in which Jewish homilists
set up Aaron as an ideal character.   There can be no question
here but that this idealisation is earlier than the Gospel criticism
of the Pharisaic indifference to "sinners."   We meet with its germ
in Malachi ii. 6, where Levi is eulogised in the words "he did
turn away many from iniquity."   These words were applied specifically to Aaron (*Aboth de R. Nathan,* i. xii.), and Hillel already has
the saying: "Be of the disciples of Aaron, loving peace and
pursuing peace, *loving mankind, and bringing them near to the
Torah*" (Mishnah Aboth, i. 12).   Here is the same spirit as "the light
of the law which was given to lighten every man" (*Testament of Levi,*
xiv.).   This "bringing men near" applies to proselytism, but in
Rabbinical literature it is again and again used of active labour in
rescuing sinners.   Nitai the Arbelite cautioned against association
with the wicked (Aboth, i. 7, on the relation between this and i. 12 see
Jewish commentaries).   But this was not the only view held.   Aaron,
we are told, would offer friendly greetings to the wicked (Johanan b.
Zakkai, we are told, Ber. 17 a, punctiliously greeted heathens in the
market-place), who would thus be shamed from their sin (*Aboth de
R. Nathan, loc. cit.*); he would go out on the roads at night, intercept
those who were about to transgress, and with soft, affectionate words
of intimate comradeship, would divert them from their intention
(Buber Tanḥuma, Numbers, p. 10), and thus "all Israel loved Aaron,
men and women."   To "bring another man near" to the Torah was
to create a soul (*Aboth de R. Nathan,* ii. xxvi.).   This ideal, pre-
Christian in Rabbinic literature, was also post-Christian.   There is the
oft-cited case of R. Meir (to whom was due a first draft of the Mishnah).
Hard by his abode lived men who were violent criminals, and they so
troubled Meir that he prayed for their extinction.   But his wife Beruria
checked him, and at her instigation he admitted that it was better to
pray for their conversion (Berachoth, 10 a).   Meir, it will be remembered,
was noted for his persistent friendship to his heretic and sinful master
and friend, Elisha ben Abuya, for whose return to the fold he so
tenderly exerted himself.   Even more to the present point is the
conduct of R. Ze'ira.   In his neighbourhood were robbers and highway-
men, but Ze'ira showed them intimate friendship, so that they might
be brought to penitence, which indeed came about in their sorrow at
the Rabbi's death (Sanhedrin, 37 a).   Pathetic, too, is the idea of

R. Joshua ben Levi that the Messiah would eventually be found at the gates of Rome, among the sick poor, binding up their wounds (Sanhedrin, 98).

And so the story might be continued. The Rabbis could see the good in all men, and might exalt above those of spotless reputation one engaged in what they considered unsavoury and demoralising occupations. Gazing over the crowd, Elijah picked out as assured of the future life a jailor, who had cared for the morals of his prisoners (Ta'anith, 22 a). On occasion of a drought in Judæa, people reported to Abbahu that they knew a man whose prayers for rain were infallible. His popular name was Pentekaka (*lit.* the man of *Five Sins*). R. Abbahu interviewed him, inquired as to his means of livelihood, whereupon Pentekaka said that his name corresponded to his profession. "I am occupied with harlots, I clean the theatre, I carry the vessels to the bath, I amuse the bathers with my jokes, and I play the flute." But, asked the Rabbi: "Have you ever done a good thing in your life?" Pentekaka answered: "Once I was sweeping out the theatre and I saw a woman standing between the pillars, bitterly weeping. I spoke to her and ascertained that her husband was a prisoner, and she could only buy his freedom by sacrificing her chastity. So I sold my bed and my pillow and all my possessions, and I gave the money to her, bidding her go ransom her husband and not sell her honour to strangers." Hearing such words from such a man, Abbahu exclaimed: "Thou art the man fit to pray for us in our hour of trouble" (Talmud Jer. Ta'anith, i. 2).

VIII. "GIVE UNTO CAESAR."

To Samuel of Nehardea (c. 165—c. 257 A.D.) belongs the honour of formulating the principle which made it possible for Jews from the early middle ages onwards to live under alien laws. Jeremiah had admonished his exiled brothers: "Seek ye the peace of the city whither I have caused you to be carried away captives, and pray unto the Lord for it; for in the peace thereof shall ye have peace." It grew necessary to become more explicit, and the Rabbis proclaimed a principle which was as influential with the synagogue as "Give unto Caesar that which is Caesar's" became with the Church. "The law of the government is law" (*dina d'malchutha dina*, T.B. *Baba Qama* 113 b; *Baba Bathra* 54 a; *Gittin* 10 b; *Nedarim* 28 a) said Samuel, and ever since it has been a religious duty for the Jews to obey and accommodate themselves as far as possible to the laws of the country in which they are settled or reside (cf. my remarks in *Encyclopaedia Britannica*, ed. 11, vol. xv. p. 404). "To Jeremiah and Mar Samuel," says Graetz, "Judaism owes its possibility of existence in a foreign country" (*Geschichte der Juden*, IV. 2, iii.).

What Mar Samuel, however, did was not to devise a new principle, but to give that principle the precision of law. Very much in the history of civilization has depended on the power of moralists to concentrate a theory into an epigram; the sayings of Jesus and Samuel are apt illustrations. Long before Samuel, however, the same attitude prevailed. At the period of the disastrous Bar Cochba insurrection, when Roman law and Roman administration were bitterly resented, the Rabbinic teachers impressed on their brethren the absolute duty of paying the taxes imposed by the Government. According to the statement of Johanan ben Zakkai (Mechilta on Exodus xix. 1, ed. Friedmann, p. 61 b top) the Romans, after the destruction of the Temple, imposed the enormous tax of fifteen shekels; and though the exact significance of this is doubtful, it may have been a tax on leases; we know that the Roman imposts were very considerable (cf. Büchler, *The Economic Conditions of Judœa after the destruction of the Second Temple*, 1912, pp. 62 seq.). Yet it was held obligatory to pay these taxes with the utmost scrupulosity, in so far as they were lawfully imposed, and were not the whimsical exactions of the publicans (T.B. *Baba Qama* 113 a; *Nedarim* 28 a; Tosefta, *Nedarim* iii. 4; *Semaḥ* ii. 9 where evasion of taxation is denounced as equivalent even to murder, idolatry, incest, and profanation of the Sabbath).

Nor does the evidence extend only to the Hadrianic period. It goes back even further. On the text in Ecclesiastes viii. 2 ("I counsel thee, Keep the king's command, and that in regard of the oath of God"), the Midrash (Tanḥuma on Genesis viii. 16, *Noah* § 10; ed. Buber, p. 33) comments thus: "The Holy One said unto Israel, I adjure you that even though the (Roman) Government decrees against you harsh decrees ye shall not rebel against it for anything that it decrees, but keep the king's command. But if it decrees against you to abandon the Torah and the commandments and deny God, then do not obey it, but say unto it: I keep the king's laws only in those things which are necessary for the government." The Midrash goes on to cite the conduct of Daniel's three friends who assure Nebuchadnezzar: "In so far as duties and taxes are concerned, in all that thou decreest upon us, we will obey, and thou art our king, but to deny God—we have no need to answer thee in this matter...we will not serve thy gods, nor worship the golden image which thou hast set up" (Daniel viii. 16). The difficulty of this compromise was twofold. First, bad government is incompatible with the Kingdom of God (Schechter, *Some Aspects of Rabbinic Theology*, p. 106), and the Roman Government was often deserving of inclusion in the category of bad government. Secondly, the tendency of Roman emperors to assert their divine status, and to found their authority on a theory somewhat approaching that of divine right, made Roman rule in general obnoxious to Jewish sentiment. Nevertheless, as Tacitus admits, the Jews were long patient under the irritation; they rebelled only when chronic irritation was transformed into specific provocation: "Duravit tamen patientia Judæis usque ad Gessium Florum procuratorem; sub eo bellum ortum." That occurred in the spring of 66 A.D. Some of the previous procurators had so far studied Jewish susceptibilities as to strike (probably employing Jewish workmen) coins of special designs for local circulation in Judæa. There were on these no figures of animate objects, but only ears of corn, palm-trees or branches (?), the cornucopia, diota, covered vase, or wreath. In 35 A.D. Pontius Pilate struck coins decorated simply with the laurel wreath and the lituus or augur's wand (T. Reinach, *Jewish Coins*, ed. Hill, p. 41). At a much later period we find a Rabbi (Naḥum b. Simai) described as remarkable for his "holiness" because "he never looked upon the form of a coin" (*Pesaḥim* 104 a and parallels in Bacher, *Agada der Palästinensischen Amoräer* III. 616); this probably refers, however, to coins on which were figures of the emperors.

Very clearly belonging to the period of the Vespasian war is the saying recorded in the Mishnah, *Aboth* iii. 2. The authority cited is Ḥaninah (Ḥananiah), the prefect of the priests, who was a contemporary of Joḥanan ben Zakkai, and like him a member of the peace party. "Pray for the peace of the kingdom," said Ḥaninah, "since but for the fear thereof men would swallow one another alive." This may allude specifically to public prayer on behalf of the ruler (see Ezra vi. 10; Baruch i. 11; I. Macc. vii. 33; Philo, *Leg. ad Caium*, xxiii., xlv.; Josephus, *War* II. x. 4; T.B. *Yoma* 69 a; I. Timothy ii. 1, 2, and cf. Schürer ii. § 24; Singer, *Transactions of the Jewish Historical Society of England* iv. 103). It is interesting to add a conjecture made by Dr Bacher. We have no record of the precise liturgical phraseology of the prayer for the Government unless Dr Bacher has discovered it in the *Aboth de Rabbi Nathan* (II. ch. xxxi. p. 68, ed. Schechter). By a slight emendation of the text, the words of the prayer would be : "May it (the Roman Government) rule over us for all time" (שתהא שולטת בנו כל הימים) Bacher, *Agada der Tannaiten*, ed. 2, vol. i. p. 52).

But though thus prepared to obey Rome and abide by all its lawful regulations, there was to be no compromise when Caesar infringed the sphere which appertained to God. This distinction we have already seen in the Midrash, but we find the same very clearly expressed in the pages of history. Josephus records several instances of the readiness of the Jews to suffer death rather than admit the images of Caesar (e.g. *War* II. ix. 3). Most nearly illustrative of the subject before us is the passage in which the historian describes what took place when Caius Caesar (who succeeded Tiberius as emperor in 37 A.D.) sent Petronius with an army to Jerusalem to place his statues in the Temple; he was to slay any who opposed this step, and to enslave the rest of the nation (*War* II. x. 1). Petronius marched from Antioch southwards towards Judæa; but when he reached Ptolemais in Galilee he was met by a deputation of Jews. Prevailed upon by the multitude of the supplicants, he summoned a meeting of all the men of note to Tiberias, where he declared unto them the power of the Romans and the threatenings of Caius, and also pronounced their petition unreasonable. "For as all the nations subject to Rome had placed the images of the emperor in their several cities among the rest of their gods, for them alone to oppose it was like the behaviour of rebels, and was insulting to the emperor." Josephus then proceeds as follows, and the passage may usefully be cited in full (§§ 4, 5) :—

And when they insisted on their law, and the custom of their country, and how it was not lawful for them to put even an image of God, much less of a man, in any profane part of their country, much less in the Temple, Petronius replied, "And am I not also bound to keep the law of my lord? For, if I transgress it and spare you, I shall justly perish. And he that sent me, and not I, will war against you; for I am under command as well as you." Thereupon the whole multitude cried out that "they were ready to suffer for their Law." Petronius then tried to quiet their noise, and said to them, "Will you then make war against the Emperor?" The Jews said that they offered sacrifices twice every day for the emperor and the Roman people; but if he would set up his statues, he must first sacrifice the whole Jewish nation; and they were ready to expose themselves to be slain with their children and wives. At this Petronius felt both astonishment and pity on account of their invincible regard to their religion, and their courage which made them ready to die for it.

Petronius yielded, and incurred the censure of Caius, but the latter's death in 41 intervened to save him from the consequences of his complacency to the Jewish steadfastness towards their God, and his own disobedience towards Caesar. Philo (*Leg. ad Caium* xxxii., xxxvi.) narrates the same circumstances at greater length; but he, too, records that the Jews willingly and even enthusiastically accepted the sovereignty of Caius, in all matters except the proposed "innovations in respect of our Temple;…the honour of the emperor is not identical with dishonour to the ancient laws (of Judaism)." Caius well represents the opposite case when he retorts (xliv.) : "Ye are haters of God, in that ye deny me the appellation of a god," though he was generous enough to attribute this blindness to the Jews as a misfortune rather than as a fault : "These men do not appear to me to be wicked so much as unfortunate and foolish, in not believing that I have been endowed with the nature of God." This misfortune and unwisdom the Jews never abandoned, and thus were always protagonists in the refusal to give unto Caesar that which is God's.

A. 5

IX.   JEWISH DIVORCE IN THE FIRST CENTURY[1].

Social conditions in Palestine at the beginning of the Christian era were bewilderingly complex.   Restricting our attention to the question of marriage, we find at the one extreme a sect (the Essenes) which advocated celibacy, and possibly at the other a sect (the Zadokites) which forbade divorce, or at all events remarriage.   Then there were the aristocrats of the court circle who had adopted Roman ways.   For instance, Josephus records two instances in which women of the Herodian house (Salome, 25 B.C., and Herodias, contemporary with John the Baptist) divorced their husbands, and paralleled the excesses denounced by Juvenal in his sixth satire (Mark x. 12 may be directed against such licentiousness).   The Pharisaic Judaism of the same period regarded marriage as the ideal state, yet freely permitted divorce.   If the ideal were shattered it seemed to accord best with the interests of morality to admit this, and afford both parties to the calamity a second chance of lawful happiness.   The marriage bond should be inviolable, but must not be indissoluble.

The progress of law and custom in Jewry tended not to modify the theoretical ease of divorce, but to increase its practical difficulties.   The Gospel view was that the Deuteronomic divorce was a concession to human weakness, a lowering of the earlier standards of Genesis which held marriage to be indissoluble.   The Rabbinic reading of history was different.   The Pentateuch introduced the formality of the written

---

[1] This Note was written at short notice, to comply with the urgent request of the late Lord Gorell, Chairman of the Royal Commission on Divorce and Matrimonial Causes.   The Note was presented to the Commission, and the author was examined on November 21, 1910.   I received valuable help from Dr M. Berlin.   For various reasons it seems best to leave the Note without substantial change.   Hence it is impossible to allude to the interesting views of Prof. L. Blau published in 1911—1912.   In his *Jüdische Ehescheidung und der jüdische Scheidebrief*, pages 45—72 of Part I are devoted to an exposition of the New Testament passages on Divorce, with Rabbinic and other parallels.

Letter of Divorce, and Rabbinism regarded this as an advance in civilization, not a retrogression. The Deuteronomic divorce was a restriction of the earlier right or power of the husband to discard his wife at will and with scant ceremony. Rabbinism contrasted the decent formalities of the Mosaic Code with the arbitrary indelicacy of primitive custom (Genesis Rabba ch. xviii.).

The Pentateuch, however, contemplates the husband as alone having the right to effect a divorce. In the Babylonian Code of Hammurabi the wife had some power of initiative, and when recently the Egyptian papyri of the fifth century B.C. were discovered, it was thought that these Aramaic documents showed the Jewish woman in possession of the same status as man in regard to initiating divorce. Closer study, however, shows that at most the woman of the papyri could *claim* a divorce, she could not *declare* one. This condition remained unaltered in the first Christian century. Josephus (*Antiq.* xv. viii. 7) distinctly asserts : "With us it is lawful for the husband to do so (*i.e.* dissolve a marriage), but a wife, if she departs from her husband, cannot marry another, unless her former husband put her away." In two cases the husband's right of divorce was abrogated by the Pentateuch (Deut. xxii.), if he ravished a virgin or if he falsely accused his wife of ante-nuptial incontinence. In the first case the man was compelled to wed the woman in an indissoluble union, in the second case he could not divorce his wife. In later Rabbinic law a divorce if pronounced was technically valid; the Biblical law, however, does not deal with such a case, and the wife was immune from divorce. But what was her position? The option rested with her. She could compel her husband to retain her, or she could accept a divorce. Philo declares (ii. 313 καὶ μένειν τε ἀπαλλάττεσθαι, this last word being Philonean for divorce) that she could divorce him, but it is not probable that the law ever agreed with Philo's view. At most the injured wife may have been entitled to move the court to compel her husband to write her a Letter of Divorce. The situation reminds one of Meredith's *Diana of the Crossways.*

We are in possession of a clear piece of evidence as to the Jewish progress in divorce law in the period preceding the Christian era. In Matthew xix. 10 the disciples after hearing Jesus' declaration on the indissolubility of marriage, object : "If the case of the man is so with his wife, it is not expedient to marry." Here, the difficulty of divorce is treated as a bar to wedlock. This is the man's point of view. What of the woman's? Now in the first century B.C. it would seem that,

from the woman's side, the facility of divorce was a bar.   In face of
the ease with which a husband could whistle off his wife, women
refused to contract marriages, and men grew grey and celibate
(T. J. Kethuboth, end of ch. viii. ; T. B. Kethuboth 82b, Tosefta xii.).
Thereupon the Pharisaic leader, Simon b. Shetah, the reputed brother of
Queen Alexandra, enacted that the wife's *Kethubah* or marriage settlement was to be merged in the husband's estate, that he might use it as
capital, but that his entire fortune, even such property of his as had
passed into other hands, should be held liable for it.   This effectively
checked hasty divorce (cf. 'Erubin 41 b), and indeed the rights of wives
under the Kethubah were throughout the ages a genuine safeguard to
their marital security.   In respect to holding property and possessing
independent estate the Jewish wife was in a position far superior to
that of English wives before the enactment of recent legislation.

Another point of great importance was this.   Jewish sentiment was
strongly opposed to the divorce of the wife of a man's youth, and men
almost invariably married young.   The facilities for divorce seem mostly
to have been applied or taken advantage of in the case of a widower's
second marriage (a widower was expected to remarry).   "What the
Lord hath joined, let no man put asunder" represented the spirit of the
Pharisaic practice in the age of Jesus, at all events with regard to a
man's first marriage.   It is rather curious that while in the Gospel so
much use is made of the phrase of Genesis "one flesh" to prove marriage
indissoluble, no reference is made to another verse in the same context
"It is not good that the man should be alone" which obviously requires
marriage and not celibacy.   It may be that Jesus, anticipating the near
approach of the Kingdom, was teaching an " interim " ethic, which
would have no relation to ordinary conditions of life (cf. the view that
Angels do not marry Enoch xv. 3—7, Mark xii. 25 and the later
Rabbinic maxim that in the world to come there is no procreation
(Berachoth 17a)).   But it is more likely that he was laying down a rule
of conduct only for his own immediate disciples, declaring that " all
men cannot receive this saying."   That, however, a belief in the divinity
of the marriage tie was compatible with a belief that the tie could be
loosened, is shown by the course of Jewish opinion.   The Rabbis held
with Jesus that marriages are made in heaven (see *Jewish Quarterly
Review*, II. 172), and several Old Testament phrases point to the same
roseate view.   Of the marriage of Isaac and Rebecca it is written "the
thing proceedeth from the Lord" (Gen. xxiv. 50).   "Houses and
Riches are the inheritance of fathers," says the author of Proverbs

(xix. 14), "but a prudent wife is from the Lord." Again, "Fear not," said the Angel to Tobias (Tobit vi. 17), "for she was prepared for thee from the beginning." The Pharisees fully accepted this amiable theory of divine fatalism. "God," said the Rabbi, "sitteth in heaven arranging marriages." Or it was more crudely put thus : "Forty days before the child is formed a heavenly voice proclaims its mate" (T. B. Moed Qaton 18b ; Soṭa 2a). In the Middle Ages, belief in the divine arrangement of marriage affected the liturgy, and on the sabbath following a wedding, the bridegroom proceeded to the synagogue with a joyous retinue, and the congregation chanted the chapter of Genesis (xxiv.) in which, as shown above, the patriarch's marriage was declared as ordained by God. Naturally this belief in the pre-ordainment of marriage must have strengthened the Jewish objection to divorce. "For I hate divorce, saith the Lord" (Malachi ii. 16) was a verse much honoured in Pharisaic thought, and Malachi's protest gave rise to the pathetic saying : "The very altar sheds tears when a man divorces the wife of his youth," and to the sterner paraphrase "He that putteth her away is hated of the Lord" (T. B. Giṭṭin 90. Cf. Prov. v. 19 ; Eccles. ix. 9 ; Ecclus. vii. 26, yet see also xxv. 26).

But though divorce is hateful, continuance of the marriage bond may be more hateful still. Perfect human nature could do without divorce, but it could also do without marriage. Adam and Eve, it has been well said, went through no marriage ceremony. The formalities of marriage are not less the result of human imperfection than is the need of divorce. Were it not for the evil in human nature, said the Rabbis (Gen. Rab. ix. ; Eccles. R. iii. 11), a man would not marry a wife—not that the married state was evil, on the contrary, it was held to be the highest moral condition—but the passions which are expressed in the marital relationship are also expressed in the lower lusts. We may also perhaps read another idea into this Rabbinic conception. X needed the marriage bond to limit his own lusts and also to ward off Y. And just as, in this sense, man's evil side requires a marriage contract, so in another sense his good side demands the cancellation of the contract, if its continuance be degrading or in-harmonious.

Hence, though the strongest moral objection was felt against divorce, and though the vast majority of Jewish marriages were terminated only by death, the Pharisaic law raised no bar to divorce by mutual consent of the parties, just as marriage, despite its sacred associations, was itself a matter of mutual consent. It should be

remembered that in the Jewish document of divorce no ground for
the act is defined, the husband simply declares his wife thenceforth
sui juris and free to re-marry.   She could, and often did, re-marry
her husband, unless he had divorced her for unchastity, or unless she
had in the meantime contracted another marriage.   In the time of
Jesus it was not necessary for a divorce by mutual consent to come
before a regular court or Beth Din of three Rabbis, as later became
the practice.   The whole ceremony could, at the earlier period, be
gone through privately, in the presence of two witnesses.   An expert
Rabbi was, however, probably required to ensure the proper drawing
up of the document, and the due fulfilment of the legal delivery to,
and acceptance by, the wife.   Thus if Joseph of Nazareth and his
betrothed bride had mutually consented to a divorce, there is no
reason in Jewish law why he should not have " put her away privily "
(Matthew i. 19).   There is little ground for thinking that such divorces
by mutual consent were either frequent or productive of social evils,
though it may be that the woman's assent was occasionally extorted
by harsh measures.   But though the Rabbis could oppose no legal
bar to divorce by mutual consent, it was their duty to exhaust every
possible expedient of moral dissuasion.   Aaron, in Hillel's phrase
(Aboth i. 12), was the type of the peace-maker, and this was tradi-
tionally explained (Aboth de R. Nathan, ch. xii.) to mean that his
life-work was, in part, the reconciliation of estranged husbands and
wives (see above, Note VII).

But the case was different when one of the parties to the divorce
was unwilling to assent, or when one party had something to gain by
treating the other party as unwilling.   From the eleventh century it
has been customary in Jewish law to require that in all cases the
wife shall assent to the divorce, except where her misconduct or failure
could be shown to be sufficient cause why the marriage might be
forcibly dissolved by the husband.   But this condition of the woman's
assent was not necessary at the beginning of the Christian era, when
neither Rabbinic sanction nor the wife's consent was obligatory.   The
rule in the first century was (Yebamoth xiv. 1): " A woman may be
divorced with or without her will, but a man only with his will."
If, however, the wife contested the divorce, it is highly probable that
the husband had to specify his reasons and bring the matter before
a regularly constituted Beth Din.   This was certainly the case if he
suspected her of adultery (Soṭa i. 3—4).   The accusing husband took
his wife before the local Beth Din or court of three, and after a first

hearing two Rabbis would conduct the accused to the Supreme Court
in Jerusalem, which alone could deal finally with such charges. If she
confessed, she forfeited her marriage settlement and was divorced;
otherwise the ordeal of the waters (Numbers v.) was applied. We
may well suppose that in other cases, especially such as involved a
stigma on the wife, the matter would be made a matter of public
inquiry if she so claimed. It is only thus that we can fully explain
the different views taken at the early period as to lawful grounds
of divorce. The schools of Hillel and Shammai differed materially
(Gittin, end): the former gave the husband the legal right to divorce
his wife for any cause. Cf. Matthew xix. 3, Josephus *Antiq.* iv. viii.
23 ("for any cause whatsoever"). Philo uses similar language (Spec.
Laws, Adultery, ch. v.). The school of Shammai limited the right to
the case in which the wife was unchaste. The "schools" or "houses"
of Hillel and Shammai belong to the first century. It is uncertain
whether this particular difference of opinion on divorce goes back to
Hillel and Shammai themselves, and thus to the very beginning of
the Christian era. It is barely possible that the teaching of Jesus
on the subject led to further discussion in the Pharisaic schools, and
that the rigid attitude of Jesus influenced the school of Shammai.
This, however, is altogether improbable, for the view of the latter
school is derived from Deuteronomy (xxiv. 1) by a process which
closely accords with the usual exegetical methods of the Shammaites.
Matthew v. 32 (as the text now stands) with its λόγου πορνείας is
certainly derived from the school of Shammai, for the text of Deut.
xxiv. 1 reads עֶרְוַת דְּבַר, and it was the school of Shammai who turned
the words round into דְּבַר עֶרְוָה (Gittin ix. 10), which corresponds
in order with the text of Matthew. Hillel's language: "even if she
spoiled his food," is of course figurative, and may point to indecent
conduct, a sense which similar metaphors sometimes bear. Hillel was
a teacher noted for his tender humaneness; it was he who popularised
in Pharisaic circles the negative form of the Golden Rule before Jesus
stated it positively. Hence, it is not just to speak of his view on
divorce as "lax" or "low," even if (as no doubt later Rabbinic
authority assumed) Hillel used this forcible language to preserve as
inalienable the ancient norm that a husband possessed complete right
to divorce his wife for any cause. For it must be observed that his
"lax" and "low" view of divorce was also a more rigid and elevated
view as to the necessity of absolute harmony in the marriage state.
Still, his view (or its interpretation) did produce a condition of sub-

jection in the woman's status, and left room for much arbitrariness on the part of the husband. Yet 'Aqiba who went beyond Hillel in maintaining the husband's arbitrary powers ("even if he find another woman more beautiful"), was in fact no friend of divorce, for he applied the severest rules in estimating the pecuniary rights of the wife under the marriage settlement. "Sell the hair of your head to pay it," said 'Aqiba (Nedarim ix. 5) to a would-be divorcer who com‐ plained that the payment of the heavy demands of the settlement would impoverish him. As D. Amram in his excellent book on the subject of *The Jewish Law of Divorce* (Philadelphia, 1896) puts it, neither Hillel nor 'Aqiba was making law, they were stating it, "regardless of their personal views or opinions" (p. 37). It is true, however, that their statement of the law helped to make and perpetuate it for future times. The injurious effect was much miti‐ gated, though never theoretically removed, by subsequent modifications. We can trace the gradual incidence of restraining enactments and customs. Already in the year 40 A.D. we find various reforms intro‐ duced by Gamaliel, who ordained *e.g.* that the *Get* or divorce letter must be subscribed by the witnesses, and withdrew from the husband the right to cancel the *Get* unless the wife or her attorney were present (Gittin iv. 2). Such cancellation was made before Gamaliel's reform; the husband would locally constitute a Beth-din of three Rabbis *ad hoc*. Though, as stated above, the divorce itself needed no Court, many questions (as to settlements etc.) arising out of the divorce would have to be brought before the Beth-din.

There were, indeed, certain grounds on which husband or wife could claim the help of the Court in effecting a divorce against the other's will. In all such cases, where the wife was concerned as the moving party, she could only demand that her husband should divorce her; the divorce was always, from first to last, in Jewish law the husband's act. The matter was not, however, always left to the parties themselves. "Joseph being a righteous man, and not willing to expose her to shame, determined to divorce her secretly." This implies that Joseph had no option as to discarding his wife. Cf. Montefiore, *Synoptic Gospels*, p. 454. This work contains an excellent analysis of the various Gospel passages on divorce, see pages 235—242, 454, 508—510, 688—692, 1000—1. To return, if the husband suspected his wife of unchastity while betrothed to him, he was compelled, as a "righteous man," to divorce her (betrothal was so binding that divorce was necessary to free a betrothed couple). His only option was between divorcing his bride privately with her consent, or formulating a charge of infidelity against her, thus subjecting her to public disgrace as well as divorce. Divorce was not in itself a disgrace, seeing that it might occur on grounds involving no moral stigma. The case was aggravated by the circumstance that Mary was with child, until Joseph, in Matthew's account, received the assurance that his whole suspicion was erroneous. The wisdom books and the Rabbinic doctors agreed in regarding adultery as peculiarly heinous when it resulted in the birth of a child (Ecclus. xxiii. 23, Ḥagiga i. 7). The offence was a three-fold sin : against God, against the husband, against the family (Hamburger, *Real-Encyclopädie des Judenthums* I. 258). In Jewish law adultery was the intercourse of a married woman with *any* man other than her husband. Though his conduct was severely reprobated, and at all events in later centuries gave his wife a right to claim a divorce, a man was not regarded as guilty of adultery unless he had intercourse with a *married* woman other than his wife. For though monogamy had become the prevalent custom in Jewish life long before the Christian era (cf. *Jewish Encyclopedia*, VIII. p. 657), the man could legally marry several wives, and sometimes did so. Thus an unmarried and un-betrothed woman with whom a married man had intercourse might become his wife; indeed such intercourse could be legally construed into a marriage. By the Pentateuchal law the penalty for adultery was death.

But this law can never have been frequently enforced. It needed eye-witnesses (hence the "taken in the very act" of John viii. 4). More-over, as Dr Büchler has pointed out, the husband would hesitate to charge his wife, and the detected adulterer would offer heavy compensation to save his own life which was forfeit. The husband could privately divorce his wife, she naturally losing all her rights under the marriage settlement. A charge of adultery would have to be public, and tried before the central court. It is not probable that the death penalty for adultery was inflicted at all in the age of Jesus. The Jewish courts had lost the general power of capital punishment in the year 30 A.D. (T. J. Sanh. 18 a, T.B. 41 a). The Mishnah cites a single case which would fall within the age of Jesus, but it does so doubtfully (Sanh. vii. 2), and Josephus' casual assertion that the penalty for adultery was death is rather an antiquarian note than a record of experience (Apion ii. 25). On the other hand it would seem that the ordeal of the bitter waters, as applied in case of suspected adultery of the wife, was still prevalent, for the Mishnah records (Soṭa ix. 9) that the ceremony was only

abolished during the Roman invasion (circa 70 A.D.), though Queen
Helena of Adiabene—a proselyte to Judaism in the first century A.D.—
sought to restore the practice (Yoma iii. 10, Tosefta Yoma ii. 3). It is
interesting to note that 'Aqiba—whose view on divorce was so "lax"—
nobly said of the ordeal: "Only when the (accusing) husband is
himself free from guilt will the waters be an effective test of his wife's
guilt or innocence" (Sifre, Nasô 21; Soṭa 47 b). With this may be
usefully compared the fine utterance (John viii. 7): "He that is
without sin among you, let him first cast a stone at her" (*Jewish
Encyclopedia*, I. 217; Hastings, *Encyclopaedia of Religion*, I. 130, from
my article there I have taken some passages). The abolition of the
ordeal is attributed by the Mishnah to the great prevalence of adultery,
and it may be that, just as on the inroad of Hellenism some unsettlement
of native morals occurred in the towns and among the wealthy (this
being all that the attacks on harlotry and unchastity in the Wisdom
Literature implies), so in the disturbed conditions due to the Roman
régime a temporary laxity of morals intruded itself. The Rabbis held
adultery in the utmost detestation. Not all a man's other virtues could
save the adulterer from Gehenna (T. B. Soṭa 4 b). Unchastity drives
away from man the Divine Presence which dwells only in the chaste
soul. It is impossible, however, to attempt to collect here the mass of
Pharisaic maxims against such offences. In the year 135 A.D., at the
crisis of the disastrous revolt against Hadrian, a meeting was held at
Lydda. The assembly was attended by several famous Rabbis (including 'Aqiba), and the question was discussed as to the extent of
conformity with Roman demands which might justifiably be made
rather than face the alternative of death. The result is a remarkable
testimony to Jewish abhorrence of unchastity. It was decided
(Sanh. 74 a) that every Jew must surrender his life rather than commit
any of the three offences: idolatry, murder, or *gillui 'arāyoth*, a phrase
which includes both adultery and incest.

The penalty for proven adultery, when the capital punishment was
abolished, was mitigated into the divorce of the woman (the husband
having no option); the wife also lost all her rights under the marriage
contract, and was not permitted to marry her paramour (Soṭa v. 1).
The husband could, nay must, divorce her on suspicion, but her settlements would be intact. It would therefore be to his advantage
sometimes to prefer a public charge against her. The male adulterer
was scourged, but was not compelled to divorce his own wife unless
she insisted. In general, when the Mishnah speaks of "compelling" the

husband to execute a Bill of Divorce, the Court could scourge, fine, imprison, and excommunicate him, and had practically unlimited power to force him to deliver the necessary document freeing his wife. By a legal fiction which undeniably had moral justification, the act would still be described as voluntary on the husband's part. But in case of his determined contumely, there would be no redress, as the Court could not of its own motion dissolve a marriage, though it could pronounce a marriage *ab initio* void. The secular courts might be used to enforce the desire of the Beth-din (Giṭṭin ix. 8). But the Beth-din could not be induced to return the compliment, and validate a divorce pronounced in a Roman Court (Giṭṭin i. 5). For the whole tenour of Jewish divorce depended on the theory that divorce was the act only and solely of the husband, and no Beth-din could validate a divorce which was the act of any court, and not of the husband, in the prescribed forms. Moreover, on matters affecting marriage and divorce the Jewish courts would be most jealous of external interference. In modern times, however, the London Beth-din would refuse to sanction or validate a divorce which had not been previously effected in the civil courts of the country.

Other consequences followed from the theory that divorce was the willing act of the husband. The divorce of the insane husband of a sane wife would be impossible (Yebamoth xiv. 1), as he could not execute the deed of divorce. Nor could the insane wife of a sane husband be divorced by him, because she stood in all the greater need of his protection. (If the insanity were proved to have existed before marriage, the marriage could be pronounced initially void, for the marriage of the insane was illegal.) It should here be pointed out that though the sane husband could divorce his sane wife on a variety of grounds, and in the first century could do so without the intermediation of a Court, he could not secure himself against the divorced wife's claims for maintenance unless he satisfied the Court that the divorce had been properly executed, and that the wife's just rights had been satisfied. In that sense, the Courts would have a power to revise his personal acts, even in the early period under review. Apart also from legal duties, the husband was expected to show every possible considerateness to his divorced wife. She was, of course, no longer under his jurisdiction, she was *sui juris*, and her husband lost the usufruct of her estate. This last fact was a constant preventive of arbitrary divorce (T. B. Pesaḥim 113 b). But the husband was expected, as a humane son of Israel, to save his divorced wife from penury. "It is related of Rabbi José the Galilean (about 100 A.D.), that after his divorced wife had remarried and was reduced to poverty, he invited her and her husband into his house and supported them, although when she was his wife she had made his life miserable, and his conduct is the subject of Rabbinical laudation. 'Do not withdraw from thy flesh,' said Isaiah (lviii. 7); this, Rabbi Jacob bar Aha interpreted to mean, 'Do not withdraw help from thy divorced wife'" (Amram, *op. cit.* p. 110). If the divorced woman retained charge of infant children, the former husband not only had to maintain her, but he was also required to pay her for her services. But, in general, as to the custody of the children, the regulations were extremely favourable to the wife, who was treated with every conceivable generosity. These regulations, however, except as concerned the infant up to the time of weaning, were not formulated so early as the first century. It is clear that a husband was very reluctant to divorce his wife if she were also the mother of his children. Though it was held a duty to divorce an "evil woman"—an incurable scold and disturber of the domestic peace—nevertheless if she were a mother, the husband would waive his right and endure his fate as best he might ('Erubin 41 b).

We have already seen that the insane husband was incompetent to deliver a Bill of Divorce. In certain other cases of disease—though not of mere infirmity—the wife could claim a divorce. If she became deaf-mute after the marriage, he could divorce her; if he contracted the same defects he could not divorce her (Yebamoth xiv.). If the husband fell a victim to leprosy the wife could claim a divorce, and in the second century the Courts could enforce a separation in such cases against the will of the parties, unless the latter satisfied the authorities that there would be no continuance of sexual intercourse. The wife could claim a divorce in other cases of loathsome disease, as well as when the husband engaged in unsavoury occupations which rendered cohabitation unreasonably irksome (Kethuboth vii. 9). In those cases the wife retained her settlements. The husband could divorce the wife with loss of her settlements if she transgressed against the moral and ritual laws of Judaism, and some Rabbis of the first century held that the same rule applied if the wife made herself notorious by her indelicate conduct in public. If he became impoverished and unable, or if he were unwilling, to support her adequately, if he denied to her conjugal rights, she could by rules adopted at various times claim the right to her freedom (Kethuboth v. 8—9), indeed such treatment on his part was a breach of the contract made in the marriage deed. Similar rights accrued to the wife—some of these concessions belong to a considerably later period—if he restricted her liberty, if he became an apostate, if he committed a crime which compelled him to fly the country, if he violently and persistently ill-treated her, if he refused marital rights, and if he were openly licentious in his life.   In case of desertion, the wife could not obtain a divorce; though, in order to presume his death, the Court would waive some of its usual strictness as to the reception of evidence.   If the whereabouts of the husband were known, the local Court would use every effort to compel him to return or grant a divorce.   The excellence of intercommunication between Jewish settlements would enable the Court to trace him.   But the Court could not grant a divorce to the wife if the husband had merely vanished and left no trace, unless they saw valid ground for presuming death.   The persecutions, to which the Jews were subjected, compelled many men to leave home in search of a livelihood, and in the Middle Ages, out of love and consideration for his wife, the husband would sometimes give her a *conditional* divorce which would become effective if he failed to appear within a stated term.   It is said that in ancient times a Jewish soldier, on going to active service, delivered such a divorce which would be valid if he died on the field.   The effect would be to save his widow from the levirate marriage, from which as a divorcee she was free.   In course of time the position of the woman was continuously improved, generation after generation of Rabbinical jurists endeavouring to secure to her an ever greater measure of justice and generosity.

The wife's barrenness, after ten years' married life, was a ground for divorce (Yebamoth 64 a); later on it was disputed whether the Court should leave the man to follow his own feeling in the matter, or whether it should *compel* him to divorce his wife, or alternatively (in countries where monogamy was not demanded by law) marry an additional wife.   Philo gives us reason to think that at the earlier period husbands were reluctant to make use of their power to divorce a barren wife.   But childless marriages were regarded as a failure, and the point gave much trouble at various epochs.   It was a religious duty to beget offspring, this was the fundamental purpose of marriage.   We very rarely come across a celibate among the well-known Pharisees. Ben-'Azzai (Tos. Yebamoth viii. 4, Soṭa 4 b etc., cf. *J. E.* ii. 672) was a rare exception.   He belongs to the beginning of the second century, and he remained unmarried though he denounced celibacy.   When a colleague remonstrated with him, pointing out the inconsistency between his conduct and his doctrine, Ben-'Azzai replied : "What shall I do ? My soul clings in love to the Torah (Law); let others contribute to the preservation of the race." But it was not believed that this prime duty to society could be vicariously performed, and every Jew was expected to be a father. The act of sexual intercourse was consciously elevated by this view from an animal function to a fulfilment of the divine plan announced at the Creation.

From this brief summary it will be seen that the Jewish law of divorce must be judged in relation to the general principles of social and domestic ethics. Rules for marriage and divorce cannot be appreciated apart from many other factors. Jewish teaching and training were directed towards producing moral sobriety, continence, purity. It did this by word and deed, by formulating moral maxims and fostering moral habits. Society usually attacks the problem at the wrong end; it penalises marital offences instead of making those offences rare. The ancient Synagogue dealt with the youth and maid in the formative period of their lives. The Jewish law of divorce applied to a society of firm domestic solidarity, it was the law of a society in which young marriages predominated, and the contracting parties entered into a life-long wedlock straight from a pious and virtuous home, a home in which harmony and happiness were the rule, and the relations between husband, wife and children were distinguished by a rarely equalled and never surpassed serenity and reverence. As a saying (certainly not later than the first century) runs (Yebamoth 62 b): "Our masters have taught, He who loves his wife as himself, and honours her more than himself; who leads his sons and daughters in the straight path, and marries them near their time of maturity;—to his house the words of Job apply (v. 24): Thou shalt know that thy tent is in peace." With much of this ideal the modern world has lost sympathy, but the Judaism of the first century maintained it, and built on it a moral structure which stands high among the manifold attempts to erect an effective discipline of life.

X. WIDOWS' HOUSES.

That in all ages, and not inconspicuously in our own, men are tempted to make undue use of their influence over wealthy women in the cause of religious institutions is a familiar fact. In the second century, in Sepphoris, the women resented the duty of supporting scholars (*Baraitha* in *Pesaḥim* 49 b). But, on the other hand, we have the testimony of Jerome that Jewish women were not only among the regular performers of this obligation, but were eulogised by him on this very ground, "Ex quo apparet eum de aliis sanctis dixisse mulieribus, quae *juxta morem Judaicum* magistris de sua substantia ministrabant, sicut legimus ipsi quoque Domino factitatum" (*Adversus Jovinianum* i. 277; cf. A. Büchler, *Sepphoris*, p. 75).

These last words of Jerome are a striking reminder of the unequal measure with which the Pharisees and their opponents are judged, not by Jerome but by more recent writers. The influence exercised by the early preachers of the Gospel over women is well attested, and held the reverse of blameworthy. When, then, Josephus complains of the "great influence over women" which a certain Pharisaic faction possessed (*Antiq.* XVII. ii. 4), it is scarcely just to endorse his condemnation, or to forget two points: (a) he distinctly speaks of a faction only (μόριον), carefully avoiding the word by which he usually designates the main body of the Pharisees (αἱρέσεις); (b) his animosity is directed against the *political* activity of this faction, who committed what to Josephus was the height of iniquity, in that "when all the rest of the people gave assurance by oath of their good-will to the Emperor and to the King's government, these very men would not swear, who were more than 6000; and when the King imposed a fine upon them, Pheroras' wife paid the fine for them."

Moreover, it must be remembered that such charges were part of the ordinary invective of controversy. In the Psalms of Solomon (see particularly Ps. iv.) the Pharisees themselves make a very similar attack on the Sadducees. In the Assumption of Moses, again, the Pharisaic author (vii. 6) assails either the zealots of his own order or the priestly caste in the words that they are "devourers of the goods of the poor," saying they do so out of mercy (misericordiam, according to Charles the word means *justice*). Colani's contention that this last phrase is to be explained by the decree of the Sanhedrin (Kethuboth 50 a) in the second century forbidding a man to give more than one-fifth of his fortune and income to the poor is monstrous. The decree of the Sanhedrin was due to the excessive generosity which led men to impoverish themselves in the cause of charity, with perhaps (as Dr Kohler ingeniously suggests) some intentional opposition to the Essenic communism and to such ideas as Matthew xix. 21 (*J. E.* III. p. 668). The Talmûd gives the former reason, and in any event the expression "devourers of the goods of the poor" cannot be explained by any such incident. Dr Charles thinks the Sadducees are attacked ; if so, one must not assume that the attack of their critics was just. The poor no doubt often felt the pressure of the taxes imposed on them, and there is a late Midrash (Shoḥar Ṭob on Ps. i., cf. Yalquṭ) in which a biting satire is put into the mouth of Korah. He adduces the case of a widow who is deprived of her crops and sheep by the many demands made on her slender resources by the priests. Certainly the Pharisees were themselves the most severe critics of the possible abuses of their own system. When, however, M. Friedländer remarks (*Die religiösen Bewegungen innerhalb des Judentums im Zeitalter Jesu*, p. 112) that the Pharisees themselves said quite as severe things as did Jesus about certain abuses ("schlimmeres wahrlich hat auch Jesus nicht von diesen Weltverderbern ausgesagt"), he misses the significance of this fact. If the Pharisees were thus critical, then it is manifestly unjust to treat the criticism as though it could apply against Pharisaism as a whole.

To justify the words "which devour widows' houses" as a description of average scribes, would require much more evidence than has ever been adduced. "Widows were known there (in Jerusalem), it appears, who had been reduced from comfort to beggary by giving up their means to religious uses at the suggestion of scribes" (Menzies on Mk xii. 38, p. 229). The text hardly requires us to make this assumption. But then there comes the incident of the Widow's mites. "She of her want did cast in all that she had, even all her living" (Mk xii. 43). This sacrifice is eulogised, and justly. Yet the acceptance of such a gift might be denounced by a hostile critic as a "devouring" of the widow's substance. Jesus, however, praises it, just as the

Pharisaic Scribe does in the story (cited by Schöttgen). A priest who had scorned a certain woman's handful of flour was rebuked in a vision overnight: "Despise her not; it is as though she offered her life" (*Leviticus Rabba* iii. § 5). It need hardly be added that the Pharisees attached much importance to the exiguous gifts of the poor (cf. the passages adduced by Schöttgen on Mark, p. 251; *Baba Bathra* 10 a; *Leviticus Rabba* iii., where the poor's offering of two doves is preferred to King Agrippa's thousand sacrifices קרבן של עני קדמך; see also Wünsche, p. 402, he quotes: *Numbers Rabba* xiv., Mishnah, *Menaḥoth* xiii. 1; and add *Pesaḥim* 118 a). On the other hand, Gould (Mark xii. 40) suggests that "the devouring of widows' houses would be under the forms of civil law, but in contravention of the Divine law of love."

But the forms of civil law were by no means harsh on widows. The prevalent custom in Jerusalem and Galilee was to allow a widow to remain in her husband's house, and be maintained from his estate during the days of her widowhood (Mishnah, *Kethuboth* iv. 12). In Judæa (apart from Jerusalem) the widow might be compelled to receive her settlement, and then leave the house. Such a rule might have pressed hard in certain cases. Strong language is used in a late passage in the Palestinian Talmud against those who help the "orphans" to take this harsh course against "widows" (T.J. *Soṭa* on iii. 4). But on the whole the widow was well protected by the Jewish civil law (see L. N. Dembitz in the *Jewish Encyclopedia*, xii. p. 514). The example of the widow of Zarephath was held up for imitation (*Cant. R.* ii. 5, § 3) and Jerome's praise would well apply to such a case. But to "devour widows' houses" was no common failing of those who based their lives as the Pharisees did on the Scriptures which so often and so pathetically plead the widow's cause. Moralists in all ages have had to repeat this urgent appeal, and there was no doubt adequate ground for such a homily in the age of Jesus. But the Pharisaic teachers were keenly alive to their duty in all periods to take up the cause of the widow. And they expressed themselves emphatically on the subject again and again; nowhere, perhaps more forcibly than in their saying *Exodus R.* ch. xxx. (כל הגוזלן כאלו גוזל להק"ב), "He who robs the widow and orphans is as though he robbed God himself."

XI. THE CLEANSING OF THE TEMPLE.

From a not unreasonable point of view the dignity and worth of the Temple in relation to national life must be considered as enhanced and not diminished by the association of that life with the Temple environment. The sacro-sanctity of the inner courts would be, as it were, humanised by the secularisation of the more remote precincts. To many a modern mind it is attractive rather than repellent to read of the popular uses to which the Temple was sometimes devoted. The famous celebration of the semi-religious function of the Water-Drawing, during the Feast of Tabernacles, with its deep spiritual significance allied to merry, carnival-like rites, is a case in point. Modern writers are too apt to confuse Pharisaism with Puritanism; more than half of the contrasts imagined between Hellenism and Hebraism arise from this same confusion. Josephus, moreover, records the holding of even more pronouncedly secular assemblages within or close to the Temple precincts (*War* I. xx; II. i, xvi; v. v). The tendency to treat the modern Synagogue as a place formally restricted to purposes of worship was a reaction which is happily breaking down, especially in America, where so many of the so-called Jewish reforms are reversions to ancient traditions.

"But indeed in those days nearly every priest must have been a trader." With these words Dr G. A. Smith concludes his brilliant account of the Temple Revenues, Properties and Finance in the first century of the Christian era (*Jerusalem*, Vol. I. p. 366). But surely the same might be said with equal validity of the governing bodies of many a Church and University in our own times, without implying that the financial side of these institutions was unduly prominent. The question always is: what is the implication? There is little ground for the supposition that the people were, in general, oppressed by the Temple financial arrangements. The Temple, again, was made a place of safe deposit for private money, but no trading was involved, and the authorities who speak of these deposits in the Temple almost explicitly state this. Thus the stores alluded to in II. Maccs. iii. were, as Dr Smith points out, "laid up for the relief of widows and fatherless children," and in part belonged to Hyrcanus son of Tobias. "It was," writes the same authority (II. Maccs. iii. 12), "altogether impossible that [by confiscating this money] such wrongs should be done unto them that had committed it to the holiness of the place, and to the majesty and inviolable sanctity of the Temple, honoured over all the world." The priests would clearly have no financial operations at all in relation to such funds, while Josephus (*War* VI. v. 2) when he says that in the Temple treasuries "the rich had built themselves store-chambers there" refers to a time of stress, when the Temple would, as a fortified place, be an obvious asylum. Again, here, however, the language of Josephus does not suggest that the priests in any way traded with the money. From the same historian's earlier account of the Parthian raid on Jerusalem (*War* I. xiii. 9) it may be gathered that private persons were not in normal times in the habit of using the Temple treasury as the store-house of their property. It is scarcely worth while citing the mass of facts available to show that sacred edifices have in many ages been used as safe-deposits, without necessarily incurring any suspicion of the taint of commercialism.

The presence in the Temple precincts of money-changers—for a full account of whose operations see S. Krauss, *Talmudische Archäologie*, 1911, II. 411—is generally conceded to have been an arrangement designed for the advantage of the pilgrims. The Temple-tax of half a shekel had to be paid in definite coinage. It could not be paid in ingots, but only in stamped coins (T.B. *Berachoth* 47 b with reference to Deut. xiv. 25; cf. *Sifrê* ad loc.). It must not be paid in inferior alloy but in high grained silver (T.B. *Bechoroth* 51 a). Again and again we are informed that the only coins accepted were *Tyrian* (Mishnah, *Bechoroth* viii. 7; Tosefta, *Kethuboth* xiii. 3, ed. Zuck. p. 275), which indeed were so emphatically the legal tender in the Temple that they were termed Jerusalemite as well as Tyrian. But it is not quite clear which Tyrian coins were meant. T. Reinach points out that among the conditions imposed on the vanquished Jews by Antiochus Sidetes was the withdrawal of the right of coining silver, though the striking of small bronze coins, intended for local circulation, was intermittently continued. This was in 134 B.C. But "very few years after the surrender of Jerusalem, in 126 B.C., when the civil war was waging between the sons of Demetrius II and the usurper Alexander Zebinas, the wealthy town of Tyre seems to have snatched from one of the pretenders to the throne the practical acknowledgment of its independence and the right to issue a silver coinage of its own. The Tyrian coinage, which lasted for almost two centuries, consists mostly of shekels (staters), bearing as types the head of the town God Heracles and the Ptolemaic eagle ; their legend *Tyre the holy and inviolable* (Τύρον ἱερὸν καὶ ἄσυλον) seems to be imitated from the *Yerushalem Kedoshah* of Simon's shekels. The dates are reckoned from the new era of 126 B.C. These coins, notwithstanding their heathen types and Greek lettering, were of so exact a weight and so good an alloy that they enjoyed a large circulation in Judæa, and were even officially adopted as sacred money, that is to say the Rabbis decided that the annual head-tax of one [half-]shekel due from every Israelite to the Temple treasury was to be paid in Tyrian money." It is strange enough that while the bronze coins circulated in Judæa should conform scrupulously to the tradition and represent nothing but inanimate objects, the payment of Temple dues should not only be accepted but required in coins containing figures on them. Reinach meets this objection by the suggestion that "once thrown into the Temple treasury, all gold and silver coins were melted down and transformed into ingots" (T. Reinach, *Jewish Coins*, ed. Hill, 1903, pp. 20—23). At all events, while the coins most current in Syria were the Roman tetradrachms and denarii (such a silver denarius is referred to in Matthew xxii. 15), the Temple demanded payment on the Phoenician standard (cf. Krauss, *op. cit.*, p. 405), and the money-changer for this (and for other reasons) was therefore an actual necessity.

In passing it may be remarked that there is no ground for supposing that the ordinary business of money-changing went on in the Temple. In the. N.T. the word κολλυβιστής is always used in describing the scene of the cleansing of the Temple, and it must be interpreted to mean the receiver of the *qolbon* (קולבון), or fee for changing other currencies into Temple currency and exclusively for Temple use. When Mark (xi. 16) adds the detail that Jesus "would not allow any one to carry a vessel through the Temple," the meaning no doubt is that he sided with those who ordained that the Temple must not be made a public thoroughfare (T.B. *Yebamoth* 6 b). Others went further, and forbade frivolous behaviour outside the Temple precincts and in the neighbourhood of the Eastern Gate (*Berachoth* 54 a). Similar rules were applied to the Synagogues (*Megillah* 27—28), and one may cite the regulation in Cambridge against carrying trade parcels through the College precincts. That Jesus is applying an established rule and not innovating is confirmed by the fact that he cites old prophetic texts (Isaiah lvi. 7, Jer. vii. 11) in support of his attitude.

Granting, then, that certain commercial operations were necessary for the maintenance of the Temple or convenient for those who had occasion to present themselves in its courts, there was nothing in such circumstances inherently censurable. If there was a sort of market within the Temple enclosure, it is impossible to assent to Dr Edersheim's easy conclusion : " It needs no comment to show how utterly the Temple would be profaned by such traffic." On the contrary, it needs much comment to show this. Equally exaggerated is Lightfoot's characterisation of the money-changer's profit as "unholy gain." Gould, in his note on Mark xi. 17, clearly sees that such attacks imply not merely an invective against an illegitimate use of the Temple, but a thorough-going antipathy to trade as such. Yet if the money-changer were necessary his profits were not "unholy." The labourer is worthy of his hire. Thus, there was considerable labour, and that of an expert kind, involved in the examination of animals to pronounce them perfect or blemished, and a fee was naturally charged (Mishnah, *Bechoroth* iv. 5). These fees as well as the profits of the money-changers were strictly limited by law and usage. Dr Edersheim seriously over-estimated the gain. " If we compute the annual Temple-tribute at about £75,000, the bankers' profits may have amounted to from £8000 to £9000, an immense sum in the circumstances of the country." We have, on the other hand, the clear statement that the profit was only one in twenty-four or one in forty-eight (Tosefta, *Sheqalim* i. 8, ed. Zuck. p. 174; Maimonides, *Sheqalim* iii. 7 ; Krauss, *Talmudische Archäologie* II. 413). Even if we take the higher estimate, that of Rabbi Meir, Edersheim has overrated the changer's earnings by three to one.

Nor is it at all certain that this profit found its way regularly into private pockets. The Babylonian Talmud (*Menaḥoth* 108 a) has no suggestion of the secular destination of the changer's gain. Maimonides (*loc. cit.*) decides that the profit was used for the Temple purposes. Here he was following the tradition of Meir. In the Jer. Talmud there is indeed an opinion expressed that the money-changer himself took the profit. But this opinion is only one among several, and very probably refers to the provincial money-changers and not to those in the Temple. From the fifteenth to the twenty-fifth of Adar the money-changers set up their "tables" in every country place (Mishnah,

Sheqalim i. 3), and it is probable that the banker received the commission of one in twenty-four for himself. Schwab, in his French translation of the Palestinian Talmud (Vol. v. p. 268) inserts the words "en province," which is a manifest impropriety, for though this may be the sense, the words do not occur in the text, which runs as follows :— "To what use were the qolbons turned? R. Meir says, they were added to the fund of the sheqalim ; R. Lazar says, they were employed for free-will offerings—nedabah ; R. Simeon of Shizur (Saijur) says, they provided with them gold-plates and covering for the Holy of Holies ; Ben Azzai says, the bankers took them as their profit; and some say they used them for the expense of keeping the roads in repair" (T.J. *Sheqalim*, chapter i. last lines). The roads were put in order at the beginning of Adar (Mishnah, *Sheqalim* i. 1). This association of the repair of the roads with Ben Azzai's view may justify the conclusion that he was referring to provincial and not Jerusalem transactions (the scene of the money-changing was transferred to the Temple on Adar the twenty-fifth ; Mishnah, *Sheqalim* i. 2). In the parallel passage in the Tosefta, however, the words about the repair of the roads are wanting. Nevertheless, the weight of evidence is in favour of the verdict that the gains of the exchange were devoted to public and not to private ends. When once the money had been paid over to the Temple treasury, it was held unlawful to use it to gain profit even for the Sanctuary (at least this was Aqiba's view, Mishnah, *Sheqalim* iv. 3); but as the qolbons were paid before the money was actually received by the Sanctuary, they would not be profit directly made by the use of the sacred funds as capital.

We may conclude that besides the ordinary traders in money-changing, there were also operators of a less commercial type. The former would not have been permitted to carry on their trade in the Temple precincts; the latter were only authorised in the outer Court of the Temple between the 25th of Adar and the 1st of Nisan, an interval of about one week (Mishnah, *Sheqalim* i. 3. Cf. D. Oppenheim, *Literaturblatt des Orients*, Vol. x. 1849, p. 555). As, in this case, the profits were destined for public and sacred uses, and the operator received no gain from the transactions, it would seem likely that the money-changing for purposes of the Temple-tax was performed by officials of the Temple, that is by the priests. This would ensure that in normal circumstances the people would be fairly treated, and it was only under the aristocratic régime of the Temple's last decades that we hear of oppression. This occurred less with regard to the money-changing than with regard to the prices of pigeons and so forth for the sacrifices, the actual buying and selling of which moreover do not seem to have been normally carried on within the Temple precincts (cf. Oppenheim, *op. cit.* p. 556). When oppression occurred, the popular defenders of the people in such cases were the Pharisaic leaders. We find on record the action of various Rabbis which lowered the prices of pigeons even to the point of modifying the law on the subject (Mishnah, *Kerithoth* i. 7, where by reducing the number of pigeons to be brought by women the price of the birds was lowered by Simeon ben Gamliel from a gold denarius to half a silver denarius—that is to one-fiftieth of the original price). An earlier Rabbi (Baba ben Buta, contemporary with Herod) actually brought in 3000 sheep so that offerers might have animals for use. But Edersheim adds to the latter story a detail absent from the source he quotes (T.J. *Ḥagigah* ii. 3). Baba ben Buta found the Temple desolated as he termed it, but not because the grasping priests had limited the supply to maintain a high price, but because it was a festival and the ruling priests held that it was not lawful for private offerings to be brought on a holy day. The question was one at issue between the Schools of Hillel and Shammai, and Baba ben Buta, though a disciple of the latter, in this detail followed the decision of the former. But there is evidence enough that certain rapacious priestly families were detested by the people (witness the case of the House of Ḥanan) and that the Pharisees themselves denounced such practices (T.B. *Pesaḥim* 57 a). While, then, it is impossible to agree that the whole of "this traffic, money-changing, selling of doves, and market for sheep and oxen was in itself, and from its attendant circumstances, a terrible desecration" (Edersheim), there might well have been occasions on which indignation such as that of Jesus would be justified. But we must not magnify an exception into the rule.

The danger always lies in this tendency to confuse a system with its abuses. This, as it seems to me, is an error made by many commentators on the Gospels, who seek to expand the often-enough just criticism of Jesus against abuses, into an unjust condemnation of the whole Pharisaic system. It is fair enough for the anti-Nomists to criticise and judge Pharisaism as a religion based on Law; but there is no justice in refusing to consider the legalistic point of view and its possible merits. Still less is it fair to confuse legalism with externalism, or to assume without close examination of each instance that the moral abuses, which seem superficially inherent in a legalistic system, were really the logical result of the system, or did actually occur in

Pharisaism as lived by those who believed and rejoiced in it. (R. Travers Herford's *Pharisaism, its Aim and its Method*, London 1912, appeared after the present volume was mostly in type. Otherwise frequent reference would have been made to this brilliant and successful attempt to do justice both to Jesus and to the Pharisees.) The Cleansing of the Temple is a good case in point. And, therefore, I venture to repeat here what I wrote at an earlier date, when pleading for a revision of this tendency where the judgment on Pharisaism is concerned (*Jewish Quarterly Review*, 1899, p. 641). "Externalism needs the most careful watching, and ritual is always in need of freshening under the inspiration of the ideas which lie behind it. But Pharisaism was not ritualism. I, and many Jews with me, have no resentment whatever against the general spirit of the criticism to which the Law was subjected by Jesus, against his healthy onslaught against externalism. When Jesus overturned the money-changers and ejected the sellers of doves from the Temple he did a service to Judaism.... But were the money-changers and the dove-sellers the only people who visited the Temple? And was everyone who bought or sold a dove a mere formalist? Last Easter I was in Jerusalem, and along the façade of the Church of the Holy Sepulchre I saw the stalls of the vendors of sacred relics, of painted beads and inscribed ribbons, of coloured candles, gilded crucifixes, and bottles of Jordan water. There these Christians babbled and swayed and bargained, a crowd of buyers and sellers in front of the Church sacred to the memory of Jesus. Would, I thought, that Jesus were come again to overthrow these false servants of his, even as he overthrew his false brothers in Israel long ago. But I will also tell you what I did not think. I did not think that the buying and selling of sacred relics was the sole motive which brought thousands of pilgrims to Jerusalem; I did not say: Here is the whole of the Gospel, this is its inevitable end, its sure outcome. I knew that there is more in Christianity than this, that there are other Christians than these. Nay, as I turned away, I thought that perhaps if I had the insight to track a dealer in relics to his inmost soul, I might after all find there a heart warm with the love of Christ."

It must finally be remembered that the payment of the Temple-tax was a privilege as well as a burden. It was the typical illustration of the democratic basis of Jewish life. The daily sacrifices being for all Israel were paid for by all Israel. "All Israel were partners in this" (*Pesiqta Rabbathi* x, ed. Friedmann, p. 33 b). An individual might not claim the privilege to pay for the whole cost of the continual offerings (see Friedmann's note *ad loc.*) : all Israel must share in the burden and the privilege.   In estimating the effect of the Temple dues on the popular life this element must not be overlooked.   It colours the whole estimate we have to form of the system.   There were amenities as well as sacrifices involved in the sacrificial institution. It was not founded on exaction nor corrupted by peculation.   These were the occasional abuses of a régime which, on the whole, secured popular enthusiasm for a beloved tradition.

XII. THE PARABLES.

"The parable became a truth, proved upon the pulses of men."
These words, used by a modern writer in another connection, aptly
characterise the abiding significance of the New Testament Parables.
A vast amount of religious and literary genius has been directed,
throughout the ages, to the worthy object of extracting the fullest
meaning from the Parables attributed to Jesus. But far more effective
has been the process by which these Parables have been "proved upon
the pulses of men."

It is generally felt that Jesus was not the originator of the method
of teaching by Parables. Even Jülicher, who advances so strenuous
a plea for the originality of the *contents* of the New Testament Parables,
does not claim—of course in presence of the Old Testament Parables
cannot claim—that the method was a new creation (*Die Gleichnisreden
Jesu*, I. 164). Bousset roundly asserts that, though as an exponent
of the Parabolic art Jesus "spoke" while the Rabbis "stammered,"
nevertheless "Jesus owed the vehicle on which he mainly relied in
his popular preaching—the Parable—to the Synagogue and the
Scribes" (*Jesus*, p. 30). And, again, "There can be no doubt that
he first learned such a manner of teaching in the Synagogue. All
that has come down to us in the way of Parables from Rabbinic
tradition—later though they undoubtedly are—bears so close a resemblance both in form and matter to the Parables of Jesus, that
no idea of accident can be entertained. And *since any influence of
Jesus upon the later Jewish Rabbinism is out of the question*, we can
only assume that Jesus caught the form of his Parabolic speech from
the Scribes in the Synagogue" (*op. cit.* p. 43). On both the points
raised in this last sentence Bousset is probably right, but he has
gone beyond the evidence in the vigour of his statement, for we know
very little as to the contemporary style of Synagogue homily. It is,
however, true that just in the case of ideas which affect the folk

influence is most likely to be exercised without the consciousness of imitation. Ziegler (*Die Königsgleichnisse des Midrasch*, 1903, Intro-duction) righ⁺ly maintains that many Parables must have been part of the common fund (*Gemeingut*) of the people, and that Jesus may have drawn upon and added to this common fund. Jesus had no need to take his Parables from other Agadists, just as other Agadists had no need to take their Parables from Jesus. But as Ziegler judiciously sums up the matter, p. xxii : " It is indeed conceivable that Jesus employed much that he had heard from his teachers ; it is also possible that sundry Parables of Jesus became popular, lived on in the mouth of the folk, and thence were taken over by later Agadists, without the least inkling on their part as to the identity of their author, just as to-day Heine is inadvertently quoted by the most pronounced Heine-phobes—yet it is out of the question to assert anything like a systematic influence of one side on the other." There must have been a large Jewish stock of fables and parables floating about long before they were set down in writing (Fiebig, *Altjüdische Gleichnisse und die Gleichnisse Jesu*, 1904, 25), and it is possible that both the Tannaim and Evangelists drew from the stock.

Close comparison of the Gospel Parables with the most similar of the Rabbinic nearly always reveals dissimilarity amid the similarity. Though in his earlier work just cited, Fiebig falls short of justice to the Rabbinic Parables as a whole, I fully agree with a conclusion which he reaches in his later work (*Die Gleichnisreden Jesu*, Tübingen, Mohr 1912), which appeared after this Note was in type. Fiebig is clearly right when he claims that the Gospel Parables are marked by characteristic features which testify to an original and exalted personality in their authorship, or at least in their adaptation. Yet the hand of the editor has been at work, and it is scarcely possible to formulate canons of criticism by which the genuine Parables of Jesus may be distinguished from the rest. It would be delightful could we accept fully the view of the Rev. J. W. Hunkin (*Journal of Theological Studies*, xvi. 381) that "the parables have been transmitted in the Synoptic tradition very nearly in the form in which they were spoken by Jesus." But without going this length, it is obvious that some of the Synoptic Parables point to a strong personality. And the same is true of the Rabbinic Parables. Amid the sameness one detects individualities. Hillel, Aqiba, Meir, Joshua b. Levi, Abbahu, are to a certain extent as distinct in their Parables and Similes as in their doctrines, and if they drew on the common stock of their people's lore,

reinforced as that stock was by accretions from the lores of other folk,
they made their borrowings, as their inventions were, personal by the
genius with which they applied them to living issues.

All authorities are agreed that there can have been no direct,
literary borrowing by the later Rabbis from the books of the New
Testament.   Thus Prof. Burkitt suggests (*J. T. S.* xv. 618) that
Matthew vii. 24—7 is the ultimate source of the Rabbinic contrast
of two forms of building in *Aboth de Rabbi Nathan* xxiv.   The parallel
is not close in detail, and an examination of the variant in the second
recension of the *Aboth* xxxv. renders it remotely possible that we have
here a confused reminiscence of some Philonean ideas on the Tower of
Babel (Mangey, I. 420).   The Rabbis were, moreover, fond of comparing
the various aspects of the study and performance of Law to firm and
infirm structure such as a tree with many and few roots (Mishnah,
Aboth iii. 22).   But if there were borrowing in the particular case
before us, Prof. Burkitt is clearly right in holding that "it was
probably second-hand, i.e. from one of the Minim," and that the
Midrash "put it down to Elisha ben Abuya [the heretic] to avoid
offence."   Similarly, if it be the case that the Talmud (*Meʿilah* 17 b)
borrowed from a Christian source the story of an exorcism, the
borrowing must have been unconscious.   (But see on this interesting
point the discussion in the *Revue des Études Juives* vii. 200, x. 60, 66,
xxxv. 285.)

Another instance of greater curiosity concerns the Parable of the
Prodigal Son.   In the literary sense this is original to Luke.   But
some of the phraseology seems traceable to Aḥiqar, and the root idea
is Philonean (G. Friedländer, *The Grace of God*, 1910).   Now, the
text of the Talmud must at one time have contained a passage
reminiscent of the Parable.   For in a Genizah MS. (published by
L. Ginzberg in *Gaonica*, New York, 1909, ii. 377) Aḥa, the famous
eighth century Gaon, quotes *Sanhedrin* 99 a in a version no longer
fully extant in the Talmud texts.   To illustrate the Pharisaic principle
that the penitent sinner stands on a higher level than the completely
righteous, Abbahu cites the parable of "a king who had two sons, one
of whom ordered his way well, while the other went out to depraved
living"

למלך שהיו לא [לו] שני בנים אחד הלך בטוב ואחד יצא לתרבות רעה

This looks like a reminiscence of Luke's Parable, and it may have been
removed from the Talmud text by scribes more cognisant than Abbahu
was of the source of the story.   Dr Ginzberg, who recognised the

similarity, takes another view. His words (*op. cit.* p. 351) are: "The source for the parable...is not known to me. Obviously R. Aḥa must have had it in his text of the Talmud....In any event, it is the short, original form of the New Testament parable of the prodigal son."

And here reference may be made to another instance. The Gospel Parable of the Sower is introduced by the medieval Jewish adapter of the Barlaam and Josaphat romance. Abraham b. Ḥisdai wrote his Hebrew version (*Ben ha-melech we-hanazir*) under the title "King's Son and Nazirite," or as moderns prefer to render the Hebrew title "Prince and Dervish," in the thirteenth century. The tenth chapter contains the Parable of the Sower at great length. The main idea, comparing the propagation of Wisdom to the Sower, must have occurred in the original Indian of Barlaam (J. Jacobs, *Barlaam and Josaphat*, 1896, p. cxi). A well-known Indian parallel, moreover, is found in the Sutta Nihata (cf. P. Carus, *Gospel of Buddha* § 74); this is clearly more primitive than the Gospel version. Yet Abraham b. Ḥisdai gives us a form, the details of which are for the most part bodily derived from the New Testament, a fact of which he was assuredly unaware. The over-working of the Indian original of Barlaam by a Christian redactor must have already occurred in the recension of the romance used by the Hebrew translator as his base. (On the problem of the relation of the Hebrew to other versions of Barlaam see M. Steinschneider, *Die hebraeischen Uebersetzungen des Mittelalters*, Berlin, 1893, § 532.) With regard to another suggestion of Rabbinic borrowing, the case is different. It has been argued that the beautiful Parable of the Blind and Lame (see below) is not Rabbinic, but Indian. The Indian parallels cannot, however, be the source of the Rabbinic Parable as it now stands. In the Indian (E. Leumann, *Die Avasyaka-Erzählungen*, Leipzig, 1897, p. 19) a lame man gets on a blind man's back and together they escape from a forest fire. This is not a *source* for the Rabbinic Parable, which differs totally in idea. Nor can I be persuaded by Dr M. James (*J.T.S.* xv. 236) that the version of the Parable (much closer to the Rabbinic than the Indian is) found in Epiphanius (ed. Dindorf, II. 683) is older than the Rabbinic. The Christian form seems to me derived from the latter. Finally I may refer to the Parable of the Three Rings, made famous by Lessing in his *Nathan der Weise*. There are many parallels to this, some using it as a vindication of Christianity, others of Italian scepticism. In the Hebrew Chronicle of Solomon ibn Verga, it is a pathetic plea for tolerance by an oppressed faith, and M. Gaston Paris firmly maintains that if not originally Jewish, the Parable is presented in its original form by the Hebrew Chronicler (*Revue des Études Juives* xi. 5).

Naturally, the preceding jottings—to which others might be added —are not designed as a formal discussion of the problem of borrowing. They may, however, serve as an indication of the vast amount of research, literary and historical, yet remaining to be undertaken before the problem can be seriously considered.   One thing is clear; the result cannot but be a triumph for humanism.   That Buddha could be made a hero for Christian and Jew is not the least of the episodes in that triumph.

Free trade in good stories corresponds to the common experience and common aspiration of mankind.   We have, in the readiness of men to adopt other men's superstitions, a sad comment on the universality of the lower elements in human nature.   But the adoption by one and all from one and all of beautiful Parables is a mark of the universality of the higher elements.   It is of itself a beautiful Parable "to preach the simple brotherhood of souls that seek the highest good."

We must try to get closer to another aspect of the historical problem. The Parable was used by Old Testament writers with perfection of art. The Tannaim, from the latter part of the first Christian century onwards, make a far more extensive use of the method.   But, in between, the later Biblical writers, the authors of the Pre-Christian Jewish Apocalypses (with the possible exception of Enoch) and such a representative Alexandrian as Philo have no parables.   In one of his early works (*Markus-Studien*, 1899, p. 11), an able Jewish scholar, H. P. Chajes, concludes that in the age of Jesus the Parable was an unusual device, and that it had not yet won the place which it afterwards filled in the Rabbinic method of popular instruction.   He even suggests that this is the original meaning of the Evangelists' discrimination between the teaching of Jesus and that of the Scribes.   "He taught as one having authority" should read "he spoke in Parable."   (Underlying the Greek text ὡς ἐξουσίαν ἔχων is the Hebrew *Ke-moshel*—כְּמֹשֵׁל—which Dr Chajes would emend to *be-mashal*—בְּמָשָׁל.)   Dr Chajes proceeds (p. 12): It will easily be retorted, How could the mere use of Parables have made so striking a sensation, seeing that the *Mashal* (Parable) plays so prominent a rôle among the Rabbis?   Yes, among the Rabbis; but it is extremely doubtful whether this was yet the case in the age of Jesus.   A real Agadic activity cannot be posited before the epoch of Hillel, and no Parable can with certainty be assigned to that teacher.

It was only at a later period, after the destruction of the Temple, that the Parable attained high honour, as we already find it to be the case with Johanan ben Zakkai, Joshua ben Hananya, and especially Meir (cf. Mishnah, *Sota*, ix. 15 ; T. B. *Sanhedrin*, 38 b, last lines).

This argument scarcely survives examination. One Rabbinic source ascribes to Hillel (and, in some readings, also to his contemporary Shammai) a mystic knowledge of the language of the hills, the trees, the beasts and the demons, and a special predilection for parables or fables (*Soferim*, xvi. 9). The authenticity of this ascription is doubted by Bacher (*Agada der Tannaiten*, I. 10, notes 3—5). But the *only* ground for this suspicion is the fact that the Talmud (T. B. *Sukkah*, 25 a) makes the same remark concerning Johanan ben Zakkai. *Soferim* seems to present the older tradition, for while it equally ascribes this knowledge to Johanan, it also carries the statement back to Hillel, whose disciple Johanan was. Weiss, the author of the History of Jewish Tradition (in Hebrew) *Dor dor vedorashav*, i. 157, throws no doubt on the trustworthiness of the passage in *Soferim*. That Hillel's thought sometimes ran in the direction indicated appears also from the Mishnah (*Aboth*, iv. 8), for Hillel said: "The more women, the more witchcraft"—he may therefore have had an academic interest in demonology as *Soferim* asserts. And it is otherwise quite clear that at all events part of the statement in *Soferim* must be true, for we have abundant evidence that Hillel was fond of Parabolical forms of speech (cf. Weiss, *op. cit.* pp. 160 seq.). That Hillel was interested in folk-lore is demonstrated by the anecdotes told of him (T.B. *Sabbath* 31 a, *Aboth de R. Nathan* xv.). Again, in the last reference, in his interview with a would-be proselyte, Hillel is recorded to have compared the study of the details of the Temple service to the etiquette at an earthly Court. This comes very near an actual Parable. So, too, there is a compressed Parable in Hillel's striking enunciation of the doctrine of retribution: "He saw a skull which floated on the face of the water, and he said to it, Because thou didst drown (others) they drowned thee, and in the end they that drowned thee shall be drowned" (Mishnah, *Aboth*, ii. 7). Another of Hillel's phrases: "He who serves himself with the tiara perishes" (*ib.*) is a figurative condemnation of the self-seeker's appropriation of the Crown of the Torah. Illustrating the covenant of love between God and Israel Hillel said: "To the place that my heart loves my feet carry me. If thou comest to My house, I will come to thine; but if thou comest not to My house I will not come to thine"

(Tosefta, *Sukkah*, iv. 3).   There are several other such sayings
recorded of Hillel; and frequent mention is made of his wide
acquaintance with popular lore as well as his readiness to enter
into familiar conversation with the common folk.   All of this goes to
confirm the authenticity of the tradition reported in *Soferim* as cited
above.   Besides this, there are quoted in Hillel's name two actual
Parables—rudimentary, but bearing unmistakably the Parabolical
stamp.   Bacher fully accepts the authenticity of these Parables
though they occur in a somewhat late Midrash (Leviticus *Rabba*,
lxxxiv.).   Chajes adduces no adequate ground for suspicion.   The first
of the two Parables referred to is as follows : Hillel's disciples were
walking with him on a certain occasion, and when he departed from
their company they enquired "Whither goest thou?"   He answered,
"I go to fulfil a religious duty."—"What duty?"—"To bathe in the
bath-house."—"Is this, then, a duty?"—"Ay," replied Hillel; "the
statues of kings which are set in theatres and circuses—he who is
appointed concerning them cleanses and polishes them; he is sustained
for the purpose, and he grows great through intercourse with the great
ones of the kingdom.   I, created in the image and likeness of God,
how much more must I keep my body clean and untainted."   Ziegler
(*op. cit.* p. 17) agrees with Weiss and Bacher in holding this passage
a genuine saying.   The authenticity is guaranteed (as Bacher argues)
on linguistic grounds, for whereas the preceding passage is in Hebrew,
the second Parable which immediately follows is in Aramaic, and this
very intermixture and interchange of Hebrew and Aramaic is characteristic of several of Hillel's best authenticated utterances.   The second
Parable is this : again Hillel is walking with his disciples (the parallel
to the journeys of Jesus in the company of his disciples may be noted);
he turns to part from them, and they ask his destination. "I go home,"
said Hillel, "to render loving service to a certain guest who sojourns in
my house."—"Hast thou then a guest ever in thy house?"—"Is not
the unhappy soul a sojourner within the body?   To-day it is here, and
to morrow it is gone!"

At this point a general remark may be interpolated.   While
rendering these and other Rabbinic Parables, the translator feels
himself severely handicapped.   Not only were the New Testament
Parables elaborated by the Evangelists far more than the Talmudic
were by the Rabbis, but the former have been rendered with inimitable
skill and felicity, while the latter have received no such accession of
charm.   Even Herder's paraphrases of Midrashim are turgid when

compared with the chaste simplicity of style and form under which the New Testament Parables appear in the Vulgate, and even more conspicuously in Luther's Bible and the Anglican versions. These versions are, from the point of view of literary beauty, actually improvements on the Greek, just as the Hebrew of the twenty-third Psalm has gained an added grace in the incomparable English rendering with which we are all familiar. No one has done as much for the gems of Rabbinic fancy. They have remained from first to last rough jewels; successive generations of artists have not provided increasingly becoming settings to enhance their splendour. But even so some modern writers have been unfairly depreciatory of the Rabbinic Parables, for while there is a considerable number of no great significance, there are some which are closely parallel to those of the New Testament, and some others which may be justly placed on the same high level. There are no more beautiful Parables than that of the blind and the lame (*Sanhedrin*, 91 a—b, Mechilta, בשלח ii.), which may be summarised thus :

A human King had a beautiful garden in which were some fine early figs. He set in it two watchmen, one lame and the other blind. Said the lame man to the blind, "I see some fine figs, carry me on your shoulders and we will get the fruit and eat it." After a time the owner of the garden came and asked after his missing figs. The lame man protested that he could not walk, the blind that he could not see. So the master put the lame man on the blind man's back and judged them together. So God brings the soul and casts it in the body (after death) and judges them together.

It is difficult to understand why the excellence of such Parables should be contested. Fiebig (p. 88) objects that it is very improbable that a king should employ the lame and the blind as watchmen. One wonders why not, seeing that in the East particularly the old and the decrepit are much used for such sedentary work. It may be that the difficult passage II. Samuel v. 6 implies the employment of the blind and lame as sentinels of the citadel. Undoubtedly the idea of the *watchmen* is necessary for the Rabbinic Parable—which is not a mere adaptation of the Parable which Dr James cites. In the Epiphanius parallel (*J. T.S. loc. cit.*) the King is described as possessing among all his subjects *only two* men unfit for military service, this is surely not less improbable than the lame and blind watchmen. Besides, there are many improbabilities in the New Testament Parables also (as e.g. the refusal of a king's invitation to a banquet, Matt. xxii. 2; in Luke xiv. 16 the banquet however is given not by a king but by "a

A. 7

certain man"). Such improbabilities are not defects in Parables at all.
We might have been spared some inept criticism of the New Testament
Parables, had due notice been taken of the wise Rabbinic maxim: Do
not apply your logic to a Midrash. Again, it is sometimes said that
the Rabbinic Parables fall below those of the New Testament in that
the latter deal with far greater subjects, Sin and Grace, Prayer, Mercy,
Love, the Kingdom of Heaven (Fiebig, p. 105). That in the enormous
mass of Rabbinic Parables many treat of trivialities in a trivial
fashion is true; but simplicity must not be confused with insignificance.
There is a quality of homeliness about many of the Rabbinic Parables,
a quality inherited from the Bible, with its Ewe-lamb and its Song of
the Vineyard. It is this quality that distinguishes the Jewish from
the ordinary Eastern Parable; the former, far less than the latter,
merely illustrates a maxim. Many Oriental Parables are expanded
Proverbs, but the Rabbinic Parables cannot as a rule be compressed
into a Proverb. As to subject matter, very many of them are directed
to most of the subjects which Fiebig enumerates, and to other fundamental problems of life and death and the hereafter. Thus the Parable
quoted above of the lame and the blind expresses the unity of body
and soul, or rather the truth that a man is a single product of dust
and spirit. The persistence in later Jewish thought of the belief in
the bodily resurrection was in part, at least, due to the impossibility
of separating body and soul, even in the aspect of immortality.

The following summary from the excellent article by Dr J. Z.
Lauterbach (*Jewish Encyclopedia*, IX. 513 a) is a just though of
course incomplete statement of the subjects of the Rabbinic Parables:

In the Talmud and Midrash almost every religious idea, moral maxim, or
ethical requirement is accompanied by a Parable which illustrates it. Among the
religious and moral tenets which are thus explained may be mentioned the following:
the existence of God (Gen. R. xxxiv. 1); his manner of retribution, and of punishing
sins both in this world and the next ('Ab. Zarah, 4 a, Yalq. Lev. 464, Sabb. 152 a);
his faithful governance ('Ab. Zarah, 55 a, Sanh. 108 a); his impatience of injustice
(Suk. 30 a); his paternal leniency (Ex. R. xlvi. 6) and his relation to Israel
(*ib.* xlvi. 4, Ber. 32 a); Israel's sufferings (Ber. 13 a); the folly of idolatry
('Ab. Zarah, 54 b—55 a); the Law as the guardian and faithful protector in life
(Soṭah, 21 a); the sin of murder (Mechilta, יתרו, 8); the resurrection (Sabb. 91 a);
the value of benevolence (B. B., 10 a); the worth of a just man for his contemporaries (Meg. 15 a); the failure of popularity as a proof of intrinsic value
(Soṭah, 40 a); the evil tendency of freedom from anxiety (Ber. 32 a); the
limitations of human knowledge and understanding (Sanh. 39 a); the advantage
frequently resulting from what seems to be evil (Niddah, 31 a); conversion
(Sabb. 153 a); purity of soul and its reward (*ib.* 152 b).

This list could be much extended, but it suffices to demonstrate that the depreciation of the Rabbinic Parables, on the ground of triviality of motive, is a mere aberration of criticism. It can, therefore, hardly be maintained with Fiebig (*op. cit.* p. 87), that "the manifold situations of human life are only sparingly and pallidly depicted" in the Rabbinic Parables. It is, on the other hand, a sound discrimination (p. 83) that there are in the Rabbinic literature a vast number of royal Parables. Hillel and Joḥanan b. Zakkai present some examples (Bacher, *Agada der Tannaiten*, I. 73, 81). Most of the royal Parables, however, belong to the period later than the fall of Bethar in 135, and they only begin to predominate with Domitian in the hands of Agadists like Meir and Simon b. Yoḥai (Ziegler, p. xxiii). By that time the interest of Jewish moralists in good government as part of the idea of the Kingdom of God (cf. Schechter, *Aspects of Rabbinic Theology*, ch. vii.) led them to portray under royal metaphors the relations of God to man, and they did this both by way of contrast and similitude. Some of the oldest Parables in which the heroes are *kings*, perhaps dealt in their original forms with ordinary *men*, and *kings* was probably substituted for *men* in some of them (both Rabbinic and Synoptic) by later redactors.

One point deserves close attention. It is not possible to assent to Fiebig's characterisation that "in comparison with the Synoptic Parables, it strikes one that the processes of Nature—sowing and harvest, growing, flowering and fruitage, were taken little account of [in the Rabbinic Parables]." In the latter, besides many Parables treating of trades, handicrafts, seafaring, school-life, domestic affairs, there are many comparisons drawn from the fields, vineyards, streams, flowers, trees, fruits, birds, beasts, and other natural objects. This is perhaps more noticeable in those phases of the Agada which do not assume the form of narrative Parables, but it is frequent in the latter also, and the Rabbinic examples agree with the Synoptic in treating of nature under cultivation rather than in a wild state. With regard to the *harvest*, Schweitzer holds that the reference in the New Testament Parables is eschatological, pointing at all events to a definite note of time; *this* particular harvest in the last year of Jesus' life is to be the last harvest on earth, and the Kingdom is to follow it immediately. In Joel iii. 13, Isaiah xvii. 5—11, as well as in the Jewish Apocalypses (e.g. Baruch lxx.), the harvest is synonymous with the judgment. This is not altogether convincing, for it is curious that the images of the sower and the mustard seed—the harvest and

the full-grown tree, processes of long maturation—should express the
idea of a sudden consummation and nothing more.

The idea of the harvest in the Synoptics is probably a composite
one, the standing corn is regarded as food for the sickle, whether it be
the sickle of an angry Master or of the human reaper of the accumulated
reward of long drawn out endeavour.   If the expression "the harvest
is large but the labourers are few" (Matt. ix. 37—38, Luke x. 2 ;
cf. John iv. 36) were the authentic exordium to the mandate to the
disciples in Q, we have here the harvest used in quite a different sense
from the Apocalyptic.   Both these uses meet us in Rabbinic.   In the first
place, with regard to the passage just cited, there is a Rabbinic parallel
nearer than is generally supposed, though so long ago as 1847 Zipser
suggested it (*Literaturblatt des Orients*, 1847, col. 752).   In the Mishnah,
Aboth ii. 19 (20), occurs a saying which in Dr Taylor's rendering runs
thus : " R. Tarphon said, ' The day is short, and the task is great, and
the workmen are sluggish, and the reward is much, and the Master of
the house is urgent.   He said, It is not for thee to finish the work,
nor art thou free to desist therefrom; if thou hast learned much Torah,
they give thee much reward ; and faithful is the Master of thy work,
who will pay thee the reward of thy work, and know that the recom-
pence of the reward of the righteous is for the time to come.' "
Dr Taylor sees in this Mishnah points of contact with the Parable
of the Vineyard in Matt. xx., " where the οἰκοδεσπότης (Master of
the house) says to the labourers whom he finds unemployed, Τί ὧδε
ἑστήκατε ὅλην τὴν ἡμέραν ἀργοί; (' Why stand ye here all day idle?')."
The first part of this Mishnah is usually taken to correspond to the
" ars longa vita brevis " of Hippocrates.   But it is a very plausible
suggestion of Zipser's that the first clause of the Hebrew has been
wrongly punctuated.   It is commonly read הַיּוֹם קָצַר (" the day is short"),
whereas the true reading should be הָיוֹם קָצֵר (" to-day is harvest"—
there is no need to emend to קָצִיר as the Gezer Calendar Stone,
published in the *Quarterly Statement* of the P. E. F., Jan. 1909,
gives us several times over the spelling קצר for "harvest").   This
is confirmed by another word in the saying, " Master of the House,"
for the Hebrew equivalent בעל הבית often means " landowner "
(cf. Dr A. Büchler, *Sepphoris*, p. 38, etc.) just as the οἰκοδεσπότης
of Matthew does (this equivalence of the Hebrew and Greek just
quoted was noted by Dr Taylor, and has been elaborated I think by
Dr Nestle).   The whole of Tarphon's saying would thus have an
agricultural setting.   It may be pointed out in passing that this is

not the only parallel between sayings of Tarphon and the New Testament. Compare the "mote" and "beam" of *'Arachin*, 16 b with Matt. vii. 3 (there seems no reason for doubting with Bacher, *Agada der Tannaiten*, I. 351 n., the authenticity of this saying as one of Tarphon's). Tarphon lived during the existence of the Temple (T. J. *Yoma*, iii. § 7, 38 d), and was thus a contemporary of the Apostles. He was a strong opponent of the Jewish Christians (*Sabbath*, 116 a), and hence his name was used by Justin Martyr (whose Tryphon = Tarphon) as a typical antagonist. It is impossible that Tarphon would have taken his similes from Christian sayings, and the parallels point unmistakably to the existence of a common and ancient source. The whole Mishnah is more elaborate than most of the passages in *Aboth* and we may conclude that Tarphon is not the author of the opening clauses but only of their interpretation in terms of studying the Law.

These opening clauses however, when juxtaposed with Matt. ix. 37--8, present under the figure of the harvest a very different idea from the Judgment. It is the goal of effort rather than the starting point of doom, the reward of life rather than the precursor of death. There is nothing apocalyptic about this, nothing catastrophic. "The king does not stand (in satisfaction) by his field when it is ploughed, or when it is hoed, or when it is sown, but he stands by it when it is full of corn for the granary," said R. Simon (Tanḥuma Miqeṣ on Gen. xxviii. 13). On the other hand there are some Rabbinic passages in which the harvest is a type of the Judgment in the sterner sense (Leviticus *Rabba*, xviii. § 3).

Several of the New Testament Parables are clearly inconsistent with a firm belief in the immediate approach of the end; there is no "interim morality" in the Parable of the Talents (Matt. xxv. 14—30, Luke xix. 12—27, cf. Mark xiii. 34—37). It is improbable, however, that the same Jesus who said "Be not therefore anxious for the morrow" (Matt. vi. 34), and "Sell all thou hast" (*ib*. xix. 21), should have cried "Well done, good and faithful servant" to those who had traded with their capital. To the idea of this story we have a Rabbinic parallel, but not in Parable form; it is cited as an incident (*Debarim Rabba*, III. § 3), and in some particulars the moral is other than in the New Testament. For, after all, the five and the two talents were risked, and might have been lost in the trade. In the Midrash incident this objection does not suggest itself. This is the incident referred to: "R. Phineas ben Jair [second half of second

century] lived in a certain city of the South [Lydda?], and certain
men went to support themselves there.   They had in their possession
two seahs of barley, which they deposited with him.   These they forgot
and left the place.   And R. Phineas ben Jair went on sowing them
year by year; he made a granary for them, and stored them.   After
seven years these companions returned to claim their seahs.   Immediately R. Phineas ben Jair recognised them, and he said to them, Come,
take your stores.   Lo, from the faithfulness of flesh and blood thou
recognizest the faithfulness of the Holy One, blessed be He."   (This
last clause reminds one of the "faithful servant.")

In Rabbinic parallels to several others of the Synoptic Parables
the inferiority is not always on the Rabbinic side as Jülicher in
particular thinks.   In the first place the parallels sometimes strike a
note which finds no exact echo in the Synoptic examples.   It is strange
that Fiebig can cite (from Mechilta *Beshallah*, ed. Friedmann, 29 b)
the following as he does (*op. cit.* p. 34) without noting that it is a
somewhat unique expression of the relation between God and man.

Rabbi Absolom the Elder says : A Parable.   To what is the matter like?   To
a man who was angry with his son, and banished him from his home.   His friend
went to beg him to restore his son to his house.   The father replied : Thou askest
of me nothing except on behalf of my son?   *I am already reconciled with my son.*
So the Omnipresent said unto him (Moses), "Wherefore criest thou unto me?"
(Exodus xiv. 15).   Long ago have I become well disposed to him (Israel).

Here then we have the idea that the Father is reconciled to his
erring son even before the latter or any intercessor makes appeal, in
accordance with the text: "Before they call I will answer" (Isaiah lxv. 24).
Compare also the similar idea in the *Pesiqta Rabbathi* ch. v. (ed.
Friedmann, p. 17 b); these expressions of the Father's love seem to go
even beyond the beautiful pathos of Luke xv. 20.

A King ordered the men of a certain district to build a palace.   They built it.
Then they stood by the gate and proclaimed : Let the King come in!   But what did
the King do?   He entered by a wicket door, and sent a herald to announce : Shout
not, for I have already come to the palace.   So, when the Tabernacle was erected,
Israel said : Let my Beloved come to his garden!   The Holy One sent and said
unto them : Why are ye anxious?   Already have I come into my garden, my sister,
my bride.

So, too, the medieval poet Jehuda Halevi sang, though he was thinking
more of the divine omnipresence :

> Longing I sought Thy presence,
> Lord, with my whole heart did I call and pray;
> And going out toward Thee,
> I found Thee coming to me on the way.

Another note of the Rabbinic Parables (which has I think no echo in
the Synoptics) is the idea of "Chastisements of love" (*Berachoth* 5 a)
which finds expression in many comparisons, among which perhaps the
following is the most characteristic (Exodus *Rabba*, xxi. § 5).   The
Midrash very pathetically puts it that God wishes Israel to cry to him,
he longs to hear Israel's voice raised in filial supplication.   Just as he
chastises Israel to discipline him, so he tortures Israel to force from
him the prayer which Israel refuses to yield while free from racking
pain.   The divine ear yearns for the human voice.   This profound,
mystical thought, is expressed with both quaintness and tenderness in
the following Parable:

> Why did God bring Israel into the extremity of danger at the Red Sea before
> saving him? Because he longed to hear Israel's prayer. Said R. Joshua ben Levi,
> To what is the matter like? To a king who was once travelling on the way, and
> a daughter of kings cried to him: "I pray thee, deliver me out of the hand of
> these robbers!" The king obeyed and rescued her. After a while he wished to
> make her his wife; he longed to hear her sweet accents again, but she was silent.
> What did the king do? He hired the robbers again to set upon the princess, to
> cause her again to cry out, that he might hear her voice. So soon as the robbers
> came upon her, she began to cry for the king. And he, hastening to her side,
> said: "This is what I yearned for, to hear thy voice." Thus was it with Israel.
> When they were in Egypt, enslaved, they began to cry out, and hang their eyes
> on God, as it is written "And it came to pass...that the children of Israel sighed
> because of their bondage...and they cried..." Then it immediately follows: "And
> God looked upon the Children of Israel." He began to take them forth thence with
> a strong hand and an outstretched arm. And God wished to hear their voice a
> second time, but they were unwilling. What did God do? He incited Pharaoh
> to pursue after them, as it is said, "And he drew Pharaoh near." Immediately
> the children of Israel cried unto the Lord. In that hour God said: "For this
> I have been seeking, to hear your voice, as it is written in the Song of Songs, My
> dove in the clefts of the rocks, let me hear thy voice; thy voice, the same voice
> which I first heard in Egypt.

Again, the following is a gracious Parable, which, were one on the
look-out for Rabbinic foils to the Gospels, might be contrasted with
Matthew xxi. 9.

> When R. Isaac parted from R. Naḥman, the latter asked for a blessing. Said
> R. Isaac: I will tell thee a Parable. A traveller was passing through a desert, and
> he was hungry, faint, and thirsty. He found a tree, whose fruit was sweet, whose
> shade was pleasant, and at whose foot there flowed a stream. He ate of the fruit,
> drank of the water, and sat in the shade. On his departure he said: O tree, O tree,
> how shall I bless thee? If I say to thee, May thy fruit be sweet, lo thy fruit is sweet
> already; that thy shade shall be pleasant, lo it is pleasant now; that a stream shall
> water thee, lo this boon is thine at present. But I will say: May all the saplings

planted from thee be like thyself! So, thou, How shall I bless thee? With Torah? Torah is thine. With wealth? Wealth is thine. With children? Children are thine. But I say: God grant that thy offspring may be like thyself! (*Ta'anith* 6 a).

Or, to turn to another idea, the following is an original note, at all events there is no full Synoptic parallel. The citation of the passage will serve also a secondary purpose; it will again illustrate the frequent Rabbinic habit of syncretising the Parable of idea with the application of historical incident.

R. Hanina bar Idi said: Why are the words of the Torah (Scriptures) likened unto water, as it is written (Isaiah lv. 1) *Ho every one that thirsteth come ye to the water?* To say unto thee: Just as water forsakes a high place and goes to a low place, so the words of the Torah find a resting-place only in a man whose character is lowly. R. Oshaya also said: Why are the words of the Torah likened to these particular liquids, water, wine, and milk, for the text continues: *Come ye, buy wine and milk without money?* To say unto thee: Just as these three liquids are kept only in the simplest of vessels, so the words of the Torah are only preserved in a man of humble spirit. It is as once the Emperor's daughter jeeringly said to R. Joshua b. Hananya: "Ho! Glorious Wisdom in a foul vessel!" He replied: "Ho! daughter of him who keeps wine in an earthen pitcher!"—"In what sort of vessel should wine be kept, then?" asked the princess.—"Important people like you should store their wine in pitchers of gold and silver."—She persuaded the Emperor to follow this course, but soon men came to him to report that the wine had turned sour. "My daughter," said the Emperor, "who told you to suggest this thing?"—She replied that her adviser was R. Joshua b. Hananya. The latter was called, and in answer to the Emperor's questions replied: "As she spake to me, so spake I unto her." (*Taanith*, 7 a; *Nedarim*, 50 b).

Various Rabbinic parallels to New Testament Parables have been detected by various scholars. One must here remark that the similarity of *idea* must not be confused with identity of Parabolical treatment. Philo has no true Parables, but several of his ideas are found later on developed into that literary type. For instance, what became a favourite Rabbinic Parable, the comparison of the creation of the world to the planning of a palace (Genesis *Rabba*, i.), a comparison associated by Bacher with the schools of Hillel and Shammai, is already found fully developed in Philo (*de opif. mundi*, 4, 5).

Leaving the study of parallels, if the Rabbinic Parables are considered absolutely, without comparative reference to those of the New Testament, it is clear that they must be allowed to rank high in literature of the kind. The Parable took a very firm root in the Jewish consciousness, though for some centuries it was not transplanted from its native soil—Palestine—to Babylonia, and Rab (died 247) scarcely presents any instances of the *Mashal* (Bacher, *Agada der babylonischen Amoräer*, 1878, p. 31). But the influence of the Palestinian Midrash prevailed, and throughout the middle ages and the modern epoch, Jewish homilies have been consistently illustrated by Parables. Now, as of old, the Parable was the instrument for popularising truths which in an abstract form were not so easily apprehensible.

Professor Bacher elsewhere describes the *Mashal* (Parable) as " one of the most important elements of the Agada." Agada must here be understood in its widest signification : the exposition of Scripture and the application of the precepts of the Law to the elucidation of principle and the regulation of conduct. The utility and even necessity of the Mashal for understanding the Torah are variously enunciated in a series of fine similes in the Midrash, and the passage (Canticles *Rabba*, I. i. 8; Genesis *Rabba*, xii. 1; Eccles. *Rabba* on ii. 11; T. B. *Erubin*, 21 b footnote) may here be paraphrased in full : " R. Naḥman said : A great palace had many doors, and whoever entered within it strayed and lost his direction (for the return). There came one of bright intelligence who [cf. Ariadne] took a clue of rope and tied one end of it to the entrance, and went in and out along the rope. Thus before Solomon arose no man could understand the words of the Torah, but all found it intelligible after the rise of this King." Further, said R. Naḥman, "It is like a wild thicket of reeds, into which no man could penetrate. But there came a clever wight who seized a scythe and cut a path, through which all men could come and go. Thus was it with Solomon." R. Jose said : " it is comparable to a great case full of fruits, but the case had no handles and no one could move it. Then there came one who made handles, and everyone could move it." R. Shila likened Solomon's service to that of a man who provided a handle to a huge cask full of hot liquid. R. Ḥanina put the same thought in these terms : "It was like a deep well, full of water, and the water was cool, sweet and wholesome, but no creature could reach it to drink. A certain one came and joined rope to rope and cord to cord; he drew water from the well and drank. Then, for the first time, all could draw and drink. Thus from word to word, from Mashal to Mashal, Solomon reached the uttermost secret of the Torah. And this he did by means of the Mashal." So, the passage continues, "The Rabbis said, Let not the Mashal be light in thine eyes, for by means of the Mashal a man can stand in the words of the Law, for it is comparable to a king who lost gold from his house, or a precious pearl, and found it by means of a clue worth a Roman *as*." There is in all this a two-fold meaning.   Solomon added certain things to the Law, the Rabbis assigned to him a number of takkanoth or new regulations which made the Law practically usable; he also popularised the Law, making it accessible to the masses by means of the Mashal.   As the Midrash continues, Solomon by means of the Mashal attained to a knowledge of legal minutiae; he also made the Law popular.   "Rabbi Judan said, Whoever speaks words of Law in public (among the many) is worthy that the Holy Spirit should rest upon him, and this thou learnest from Solomon."

In this analytical passage, the term *Mashal* is used in a very wide sense, and includes all forms of applied morality.   Parable thus becomes part and parcel of the instrument for arriving at truth and for making truth prevail.   Truth, to Pharisee and Evangelist alike, is the will of God, and the Parable was at its highest when seeking to understand and to do that will.   The Parables of Talmud and Gospels are (so Zipser put it) derived from a common source, the systematised teaching of Hillel and Shammai.   Parables were not merely an entertainment, they were not merely designed to interest the people.   They were the method by which the mysteries of providence and the incidences of duty were posted and illustrated. Sometimes these mysteries and incidences are beyond understanding and when then Mark (iv. 11) describes the Parable as actually employed by Jesus to prevent men from understanding, the description is happily characterised by Bousset when he calls it "preposterous," and dismisses it as "the dogmatic pedantry of a later age."   The same idea is found in all the Synoptics and cannot be dismissed in this easy way.   What is "preposterous" is the supposition that Jesus taught in Parable *in order* that men might misunderstand.   This is to mistake an Oriental process of thought by which consequences are often confused with motives. (Cf. Skinner on Isaiah vi. 10.) The Parable has this danger that it may imply more than it says, and may leave behind it more puzzles than it solves.   It is not an exact instrument; it works without precision.   The *consequence* of a Parable may be misunderstanding, or what is equivalent, partial understanding, and it is certain from the language of the evangelists that the Parables ascribed to Jesus were liable to this consequence.   Hence, as it was improper to admit that Jesus used an imperfect form imperfectly, consequence was translated into intention, and the misunderstanding was described as

designed in order to prevent the Jews from turning and finding forgiveness.   Later on, when the eschatological element in the teaching
of Jesus was forced into greater prominence, the supposition that the
Parable was used in order to veil a Messianic secret may easily have
arisen.   The latter, however, cannot be the original force of the
reference, for it is plain enough that many of the New Testament
Parables, different though they be to explain in all their details, are
absolutely simple inculcations of moral and religious truths, profound
but not mysterious.

XIII. DISEASE AND MIRACLE.

Rabbinic Judaism took over from the Old Testament a belief that disease was a consequence of sin (Leviticus xxvi. and parallels in Deuteronomy). This theory was especially held to explain general epidemics, and also those afflictions the origin of which was at once most obscure and their effects most dreaded—such as leprosy. It is not necessary to do more than recall the cases of Miriam, Joab, Gehazi, and Job.

The Rabbinic sources contain many assertions as to the relation between sin and disease. (Cf. the valuable discussion in the Tosafoth to Aboth iv. 11.) "Measure for Measure" applied here as in other aspects of Rabbinic theology (Mishnah, Aboth v. 11—14). R. Ammi (of the third century, but his view was shared by earlier authorities) asserted *sans phrase* that there was no affliction without previous sin (Sabbath, 55 a). R. Jonathan said: "Diseases (נגעים) come for seven sins: for slander, shedding blood, false oaths, unchastity, arrogance, robbery, and envy" ('Erachin, 16 a). In particular leprosy was the result of slander (Leviticus Rabba, xviii. § 4). On the other hand, "When Israel stood round Sinai and said, All that the Lord has spoken we will do, there was among the people no one who was a leper, or blind, or halt, or deaf," and so forth (*ibid.*; Sifrê 1 b, the sin of the golden calf, like other acts of rebellion, caused leprosy and other diseases, Pesiqta Rabbathi vii., ed. Friedmann p. 28). Thus obedience prevented disease, just as disobedience produced it. This, to a large extent, moralised the idea: it set up the moral life as the real prophylactic. In general the principle enunciated in Exodus xv. 26 was adopted by the Rabbis, though it must be remembered that so great an authority as R. Meir altogether disputed the theory as to the connection between suffering and transgression. God's dealing with men, he held, was an unfathomable mystery. Leprosy, again, like other diseases might, in another view, merely be the beneficent earthly penalty designed to save the sufferer from tribulations in the future (Lev. R. xvii.).

To exemplify the application of the " Measure for Measure " idea, the case of blindness will suffice. Naḥum of Gimzu (first century) explained his blindness as the consequence of his inhumanity to a poor sufferer (Ta'anith, 21 a). The man who accepted bribery and perverted justice would not pass from the world unless he suffered the infliction of physical blindness corresponding to his moral lapse (Mechilta, Mishpaṭim, § 20, p. 100 a, Sifrê, on Deuteronomy, § 144). The case of one blind from birth was more difficult to fit into the theory, and in John ix. 1 Jesus denies that such an affliction was due to sin at all. It is there explained that the congenital blindness had been imposed that it might be cured, so "that the works of God should be made manifest in him." This explanation is identical with that of Ecclesiasticus xxxviii, except that Sirach applies it to the doctor's art. " The Lord hath given men skill, that he might be honoured in his miraculous works." Disease—more particularly pestilence—was ascribed also to sins which were not punished by human tribunals.   In general it was thought that sin left its material impress, and the later mystics put it that it disfigured the image of God (Schechter, *Studies in Judaism*, II. 274).

Two points only must be further indicated ; the legal position of the leper in Rabbinic law is sufficiently indicated in the *Jewish Encyclopedia* VIII, 10 a. ("Leprosy was not considered contagious.") The first point is that the moral stigma attaching to disease soon took a more amiable form.   As Dr Schechter well puts it (*Studies in Judaism*, I. 269) : ' The only practical conclusion that the Rabbis drew from such theories as identify suffering with sin was for the sufferer himself, who otherwise might be inclined to blame Providence, or even to blaspheme, but would now look upon his affliction as a reminder from heaven that there is something wrong in his moral state.   Thus we read in tractate Berachoth (5 a) : "If a man sees that affliction comes upon him, he ought to inquire into his actions, as it is said, Let us search and try our ways, and turn again to the Lord (Lam. iii. 40). This means to say that the sufferer will find that he has been guilty of some offence." '

The second point is that though leprosy was regarded as the punishment for the worst crimes, it was not thought lawful or right to leave the leper to his fate. Sympathy with suffering was not diminished by any theories as to the origin of the suffering. In Ecclesiasticus Rabba (on ix. 7) is told the touching story of Abba Taḥna. As the sun was near its setting on a Friday afternoon, Abba Taḥna was going home with all his worldly goods in a bag on his shoulders. At the cross-road he saw a man smitten with leprosy. The latter entreated the Rabbi in these terms: "My master, show me charity and carry me to the city." The perplexed Rabbi said: "If I leave my goods, how shall I sustain myself and my household? and if I leave this leper I shall commit a mortal sin." Abba Taḥna conquered the suggestion of his evil inclination, left his bag, and bore the leper into the town. In the end he did not suffer for his action. But the whole passage is an effective comment on Luke x. 30.

Demoniac "possession" as a cause of disease, and "exorcism" as its cure, were well known to the Rabbis. But it is certain that these beliefs and practices were uncommon in Palestine at the time of Jesus. The easy assumption to the contrary has no foundation. Though the Enoch and other apocalyptic literature has a developed demonology, and Acts xxiii. 8 implies a Pharisaic angelology, there is a remarkable infrequency of references to the subject in the Mishnah and the Tannaite literature (L. Blau, *Das altjüdische Zauberwesen*, p. 23). Quite early was the power attached to prayers for rain. The fact that Onias (on whom see *Jewish Encyclopedia* IX. 410 and refs.) stood in a ring while praying for rain has a "magical" look, but it is not clearly a charm. There is nothing of the magician or spell-worker in the picture of Onias drawn in Josephus (*Antiq.* XIV. 2, 1). Hillel (p. 95 above) was a student of demon-lore, perhaps under Parsic influence— he was by birth Babylonian. Compare the prayer cures of Ḥaninah b. Dosa (first century)—he had magical leanings (see *J.E.* VI. 214), but the female demon Agrat mentioned in his case was Persian. Persian influence reached Palestine in the first century (Darmesteter in *Revue des Etudes Juives* I. 195) but became more pronounced after the Palestinian schools were superseded by the Babylonian early in the third century. Members of the Sanhedrin were expected to understand magic in order to deal with causes in which the question arose (Sanhedrin 17 a. See refs. in Taylor, *Aboth* v. 9). The same Mishnah (v. 9) refers to demons, but this like Ḥagigah 16 a apparently belongs to the late second century. It is in the Babylonian Talmud that we find an appalling mass of demonology which, though it stands in relation to earlier beliefs,—Biblical, Apocalyptic and Rabbinical—cannot properly be cited as applicable to the time of Jesus in the Holy Land

(Perles on Bousset, p. 35. Bousset frankly admits the validity of Perles' objection in the second edition of his *Religion des Judentums*, p. 388, n. 4, but hardly corrects his general statements in accordance with the admission). Probably, therefore, the Pharisees were amazed at the attitude and actions of Jesus, so that it is intelligible that Jesus was afterwards called a "magician" (Sabbath, 104 b), though subsequent schools of Pharisaism would have been less amazed than his contemporaries were. It may be, indeed, the fact that the Essenes were (as Geiger supposes) "healers," in which case we should have a further bond between Jesus and this sect. There was between the years 150 and 450 a great increase in Jewish circles in the belief in demons and their influence. (Cf. Conybeare, *Jewish Quarterly Review*, ix. 87.) It is undeniable, however, that some cases of exorcism are recorded earlier. But it is curious that they are all associated with the Roman imperial family. Josephus, who makes indeed a general assertion as to demoniac possession (*Wars* VII. vi. 3), only recites an actual cure by exorcism performed in the presence of Vespasian (*Antiquities* VIII. ii. 5). So, too, the notorious instance of exorcism reported of a second century Rabbi, Simon b. Yoḥai, was not only performed in the case of a Roman lady of the imperial family, but actually occurred in Rome, if it be not indeed a mere reproduction of a Christian story (see p. 92 above). Again, though the Jewish exorcists (Acts xix. 13) were "strollers," yet the scene of their exploits is not Judæa but Ephesus and the impression conveyed is that they were playing with foreign fire. It does not seem, therefore, appropriate to the purpose of these Notes to enter at large into the Rabbinic parallels to New Testament ideas on demonology. (See, besides the literature already referred to, Kohler in *Jewish Encyclopedia*, IV. 517 b.)

In the earlier period we find the physician held in high repute (Ecclus. xxxviii. 1 seq.), though Sirach accepts the theory that disease is connected with sin. The "confections" of the apothecary are associated with prayer in effecting a cure. Moses prays for Miriam's relief, and God is the "Healer." The prayer for such divine healing found a place in the oldest part of the Synagogue liturgy, the eighteen benedictions, the words used being derived in part from Jeremiah xvii. 14. This two-fold conception always finds expression in Jewish thought. Prayers for the sick go side by side with the demand that every community shall have its doctors (Sanhedrin, 17 ; Maimonides

Sanh. i. 10). Rabbinic "medicine" has very much of the "sympathetic" and the folk-cure and the exorcist about it, but there is no ground whatever for Bousset's assumption that the Rabbinic demonology arose from any supposed surrender of the divine omnipotence, and the yielding of part of his powers to demons and the like. The Rabbis considered, in one sense, every recovery from sickness as a "miracle." Said they: "Greater is the miracle that occurs when a sick person escapes from a perilous disease than that which happened when Hananiah, Mishael and Azariah escaped from the fiery furnace" (Nedarim, 41 a).

XIV. POVERTY AND WEALTH.

The twelve were sent forth "two by two," just as was the rule with the Jewish collectors of alms (T.B. *B. Bathra* 8 b); indeed *solitary* travelling, especially at night, was altogether antipathetic to Jewish feeling. According to all three synoptics (Mark vi. 7, Matt. x. 10, Luke ix. 3) the disciples were to take nothing for their journey, no provisions, no wallet, no money. Even so did the Essenes travel, according to the report of Josephus (*War* ii. viii. 4): "They carry nothing at all with them when they travel." The twelve were to accept hospitality wherever it was offered, and the Essenes "go (on their journeys) into the houses of those whom they never knew before," the houses, however, belong to brother Essenes. The Essenes carried weapons with them, while Matthew and Luke distinctly assert that the twelve were not even to carry a staff. This seems an improbable restriction, for the staff ($\dot{\rho}\dot{\alpha}\beta\delta o\varsigma$) was a common necessary for the traveller, serving at the same time as a help to walking and as a weapon. The ordinary Jewish traveller carried a staff and a bag (see Dictionaries s.v. תרמיל). Mark distinctly states that the twelve *were* to carry a staff ($\epsilon i\ \mu\dot{\eta}\ \dot{\rho}\dot{\alpha}\beta\delta o\nu\ \mu\acute{o}\nu o\nu$), and later on we find one or two of the disciples in possession of weapons (Mk xiv. 47, Matt. xxvi. 51). Luke (xxii. 38) reports that there were two swords. Luke seems to feel the contradiction between the earlier commission and this, and so inserts the passage (xxii. 35, 36) to explain the divergence.

The Essenes were "despisers of riches" (Josephus, *loc. cit.* § 3) but they were not worshippers of poverty. "Among them all there is no appearance of abject poverty, or excess of riches," says Josephus. Theirs was a rule of equality, a régime of simple sufficiency not of common insufficiency. A life of such poverty was the natural corollary of life in a society aiming at a holy life, and we find a similar rule among the Therapeutae described by Philo; though the Therapeutae were closer to the later Christian monastics than were the Essenes.

That the pursuit of certain ideals was incompatible with the desire to amass material wealth is, however, a common thought of the Rabbis: "This is the path to the Torah: A morsel with salt shalt thou eat, thou shalt drink also water by measure, and shalt sleep upon the ground, and live a life of trouble the while thou toilest in the Torah. If thou doest this, happy shalt thou be and it shall be well with thee (Ps. cxxviii. 2); happy shalt thou be in this world, and it shall be well with thee in the world to come" (Mishnah, *Aboth* vi. 4).

But this implies no cult of poverty. Among the blessings prayed for by Abba Areka were "wealth and honour" (*Berachoth* 16 b). From time to time, ascetic movements have arisen in Judaism (cf. *Jewish Encyclopedia* ii. 167), and the value of such movements cannot be denied (cf. C. G. Montefiore *Truth in Religion* pp. 191 seq.). On the whole, however, Pharisaic Judaism had, on the one hand, too full a belief in calm joyousness as a fundamental and generally attainable ideal of life, and on the other hand too acute and recurrent an experience of the actualities of destitution, for it to regard poverty as in itself a good. (Cf. Note XVI below.) Even in the pursuit of the Torah, there comes a point where poverty is a preventive rather than a help. Eleazar ben 'Azariah, who succeeded the second Gamaliel as President of the Sanhedrin, and was himself wealthy (*Qiddushin* 49 b), summed the truth up in his epigram: "Without food, no Torah; without Torah, no food" (*Aboth* iii. 26). That destitution may be a bar to the ideal is an experience of many an idealist. After the Bar Cochba war, there was so general an impoverishment in Palestine, that the study of the Torah was intermitted. (Cf. the lurid picture drawn by Dr A. Büchler in his essay on *Sepphoris in the Second and Third Centuries*, pp. 70 seq.) "God weeps daily alike over the man who could study Torah but omits to seize his opportunity, and over the man who cannot study yet continues to do it" (T.B. *Hagigah* 5 b). In other ways, too, the Rabbis recognised that poverty was an evil. "Poverty in the house of a man is more distressful than fifty plagues" (T.B. *Baba Bathra* 116). The sufferings endured are so intense that they save a man from seeing Gehinnom ('*Erub.* 41 b, cf. *Yebamoth* 102 b). Poverty is an affliction equal in severity to all the curses in Deuteronomy combined (*Exod. Rabba* xxxi.). The contrast between the earthly lot of rich and poor is found in well-known passages of the Wisdom literature. Very pregnant is the saying attributed in the Talmud to Sirach, though the passage is not found in any known text of the apocryphal book. It runs thus (*Sanh.* 100 b):

"All the days of the poor are evil (Prov. xv. 5): Ben Sira said, the nights also. The lowest roof is his roof, and on the highest hill is his vineyard. The rain off (other) roofs (falls) on his roof, and the soil from his vineyard on (other) vineyards"—another illustration of the truth that to him that hath shall be given, and from him that hath not even his little shall be taken away. Poverty dogs the footsteps of the poor, putting him at a constant disadvantage (T.B. *Baba Qama* 92 a). Poverty even affects the personal appearance. "Beautiful are the daughters of Israel, but poverty mars their face" (*Nedarim* 66 a).

But though an evil, poverty was not the consequence of sin, unless that sin be the misuse of wealth (*Leviticus R.* xxxiv.). There is a wheel revolving in the world, and wealth ill-spent ends in poverty (*Exod. Rabba* xxxi.; T.B. *Sabbath* 151 b). But the poor though deserving of human pity have no right to complain of the Divine justice. As Philo says : "Poverty by itself claims compassion, in order to correct its deficiencies, but when it comes to judgment...the judgment of God is just" (*Fragments*, Mang. ii. 678). In fact the Rabbinic analysis goes deeper, and makes it necessary for us to qualify the general statement that Poverty is an evil. "There is no destitution but poverty of mind" (אין עני אלא בדיעה *Nedarim* 41 a). Compare with this the sarcastic allusion to "the poor man who hungers but knows not whether he is hungry or not" (*Megillah* 16)—this is the real poverty, the lack of original insight, the absence of self-sufficiency in character. Poverty, as we have seen, may be so crushing as to destroy the victim's ideals. Far be it for an arm-chair moralist to inveigh against those who listen not to a Moses because the iron of misery has entered into their souls, so that they cannot hear for anguish of spirit, and for cruel bondage. But the excuse cannot be accepted. There was none so poor as Hillel, yet he worked for a half-dinar a day and paid a moiety to the door-keeper for admission to the house of study, sometimes braving the winter snow. Thus the cares of poverty are no defence against the charge of neglecting the Torah. And, continues the same Talmudic passage (T.B. *Yoma* 25 b), there was none so wealthy as R. Eleazar ben Harsom, yet he forsook his wealth, and with a skin of flour spent his days in the house of study. The cares of wealth are no defence. Man must rise superior to either. As the Midrash puts it (*Exod. R.* xxxi.): Happy is the man that can endure his trial, for there is none whom the Holy One trieth not. The rich God tries whether his hand be open to the poor, the poor He tries whether he can calmly endure affliction. If the rich man sustain his trial, and worketh righteousness, lo, he eateth his money in this world and the capital endureth for the world to come and God delivereth him from Gehinnom.   And if the poor man sustain his trial and kick not against it, lo! he receives a double portion in the world to come.   Then the Midrash proceeds to distinguish between the wealth which doeth evil to its owner and the wealth that doeth good to him, and so with the qualities of strength and wisdom.   Suffering, indeed, was the lot of rich and poor alike.   A life of unbroken prosperity was the reverse of a boon.   An old baraitha (of the school of R. Ishmael) asserts that "he who has passed forty days without adversity has already received his world in this life" (*'Erachin* 16 b foot); one who was not afflicted would not belong to the category of Israel at all (*Ḥagiga* 5 a).   Here we read the note of experience. It was Israel's lot so to suffer that it was forced to fall back on the theory that only by "chastisements of love" (*Berachoth* 5 a) might he obtain purification and atonement (Sifrê 73 b).   So, too, in another sense, the difference between men's condition—not an absolute difference, for wealth was accessible to all possessed of knowledge, i.e. virtue (*Sanhedrin* 92 a on the basis of Proverbs xxiv. 4), while there was a ladder in men's affairs up which the poor rise and the rich descend (*Pesiqta* ed. Buber 12 a) or a wheel revolving to similar effect (*Sabbath* 151 b)—was a means of atonement when sacrifices ceased (see quotations p. 128 below).

There is no cult of poverty neither is there a cult of wealth.   Both are conditions of good and ill rather than good or ill themselves.   Not the possession of wealth but too absolute a devotion to its acquisition and too ready a surrender to its temptations were feared.   It was the gold and silver showered on Israel by a bountiful God that provided the material for the golden calf (*Berachoth* 32 a).   Hillel held that increase of property meant increase of anxiety (*Aboth* ii. 7).   Yet Rabbi Judah honoured the rich, and so did Aqiba (T.B. *'Erubin* 86 a), for the rich maintain the order of the world when they turn their possessions to the service of their fellows : the rich support the poor, and the poor support the world, says the Talmud (*loc. cit.*)—a not inept statement of the relations between capital and labour as understood until the inroad of recent economic theories.   Equality, whether in the degree of wealth or poverty, was regarded as destructive of the virtue of charity.   If all men were equal, all rich or all poor, who would perform *the loving kindness of truth* of Psalm lxi.?

(Tanḥuma, Mishpaṭim ix. אם אעשה עולמי שוה חסד ואמת מן יוצרוהו)

Thus, there must be inequality.   This theory, that the poor are
necessary to the rich, runs through the Jewish theory of alms-giving
and charity in all subsequent ages.   Wealth becomes an evil when
it is made the instrument of oppression (*Aboth de R. Nathan* II. xxxi.),
or when the acquisition of it leads to the neglect of the Torah.   The
poor are God's people (*Exod. R. loc. cit.*) and "poverty becomes Israel
as a red halter a white horse" (*Ḥagiga* 9 b)—it sets off and augments
the beauty in each case.   And it moreover acts as a restraint against
the abuses which luxury may induce.   Extreme wealth is hard to bear
(*Giṭṭin* 70 a), yet charity is its salt (*Kethuboth* 66 b), and is more
efficacious than any of the sacrifices (*Succah* 29 b).   Yet, if wealth
often leads to a materialistic life, poverty may impel to unworthy
pursuits (*Kiddushin* 40 a).   The wealthy man may win Paradise like
Monobazus, storing up wealth in heaven by generous use of his riches
on earth (T.B. *Baba Bathra* 11 a).   The poor man is equally able to
attain bliss.   Most of the Rabbis were poor artizans, but some were
rich (*Nedarim* 50 a seq.).   The wealthy among them scorned the idea
that wealth, as such, made up any part of the man's real account
(*Pesaḥim* 50 a).

For, "when Solomon built the Temple, he said to the Holy One in
his prayer : Master of the Universe, if a man pray to thee for wealth,
and thou knowest that it would be bad for him, give it not.   But if
thou seest that the man would be comely in his wealth (נאה בעשרו),
grant wealth unto him" (*Exodus Rabba* xxxi. § 5).   To sum, again,
poverty and wealth are conditions not ends.   Hence the test of wealth
is subjective, not objective.   Who is rich ?   In the Mishnah (*Aboth* iii. 3),
contentment is the definition of wealth.   "Who is rich? he who is
contented with (literally, he who rejoices in) his lot ; for it is said,
when thou eatest the labour of thine hands, happy art thou, and it
shall be well with thee (Ps. cxxviii. 2), happy art thou in this world
and it shall be well with thee in the world to come."   It may be
difficult but it is not impossible for one and the same person to eat
at the two tables.

XV. THE CHILDREN.

The passages depicting Jesus' love for children are marked by
a singular tenderness and beauty. In several points there is contact
here with the stories of Elijah and Elisha. There is, however, a painful
contrast between the Synoptics (Mark x. 13—16 and parallels) and
the incident of Elisha and the bears (2 Kings ii. 23). But this is a
good illustration of the need to examine the judgment passed by the
Pharisees on certain Old Testament incidents. What did the Pharisees
make of Elisha's conduct? From the text (2 Kings xiii. 14), "Now
Elisha fell sick of the disease *of which he died*," the inference was
drawn that the prophet must previously have suffered from diseases of
which he did *not* die. "The Rabbis have taught (in a baraitha),
Elisha suffered three illnesses, one because he thrust Gehazi off with
both his hands, *one because he incited the bears against the children*, and
the one of which he died" (T.B. *Soṭa* 47 a, *Baba Mezia* 87 a).

Simplicity of faith, such as characterises the child's confidence in
its parent, is the motive of Psalm cxxxi. "Lord, my heart is not
haughty...Surely I have stilled and quieted my soul like a weaned child
with his mother." The weaned child in the Orient would be old
enough to run alone. Cf. I. Samuel i. 22. In 2 Macc. vii. 27 the mother
of the seven martyrs speaks of suckling her child for three years,
and in the Rabbinic period the average age for weaning was between
the second and third year (cf. Krauss *Talmudische Archäologie* ii.
p. 9 and notes p. 436). Young pupils were termed sucklings
(Taanith 9 a). Hence the Psalmist's point of comparison is not the
helplessness of the child, nor its contentment in spite of the loss of
what once seemed indispensable; but its natural readiness to return to
its mother despite the fact that it no longer needed her. This Psalm
(though the particular metaphor is differently explained) is thus the
model for man's attitude towards God (Midrash on the Psalm quoted).
David made it the guide of his life in all his vicissitudes (*ibid.*; cf.

T.B. *Sota* 10 b). Just as only the man could enter the Kingdom who sought it as a child (Mark x. 15), so he who makes himself small (perhaps as a child המקטין) in this world is made great (perhaps "grown up" גדול) in the world to come, and he who holds himself as a slave for the Torah here is made free hereafter (*Baba Mezia* 85 b). In the Old Testament God's relation to Israel is compared to the relation between a father and his young child. This relation was much treasured in the Midrash (see *Yalquṭ* on Jeremiah i. 5 and Hosea xi. 3 and parallels). God's nearness to the child is expressed also by the thoughts (1) that the young is without sin (בן שנה שלא טעם טעם חטא *Yoma* 22 b, cf. *Niddah* 30 b, Löw *Lebensalter* p. 65); and (2) that the Shechinah is with the young. The whole passage which follows has several other striking ideas which lead up to the most striking of all: "Rabbi used to despatch R. Assi and R. Ammi to visit the towns of Palestine in order to see that local affairs were well ordered. Once they went to a place and asked to see its Guardians. They were confronted with the Chiefs of the Soldiery. These, said the Rabbis, are not the Guardians of the town, they are its destroyers.—Who, then, are the true Guardians?—The teachers of the children....The nations asked, Can we prevail against Israel? The answer was given, Not if you hear the voices of the children babbling over their books in the Synagogues...See how deeply loved of God the children are. The Sanhedrin was exiled, but the Shechinah (Divine Presence) did not accompany its members into exile; the Priests were exiled, but still the Shechinah remained behind. But when the children were exiled, forth went the Shechinah with them. For it is written (Lam. i. 5): Her children are gone into captivity, and immediately afterwards: And from the daughter of Zion all her beauty is departed" (*Echa Rabba* Introd. and 1, 32).

The antiquity of the custom of blessing children by laying on of hands is attested by Genesis xlviii. 14. The same passage (the very words of verse 21 are used) was the source of the modern Jewish custom of blessing the children especially in the home and on the Sabbath eve. "Before the children can walk, they should be carried on Sabbaths and holidays to the father and mother to be blessed; after they are able to walk they shall go of their own accord with bowed body and shall incline their heads and receive the blessing." This is from a book published in 1602 (Moses Henochs' *Brautspiegel* ch. xliii.). Similarly the children are taken to the Rabbi, who places his hand on the head of the children in the Synagogue and blesses them, especially on Friday nights.   It is not easy to say how old these customs are.   From Biblical times onwards the teacher regarded his pupils as his children, and constantly called them so.   (For the part assigned to children in public worship see p. 4 above, and my *Jewish Life in the Middle Ages*, pp. 31–2.   Very beautiful is the passage in *Soṭa* 30 b, in which is related how the infant on its mother's knee, and the babe at the breast, no sooner saw the Shechinah at the Red Sea, than the one raised its head, the other took its lips from the breast and exclaimed : This is my God and I will glorify him.)   Such customs as just described do not always find their way into literature (cf. D. Philipson in *Jewish Encyclopedia* iii. p. 243), and they are often far older than their earliest record.   They suffice to show how fully in accord with the Jewish spirit was Jesus' loving regard for the young. In olden times, the Jewish child began to learn the Pentateuch with the Book of Leviticus.   Why ?   Because the sacrifices are pure and the children are pure.   Said R. Assi, " Let the pure come and occupy themselves with what is pure " (*Leviticus Rabba* vii.).

XVI. FASTING.

Philo did not represent Pharisaic teaching as to the relation between body and soul; he held that they formed a dualism, while the Rabbinic view was that they constituted a unity. "Righteousness," he says, "and every virtue love the soul, unrighteousness and every vice the body" (I. 507; cf. Drummond, *Philo-Judaeus* i. 23). Pharisaism, on the other hand, placed the seat of good and evil, virtue and vice, equally in the heart (cf. Porter, *op. cit.* p. 52 above). But on the subject of asceticism Philo and the Rabbis were at one. His theory would naturally lead, on the contemplative side, to such developments as the societies of the Essenes and Therapeutae, which belong, just as the medieval and modern Ḥassidic asceticisms belong, to Judaism quite as much as do any of its more normal institutions. Yet, despite his admiration for these societies, Philo steered a sane course between extremes, and so on the whole did Pharisaism. He, like them, had no love for excesses in table luxury; he, like them, thought that enjoyment was possible and laudable without excess. Philo disapproved of the sumptuous Alexandrian banquets which took toll of the world to supply rare dainties (I. 81), but, he adds, "Do not turn to the opposite course and immediately pursue poverty and abasement, and an austere and solitary life." And, as Drummond (i. 24) summarises Philo's conclusion (on the basis of the passages quoted and of I. 549—51), the philosopher counselled: "On the contrary, show how wealth ought to be used for the benefit of others; accept posts of honour and distinction, and take advantage of your position to share your glory with those who are worthy, to provide safety for the good, and to improve the bad by admonition; and instead of fleeing from the banquet-table exhibit there the virtue of temperance." Cf. F. C. Conybeare, *Philo about the Contemplative Life*, 1895, p. 270. This became precisely the predominant Jewish view. Maimonides (*Eight Chapters* iv., ed. Gorfinkle, pp. 62, 65) concedes that Jewish pietists at various periods deviated into extremes of asceticism, but he diagnoses their conduct as a medicine against disease, the medicine being noxious to the healthy. "The perfect Law which leads to perfection recommends none of these things. It rather aims at man's following the path of moderation"; but in order "that we should keep entirely from the extreme of the inordinate indulgence of the passions, we should depart from the exact medium, inclining somewhat towards self-denial, so that there may be firmly rooted in our souls the disposition for moderation" (cf. *Guide* iii. 35). Self-discipline is not self-torture, and man's right and duty to participate in all lawful happiness is illustrated in such remarks as that of Abba Areka in the famous Talmudic passage: "On the day of reckoning man will have to give account for every good which his eyes beheld and which he did not enjoy" (T.J. *Qiddushin*, last lines).

In the first century we find, however, an unsettled condition of opinion. Whether or not it belong to the original source (it is absent from Mark), yet the outburst in Matt. xi. 18, Luke vii. 33 is an apt summary of the conflict of views. John was addicted to fasting—he had a devil!; Jesus was not so ascetic, therefore he was a glutton and a wine-bibber! These passages suggest also another contrast, that presented by II. Samuel xii. 21—23, and Mark ii. 19, 20 (incidentally it may be remarked that the custom of a bridal pair fasting on the wedding-morn is only imperfectly traceable to a baraitha in T.J. *Bikkurim* iii. 65 c).

II. Samuel xii. 21—23.	Mark ii. 19, 20.
Then said his servants unto him [David], What thing is this that thou hast done? thou didst fast and weep for the child, while it was alive; but when the child was dead, thou didst rise and eat bread. And he said, While the child was yet alive, I fasted and wept, for I said, Who knoweth whether the Lord will not be gracious unto me, that the child may live? *But now he is dead, wherefore should I fast?* can I bring him back again? I shall go to him, but he shall not return to me.	And John's disciples and the Pharisees were fasting: and they come and say unto him, Why do John's disciples and the disciples of the Pharisees fast, but thy disciples fast not? And Jesus said unto them, Can the sons of the bride-chamber fast, while the bridegroom is with them? as long as they have the bridegroom with them they cannot fast. But the days will come *when the bridegroom shall be taken from them, and then will they fast* in that day.

These passages are interesting from another point of view. They suggest (in David's saying) the addiction to fasting as a form of supplication, and (in the saying of Jesus) as a form of mourning. Both of these ideas are abundantly illustrated by the Old and New Testaments, and also by other evidence available from the beginning of the Christian era. Thus R. Zadok fasted for forty years to ward off the destruction of the Temple (T.B. *Gittin* 56 a). Fasting was always thought one of the means of causing an alleviation of calamity (T.J. *Ta'anith* ii. 65 b top ; cf. Mishnah, *Aboth* iv. 11), but this, as we shall see, was only admitted by the moralists with the condition that such fasting be associated with true repentance. In time of drought and other exceptional natural visitations public fasts were decreed during Temple times (see Mishnah, *Ta'anith* passim ; the rule was not, however, continued in Babylonia, T.B. *Pesaḥim* 54 b), just as was done in the Maccabean age under the stress of political crises (I. Macc. iii. 47 ; II. Macc. xiii. 12, cf. the Elephantine Papyrus ed. Sachau i. 15, p. 7). Before starting on his journey from Babylon to Jerusalem, a journey likely to be attended with danger, Ezra, thinking it unbecoming to ask for a mounted guard, calls a fast, and this is efficacious as protection (Ezra viii. 23). Such examples would naturally be long imitated. When, at the beginning of the fourth century A.D., Zeira was about to travel also from Babylon to Palestine, he fasted 100 days (T.B. *Baba Mezi'a* 85 a. The number is no doubt exaggerated, the Jerusalem Talmud, *Ta'anith* 66 a, speaks of Zeira's 300 fasts. Cf. Bacher, *Agada der Palästinensischen Amoräer* iii. 6). It is unnecessary to illustrate the prevalence of fasting as a mourning rite (cf. the fast decreed on the death of R. Judah, T.B. *Kethuboth* 104 a) ; David's action stands out from the normal idea. So, on the opposite side, does Judith's ; with certain (rather numerous) exceptions, she fasted all the days of her widowhood (Judith viii. 6. For the medieval Jewish custom of fasting on the anniversary of a parent's death see Shulḥan Aruch, *Yoreh Deah* 402, § 12, gloss).

Fasting as a penitential rite was, in the Rabbinic view, allied to sacrifice. But this idea only came to the front after the destruction of the Temple. The Talmud (T.B. *Berachoth* 17 a) records that R. Shesheth (third century A.D.) on fast days was wont to pray: "Master of the Universe, it is revealed before thee that while the Temple stood, a man sinned and brought a sacrifice, of which only the fat and blood was offered, and this atoned for him ; and now I have sat fasting and my fat and blood has been diminished. May it be thy will that it may be accounted unto me as though I had offered it on the altar, and do thou accept it from me with favour." According to some Mishnaic texts, at an earlier period, while the Temple was in existence, the delegation (*ma'amad*) of Israelites who were appointed in association with the priests officiating in Jerusalem, remained in their cities and fasted four times a week during their sacrificial term (Mishnah, *Ta'anith* iv. 3); but this passage is missing in the best texts (including the Cambridge Mishnah, and the Munich codex, on which see Rabbinovicz, *Variae Lectiones*, Ta'anith, p. 160) and cannot therefore be relied upon.   One may perceive a trace of the same idea in the preference given to fasting over alms-giving as a means of expiation; alms-giving is a sacrifice of money, fasting of one's body (T.B. *Berachoth* 32 b, top).   Yet it must not be forgotten that according to Mar Zutra the value of fasting lay in the accompanying alms-giving (*Berachoth* 6 b).   Far older and more continuous than the idea of fasting as sacrifice is the association of fasting with initiation and the reception of sacred messages.   The Talmud (*Sanhedrin* 65 b) speaks of the one who fasts in order that the spirit of purity may rest upon him (cf. Exodus xxxiv. 28; Deut. ix. 9, 18; Daniel ix. 3).   In early Christianity this idea was more fully developed than in the Pharisaic system, for there is no exact Rabbinic parallel to Acts xiii. 2, xiv. 23. But from the Apocalypse of Baruch (v. 7, ix. 2) it is clear that in the latter part of the first century fasting was the "usual preparation for the reception of supernatural communications" (cf. Daniel ix. 3, and several instances in IV. Esdras; see Charles on the Baruch passages). Jesus fasts for 40 days (Matt. iv. 2) as a preparation to his ministry. In later centuries Jewish mystics practised fasting in hope of close communion with God, in the third century already Joshua b. Levi fasted much whereupon Elijah resumed his interrupted visits (see refs. in Bacher, *Agada der Palästinensischen Amoräer* i. 189).   On the other hand, though fasting might be regarded as a specific for the preservation of the knowledge of the Torah in a pietist's progeny (see *Baba Mezi'a* 85 a), nevertheless religious joy rather than a mood of sadness was the pre-requisite for the reception of the Shechinah (T.B. *Pesaḥim* 117 a), as also for entering on prayer (*Berachoth* 31 a). This idea must be set against the assumption that Pharisaic fasting was conducted in a dismal manner or with a sad countenance (on the basis of Matt. vi. 17).   In the *Testament of Joseph* (iii. 4), the patriarch declares: "I fasted in those seven years, and I appeared unto the Egyptians as one living delicately, for they that fast for God's sake receive beauty of face" (cf. Daniel i. 15).   The Day of Atonement was a day of joy (Mishnah, *Ta'anith* iv. 8).   How uncharacteristic of

Pharisaic piety, moreover, is the public display of fasting, may be seen from the categorical statement of the Code (Shulḥan Aruch, *O. Ḥ.* 565, 6): "He who fasts and makes a display of himself to others, to boast of his fasting, is punished for this." On occasions of public fasts, naturally the fasting was public, for all the community assembled at devotions in the public ways (Mishnah, *Ta'anith* ii. 1); it was indeed an offence for an individual to dissociate himself from the community on such occasions, perhaps because he was not personally affected by the calamity which had called forth the general fast (T.B. *Ta'anith* 11 a). But on private fasts it was the duty of the pietist to avoid publicity. It is not easy to decide the extent to which private fasts were developed at the beginning of the Christian era. In later times they became very frequent; against bad dreams fasting was declared by Abba Areka as efficacious as fire is against flax (T.B. *Sabbath* 11 a). Excessive private fasting was, however, discountenanced in the second century by Jose ben Ḥalafta, though apparently it was permitted by the general opinion (*Ta'anith* 22 b). From a passage in the Psalms of Solomon iii. 8, 9, it would seem that in the homes of pietists private fasting was common: "The righteous man maketh inquisition continually in his own house to the end to put away iniquity; with his trespass offering he maketh atonement for that wherein he erreth unwittingly, and with fasting he afflicteth his soul." ' But this may refer to the Day of Atonement. The statement in Luke xviii. 12 has been held to prove that the Pharisees fasted every Monday and Thursday, but it is plausible to explain this as exceptional. "The simplest view seems to be that Luke xviii. 12 (as well as Matthew vi. 1–6, Mark ii. 11, etc.) refers to the exceptional fasts during October—November, when severe pietists fasted on Mondays and Thursdays if the rain failed. At the close of the period every one was required to fast, but the Pharisee of Luke puts himself forward as a specially strict observer of the rite, and such pietists (yeḥidim) fasted several Mondays and Thursdays during the drought (T.B. *Ta'anith* 10 a and b). Didache viii. 1 has the same autumn fasts in mind" (Büchler, *Journal of Theological Studies*, x. 268. Similarly, the trumpet-blowing before giving alms, Matthew vi. 2 etc., refers to the public fasts; the Pharisees were much opposed to public alms-giving and took various measures to prevent the identity of the donor becoming known to the recipient— *Baba Bathra* 10). The Monday and Thursday fasts became more regular later on (*Ta'anith* 12 a), and it is possible that they go back to the age of Luke. After the destruction of the Temple, private fasts became frequent, though the cases of those who fasted constantly must have remained exceptional, as their cases are specifically cited (cf. *Ḥagiga* 22 b; *Nazir* 52 b; *Pesaḥim* 68 b). And opinion was much divided as to the laudability of the habit. Meir held that Adam was a saint in that he fasted for many years and imposed other austerities on himself (*'Erubin* 18 b), while Mar Samuel declared the constant faster a sinner (*Ta'anith* 11 a, foot). A student (talmid ḥacham) was forbidden to fast overmuch as it rendered him physically unfit for "the work of heaven" (*ibid.* 11 b, top). And even in the bitter sorrow which followed immediately on the destruction of the Sanctuary by Titus, Joshua b. Ḥananiah, a disciple of Joḥanan ben Zakkai, opposed excessive asceticism, though actual fasting is not named (Tosefta, *Soṭah*, end; T.B. *Baba Bathra* 60 b). It is also probable that when Paul (II. Cor. xi. 2) refers to frequent fastings, he was referring to that kind of self-denial which is so pathetically described in the Mishnah (Meir—vi. 4 quoted above p. 114).

On the most important aspect of fasting the Pharisaic record is peculiarly clear, though they are habitually assailed on the very subject. If there is one thing evident from the continuous record of Judaism, it is the determined effort made by prophet and scribe to prevent the fast becoming a merely external rite. The fifty-eighth chapter of Isaiah remains, of course, the most spirited homily enforcing the true significance of fasting. But there are several powerful reinforcements of the prophet's protest.

Ecclus. xxxiv. 25, 26.	Tosefta, Ta'anith i. 8.
He that washeth himself after touching a dead body, and toucheth it again, What profit hath he in his washing?	If a man keep the object of defilement (sheres) in his hand, though he bathe in the waters of Siloam and in all the waters on earth he is not clean.
Even so a man fasting for his sins, And going again, and doing the same; Who will listen to his prayer? And what profit hath he in his humiliation?	Mishnah, Yoma viii. 9. He who says I will sin and repent, I will sin and repent, he hath no power of repentance.

The passage quoted from the Tosefta also occurs in the Jerusalem Talmud (*Ta'anith* ii. 65 b) in an interesting context. We have there recorded a series of actual homilies spoken on fast days. Before citing some of these, reference must be made to a more familiar instance. The Mishnah (*Ta'anith* ii. 1) ordains that on a fast after a continued

drought, all having assembled with the Ark containing the Pentateuchal Scroll in the public thoroughfare, and having sprinkled
themselves (and the Ark) with ashes, the oldest present is to address
the assembly in these terms: "Our brethren: it is not said of the
men of Nineveh that he saw their sackcloth and their fast, but he saw
their acts, that they turned from their evil way (Jonah iii. 10), and in
the prophet (Joel ii. 13) it is said: Rend your heart and not your
garments." In the Jerusalem Talmud (*loc. cit.*), besides the homily
referred to above, we have the address of R. Tanḥum bar Illai, on the
text (II. Chron. xii. 6, 7): "Then the princes of Israel and the king
humbled themselves, and they said, The Lord is righteous. And when
the Lord saw that they humbled themselves, the word of the Lord
came to Shemaiah, saying, They have humbled themselves, I will not
destroy them." On which the Rabbi comments: "It is not written
here *they fasted*, but *they humbled themselves, I will not destroy them.*"
Of R. Ḥaggai the same passage tells us that he always cited on every
fast day the saying of R. Eliezer: "Three things annul the decree:
prayer, alms-giving and repentance, and all three are derived from the
same text (II. Chron. vii. 14): 'If my people, which are called by my
name, shall humble themselves, and pray, and seek my face, and turn
from their wicked ways, then will I hear from heaven, and will forgive
their sin, and heal their land'" (*seek my face* is defined to mean
alms-giving on the basis of Psalm xvii. 15). It is manifestly unjust
to charge with ritualism fasts on which such homilies were a regular
feature.

The main point was that neither fasting nor confessing sufficed
unless with it went a practical amendment of conduct (T.B. *Ta'anith*
16 a). No doubt alms-giving may degenerate into an external and
mechanical rite, but it was sought to so combine it with an inward
sense of sin and a conscientious aspiration towards amendment that
the danger of degeneration was lessened. It was an old theory, and
Tobit (xii. 8) already expresses it: "Good is prayer with fasting and
alms and righteousness." A fine turn was given to the idea when the
alms-giving was not regarded as a direct agent in turning away
the divine disfavour, but as an imitation of the divine nature.
R. Tanḥuma (*Genesis Rabbah* xxxiii. 3) addressed his assembled
brethren on a fast day in these terms: "My children, fill yourselves
with compassion towards one another, and the Holy One blessed
be he will be full of compassion towards you." It must moreover
be remembered that, after the fall of the Temple, Joḥanan ben

Zakkai comforted his mourning disciples with the saying that the loss of the Sanctuary by removing the sacrifices had not deprived Israel of the means of atonement.   Charity remained.   And the word used by Johanan for charity is not alms-giving but the bestowal of loving-kindness (נמילות חסדים) and the Rabbi cites the text (Hosea vi. 6): I desire loving-kindness and not sacrifice (*Aboth de R. Nathan*, ch. iv., ed. Schechter, p. 11).   It was the same Rabbi who before the destruction of the Temple had said : "Just as the sin-offering atones for Israel, so charity (צדקה) atones for the Gentiles" (T.B. *Baba Bathra* 10 b).

XVII. THE SABBATH.

In no other detail of the differences of the Gospels with the Pharisees do the latter appear to more advantage than in their attitude towards the Sabbath. As against his critics Jesus, indeed, sums up his position in the reasonable epigram : "The Sabbath was made for man, not man for the Sabbath " (Mark ii. 27), but the Pharisees would have done, nay, did do, the same. In the higher sense, it is true, this principle cannot be maintained. The Philonean conception of Sabbath was that of the divine effortless activity (*De Cherub.* xxvi., 1. 154), and man was most closely imitating the divine exemplar when he made the approach to such a state the ideal purpose of his being. So the Rabbis also taught. The observance of the Sabbath constitutes a man the partner of God in the creation of the world (T.B. *Sabbath* 119 b); if he keep the Sabbath man *makes* it (Mechilta on Exod. xxxi. 16, ed. Friedmann, p. 104); by hallowing the Sabbath, Israel brings redemption to the world (T.B. *Sabbath* 118); and by fulfilling the Sabbatical precepts, man bears testimony to the divine ordering of the Universe (Mechilta on Exod. xx. 17, ed. Fr., p. 70 b). In this higher sense then, man was made for the Sabbath, the destined purpose of his being was the establishment of harmony with the divine. God kept the Sabbath before man kept it (*Jubilees* ii. 18 seq.), and man was made that he might fulfil on earth the custom of heaven.

But in its practical application to ordinary human life, the Gospel rule is salutary. Life must be fitted to religion, not religion to life ; but there can be neither religion nor life when the one is allowed to crush out the other. And this the Rabbis felt. The commandments were given that man might live by them (וחי בהם Levit. xviii. 5), and this text was the basic ground of the Rabbinic permission of many acts which, in themselves, and apart from their necessity for the preservation of human life, were more or less flagrant invasions of the Sabbatical rest (T.B. *Yoma* 85 b). The parallel between the view of

Jesus and that of the Pharisees is, however, still closer. For, as is
well known, a principle almost verbally identical with that of Mark
ii. 27 is found in the name variously of R. Simon b. Menasya (Mechilta
on Exod. xxxi. 13, ed. Fr., p. 103 b) and of R. Jonathan b. Joseph
(T.B. *Yoma, loc. cit.*).   Both these authorities were Tannaim, the latter
belonging to the beginning, the former to the end of the second century.
The variation in assigned authorship suggests that the saying originated
with neither, but was an older tradition.   For the principle that
the Sabbath law was in certain emergencies to be disregarded was
universally admitted (T.B. *Yoma* 85 a), the only dispute was as to the
precise Pentateuchal text by which this laxity might be justified.
Such discussions always point to the fact that a law is older than the
dispute as to its foundation.   One Rabbi bases the principle on the
text (Leviticus xviii. 5) already cited ; another—in the Talmud, Simon
b. Menasya—on the text : "Wherefore the children of Israel shall
keep the Sabbath *to observe the Sabbath throughout their generations* "
(Exod. xxxi. 16), and the Rabbi argued that one may profane a
particular Sabbath to preserve a man for keeping many Sabbaths.
Then follows another suggested justification : " The Sabbath ; holy *unto
you* " (Exod. xxxi. 14) : *unto you* is the Sabbath given over, and ye are
not given over to the Sabbath " (לכם שבת מסורה ואי אתם מסורים לשבת).
As I have previously contended (*Cambridge Biblical Essays*, p. 186),
the wording of the Hebrew saying is noteworthy.   *Given over* is from
masar (= *to deliver up*).   The maxim seems to go back to Mattathias.
War was prohibited on the Sabbath (*Jubilees* ii. 12) but the father of
the Maccabee, under the stress of practical necessity, established the
principle (1 Macc. ii. 39) that self-defence was lawful on the Sabbath
day, for to hold otherwise was to "deliver up" man, life and soul, to
the Sabbath.   In the age of Josephus, Jewish soldiers would not
march, bear arms, or forage on the Sabbath (*Antiquities* xiv. x. 12), just
as at an earlier period they would not continue the pursuit of a
defeated enemy late on a Friday afternoon (2 Macc. viii. 26).   But
these acts were not necessary, in a primary sense, and therefore were
avoidable ; self-defence fell into a different category, and Josephus
attests (*Antiquities* xii. vi. 2) that "this rule continues among us to
this day, that if there be necessity, we may fight on the Sabbath days."
The distinction, however, between offensive and defensive warfare was
not without its dangers (see Josephus *Antiquities* xiv. iv. 1 ; *Wars* I.
vii. 1 ; II. xi. 4), and the Judæans suffered from the distinction when
Pompey took advantage of it.   Shammai held that though offensive

warfare might not be initiated, an offensive already in progress might
be continued (*Sabbath* 19 a).   Thus though Shammai and his school
took a severer view than did Hillel and his followers, the former made
concessions to necessity.

The exact limits within which the early halacha permitted the
infringement of the Sabbath law are not easily defined, for no subject
is more intricate than the history of the principle of the subordination
(דחייה) of Sabbatarian rigidity.   It has been maintained (*e.g.* by
F. Rosenthal in the Breslau *Monatsschrift*, 1894, pp. 97 seq.) that the
earlier law was the more lenient, and that custom became continuously
more severe.   But this is not accurate.   It is only necessary to compare
the prescriptions of the *Book of Jubilees* with the later halacha to see
that there was evolution in lenity as well as in severity.   Compare,
for instance, the asceticism in the marital life of *Jubilees* (xlix. 8) with
the very opposite attitude in T.B. *Kethuboth* 82 b (and commentaries
on *Nedarim* viii. 6).   The Essenes (Josephus, *War* II. viii. 9) avoided
other bodily necessities on the Sabbath, but such rigidity was quite
opposed to the Pharisaic view (*Sabbath* 81 a).   Or again, the *Book of
Jubilees* is firm in its refusal to admit the presence of heathens at the
Sabbath meals of Jews: "the Creator of all things blessed it [the
Sabbath], but he did not sanctify all peoples and nations to keep
Sabbath thereon, but Israel alone: *them alone he permitted to eat and
drink* and to keep Sabbath thereon on the earth" (*Jubilees* ii. 31).
The later halacha radically modified this attitude, for not only might
meals be provided for heathens on the Sabbath (T.B. *Beza* 21 b), but
the very compiler of the Mishnah himself gave a banquet in honour of
Antoninus on the Sabbath (Genesis, *Rabba* xi. § 4).   It is even open
to question whether the halacha, as developed by Hillel, did not
introduce the important rule which permitted the bringing of the
paschal lamb on a Sabbath (פסח דוחה שבת).

It is clear, then, that the later halacha permitted certain relaxations
of the Sabbath law.   From this, however, it cannot be inferred that in
the time of Jesus there was such rigidity as would account for his
antagonism to the Pharisees.   It may well be that greater severity
prevailed in Galilee and the North than in Judæa and the South (see
some references by J. Mann in the *Jewish Review*, iv. 526).   In that
case, and if the dispute really occurred in Galilee, the controversy
between Jesus and his opponents was *local*, and has no relevancy to
the Sabbath law as established by the school of Hillel.   For it is just
on the points in which the conflict occurred that the Pharisaic law

must already have reached its humane position in the first century at
latest.   The controversies between the schools of Hillel and Shammai
are concerned with some details of Sabbath observance, but in no case
do these controversies touch the points raised by Jesus.   The established general rule was that the Sabbatical regulations might be, nay
must be, waived in order to save life, and this is throughout implied
in the Synoptic incidents.   The Rabbinic phrase expressing this
general rule (*Yoma* 85 a פקוח נפש דוחה שבת) was derived from a
special case, that of removing a person from under a fallen mass of
débris (פקוח נפש), whence the term came to apply, in general, to all
acts necessary for saving an endangered life (see dictionaries *s.v.* פקוח).
The Mishnah treats the rule as well established even in case of doubt :
"Any case in which there is a *possibility* that life is in danger thrusts
aside the Sabbath law " (Mishnah, *Yoma* viii. 6, Tosefta, *Sabbath* xv. 16).
A generous inclusiveness marked the limits of this bare possibility.
No Sabbatical considerations would have prevented the actual preparation of food for those in danger of actual starvation.   Ears of corn
might not be plucked and ground on the Sabbath under normal
circumstances, but so soon as the element of danger to life entered,
such and any other acts requisite for saving that life became freely
admissible (cf. the collation of the early Rabbinic laws in Maimonides,
Hilchoth *Sabbath* ch. ii.).   "And such things " (says the Baraitha,
T.B. *Yoma* 84 b and Tosefta, *Sabbath* xvi. 12, of all active infringements
of the Sabbath law in cases of emergency) "are not done by heathens
but by the great men of Israel " (ע"י גדולי ישראל)—*i.e.* these breaches
of the law were to be performed personally by the leading upholders of
the law.   So, too, in the similar case of the Day of Atonement, the
Mishnah (*Yoma* viii. 5) allows a sick man to be fed on the fast at his
own desire, in the absence of doctors, or in their presence even if they
thought the patient's need not pressing, but in the case of the presence
of experts, the patient might be fed if they recognised the necessity.
The Talmud (T.B. *Yoma* 83 a) explains this to mean that whereas the
patient, who himself desired it, was on his own demand to be fed,
whether experts were present or not, he was to be fed, even against
his own inclination, if experts declared him in danger.   Thus even
though the ministrations of the doctors involved *them* in a profanation
of the Sabbath (for the Day of Atonement was also a Sabbath) they
were required to compel the patient to accept those ministrations,
however unwelcome it might be to him.

On the other side the case is different with unnecessary interruption of the Sabbath rest. Normally, food eaten on the Sabbath must be provided on the Friday. On this rule the older and the later halacha agree. *Jubilees* (ii. 29, l. 9) already lays this down with emphasis : "they shall not prepare *thereon* anything to be eaten or drunk." This restriction might easily be derived from an expanded application of the Pentateuchal law concerning the manna (Exod. xvi. 23, 25), and from the direct prohibition against kindling fire on the Sabbath (Exod. xxxv. 3). It is scarcely doubtful but that the prohibition of preparing food on the Sabbath, involving as it must a variety of more or less laborious operations, was essential to any real observance of the day of rest. Even so, certain work, such as the removal of heavy boxes of produce, might be performed on the Sabbath to make room for the reception of wayfarers (Mishnah, *Sabbath* xviii. 1), but whatever could be done on Friday was to be done on that day (*ibid.* xix. 1, specifically of the circumcision rite, according to Aqiba). Friday is therefore called in the Greek sources *the day of preparation* (παρασκευή), a title authenticated by Josephus (*Antiquities* xvi. vi. 2) as well as by the Synoptics (Mk xv. 42 ; Mt. xxvii. 62 ; Luke xxiii. 54 ; cf. John xix. 14 with reference to the Passover). There is no exact Hebrew or Aramaic term corresponding to this, but later on, at all events, the technical word הכנה (T.B. *Beṣa* 2 b) seems to show that παρασκευή must have been the paraphrase of some such older phrase. At all events substantially the Greek word represents the fact. An important element of this preparation was the provision of ample Sabbath meals for needy wayfarers (Mishnah, *Peah* viii. 7). Such entertainment was not to be accepted lightly, and those who refused to avail themselves of this relief were praised (*ibid.* § 9). On the other hand, one who, if absolutely destitute, declined the food provided (not on Sabbath only) was esteemed a self-murderer (כאילו שופך דמים). Fasting, moreover, was forbidden on the Sabbath, this was an old and continuously observed rule (*Jubilees* l. 11, *Judith* viii. 6). It has been ingeniously suggested (E. G. Hirsch in *Jewish Encyclopedia* x. 597) that Jesus practically charges his critics with having neglected charity, in not providing Sabbath meals for the needy. "Thus he answers their charge with another. For the act of his disciples there was some excuse; for their neglect to provide the Sabbath meals there was none." But this view, arrestive as it is, hardly fits the language of the Synoptics. The argument turns on the lawfulness or unlawfulness of certain acts on the Sabbath. It cannot be, on the other hand, that Jesus alleges that even the Galilean Pharisees would admit *no* abrogation

of the Sabbath law to meet a pressing necessity, for his whole contention assumes that certain abrogations *were* permitted.   The incidental
question as to travelling on the Sabbath does not arise, for in the
Gospels this aspect is ignored, and we must suppose that the disciples
had not engaged on a long journey, for such a proceeding would
constitute an entire breach with the spirit of the Sabbath rest.   If
the disciples were in imminent danger of starvation, then the Pharisees
must have admitted the lawfulness of their act under the pressure of
circumstances.   But it is scarcely asserted in the Gospels that the
necessity was so absolute as this.   The citation of the precedent of
David does not involve this.   Though there are variations in detail in
the accounts of the Synoptics they all agree in the reference to David
(Mark ii. 25, Matt. xii. 3, Luke vi. 3).   "When he (David) had need
and was an hungered" says Mark, and the other Gospels say much
the same thing : in 1 Sam. xxi. it is not specifically said that David's
young men were in a condition of starvation, for the context implies
haste rather than destitution as the ground for using the holy bread.
The Midrash (*Yalqut ad loc.*), however, clearly asserts that it was a
case of danger to life.   (It may be remarked incidentally that the
Midrash supposes the David incident to have occurred on a Sabbath,
and this would make the Synoptic citation of the parallel more pointed.)

All things considered, it would seem that Jesus differed funda-
mentally from the Pharisees in that he asserted a general right to
abrogate the Sabbath law for man's ordinary convenience, while the
Rabbis limited the licence to cases of danger to life.   The difference is
shown, too, in the citation of Temple analogies.   The Pharisees thought
that work permitted in the Temple was to be specially avoided in
general life on the Sabbath (T.B. *Sabbath* 74 a), but Jesus cites the
Sabbath work of the Temple as a precedent for common use (Matt.
xii. 5).   But the real difference lay in the limitation assigned by the
Pharisees, according to whom all labour, not pressing and postponable,
was forbidden on the Sabbath.   That this is the true explanation is
confirmed by the cases of healing, and is indeed forcibly suggested in
Luke xiii. 14 : "There are six days in which men ought to work, in them
therefore come and be healed, and not on the day of the Sabbath."
And this argument of the ruler of the synagogue remains unanswered ;
it is regrettable that the Synoptics do not in other cases present the
Pharisaic case so precisely.   Pharisaism speaks with no uncertain
voice, and it is the voice of moderation and humanity.   Every remedy
for saving life or relieving acute pain, such as those of child-birth

(Mishnah, *Sabbath* xviii. 3), the curing of snake-bites (Tosefta, *Sabbath*
xv. 14), the relief of various pains (T.B. *Yoma* 84), cooking for the
sick (Tosefta, *ibid.* § 15), these and many other matters are detailed in
various parts of the old halacha (see the collation of these passages in
Maimonides, Hilchoth, *Sabbath* ch. ii.). It is interesting to note that
John vii. 22 reports Jesus as defending his general position from the
analogy of circumcision. Here we have yet another instance of the
Fourth Gospel's close acquaintance with Hebraic traditions, for the
most notable relaxation of the Sabbath law was just in cases of
circumcision (see Mishnah and Talmud, *Sabbath* ch. xix.). In *Yoma* 85 b
the very words of John vii. 23 are paralleled, and the saving of life
derived by an à *fortiori* argument from the rite of circumcision. Jesus,
however, traverses the Pharisaic position, in that he had no objection
to treat long-standing diseases, lingering maladies, and in general
cases where the treatment could be postponed without fear of dangerous
consequences. Jesus concedes, nay his argument is based on the
assertion that the Pharisees would permit the relief of an animal's
distress on the Sabbath—indeed the principle was laid down in various
places (Tosefta, *Sabbath* xv., T.B. *Sabbath* 128 b צער בעל חיים דאורייתא).
But Jesus went further. No act of mercy, whether the need pressed
or not, was to be intermitted because of the Sabbath. This is an
intelligible position, but the Pharisaic position was as intelligible, and
it was consonant with the whole idea of the Sabbath rest. For there
are many categories of acts, clearly servile, and yet which might be
brought within the definition of the merciful, thus first invading, and
finally destroying, the day set aside for repose and communion with
God. The Pharisees permitted, nay required, the performance of all
necessary works of mercy, but refused to extend the licence too
indiscriminately, and never reconciled themselves to the theory that in
general the performance of a duty justified the infringement of a
prohibition. Whatever may be urged from other points of view
against the Rabbinic treatment of the Sabbath, and much may be so
urged, it is just on the subjects in dispute in the Gospels (cf. *Orient*
ix. 62) that their withers are entirely unwrung.

XVIII. THE PERSONAL USE OF THE TERM "MESSIAH."

In the Hebrew Bible there is no indubitable instance of the use of the term Messiah (Greek χριστός) as a personal description of the instrument of the future redemption. There are several passages which tend in that direction, but as Dalman remarks no single passage can be made responsible for the use of the title. Dalman's discussion of the whole subject is full, and, in the main, satisfactory (*The Words of Jesus*, Edinburgh, Clark, 1902, pp. 268 ff., 289 ff.). The reader may be referred to Dalman for much careful information on the Rabbinic uses of the term Messiah. That, as applied to the future salvation, the term is pre-Christian is shown by the Psalms of Solomon (between 70 and 40 B.C.), where however it has been doubted whether the reading (xvii. 36) χριστὸς κύριος is right or merely a mistranslation of משיח יהוה. It should be mentioned that earlier Jewish critics have altogether doubted the Jewish provenance of this passage; Geiger held that the Greek translator, Graetz (*Geschichte der Juden*, III. ed. 2, p. 439) that the author, was a Christian, because of this very phrase (Ryle and James, *Psalms of the Pharisees*, Cambridge, 1891, pp. 141—143, notes). A similar remark applies to the use of the phrase in Pss. of Solomon xviii. 6—8. But for this suspicion there seems no sufficient ground, for in the passages cited (especially xvii. 36) the Messiah is a scion of King David in contradistinction to the Hasmonean kings. This falls well in line with the developed Pharisaic tradition in which David becomes almost inseparably associated with the Messiah. Almost, but not absolutely, for Aqiba recognised Bar Cochba as Messiah, though there is no claim in the sources that he was of Davidic descent. It is not possible to regard the non-Davidic origin of the Messiah in any document as, of itself, evidence that the document is Sadducean.

The simplest view seems to be that when a name was sought for the king of salvation, the old phrase used of the royal dignitary משיח יהוה Ar. משיחא דיי "the Anointed of the Lord" was appropriated. The transference would be helped by the Apocalyptic literature, and it may be also by the existence of a military official the "Anointed of War" (משוח מלחמה, Mishnah Soṭa viii. 1). This office was probably filled by Judas Maccabeus. As regards the mere name, the word Messiah, with or without the article, is the common appellation in the Babylonian Talmud for the personal Messiah. Dalman (*op. cit.* p. 293) thinks that "the Babylonian custom of using משיח as a proper name is incapable of being verified in regard to Palestine. It cannot, therefore, be regarded as old, or as having had a determining influence in Christian phraseology." This distinction, however, is one hard to draw. What may be asserted is that the name Messiah does not become common in Rabbinic usage till after the destruction of the Temple. Its application to Jesus occurs at the moment when the name began to be widely used, and the New Testament usage here, as in many other points, is parallel to Rabbinic development and forms a link in the chain. After the Bar Cochba war (135 A.D.) the name was well established.

Assuming then that the older phrase-form was משיח יהוה, it remains to account for the dropping of the word "Lord." In Daniel ix. 25—6 the term is used absolutely, "an anointed one"; and in the *Zadokite Fragment* (ed. Schechter) we find "his anointed," and also "an anointed from Aaron—Israel" (p. 20, l. 1). In another place the text has "anointed of Aaron" (12, l. 1). Dalman (p. 291) urges that "as the Tetragrammaton was not pronounced, and as there was a reluctance to name God [a reluctance which Dalman thinks, p. 196, was shared by Jesus], so here, as in other commonly used titles, the name of God was omitted and only המשיח Aram. משיחא was said." But though this explanation has cogency, it must be supported by another consideration which Dalman omits. It rather seems that it was a Hebrew tendency to omit the qualifying noun in titles, whether the qualifying noun was the name of God or not. We have an instance in Sirach. The Hebrew text of ch. xliv. is headed שבח אבות העולם "Praise of the Fathers of the World," whereas the later Greek translator abbreviates this into πατέρων ὕμνος, "Praise of the Fathers." Then later again the term "Fathers" was used

to mean the older Rabbis without any qualifying noun. We see
the same process in two famous titles which subsequently were much
used.   These were Nagid (probably abbreviated from נגיד עם אל, cf.
שר עם אל of 1 Macc. xiv. 28) and Gaon (abbreviated from גאון יעקב
Psalm xlvii. 5).   At a far older period Nasi (נשיא) seems an abbre-
viation of a longer expression.   It may be noted in passing that the
term Nasi like Messiah was transferred from a political to a spiritual
function, and that at an earlier period than we can definitely trace
the same reference in the case of Messiah.

XIX. GOD'S FORGIVENESS.

Rabbinic Judaism rested its confidence in the divine forgiveness on God's justice—based on his knowledge of human nature, and on his mercy—based on his love. Divine pardon is the logical correlative of human frailty. "He knoweth our frame"—as the Rabbis translated it "our yeṣer, our evil propensities"—"he remembereth that we are dust" (Psalm ciii. 13). Hence, Repentance forestalled sin in the order of creation; the means of grace was premundane; the remedy preceded the disease (*Aboth*, ii. 4). All moral basis for the world was lacking until this pillar of Repentance was set firm in place (*Pesaḥim*, 54 a; *Pirke R. Eliezer*, iii.; *Genesis Rabba*, i. 4. Cf. Schechter, *Rabbinic Theology*, 128, 314). This idea of premundane grace was deftly supported by the citation of two juxtaposed verses of Psalm xc.: "Before the mountains were brought forth, or ever thou gavest birth to the world...thou didst turn man back to dust, saying, Return, ye children of man." Again, God desires man's reverence, and to this end he forgives. "There is forgiveness with thee, that thou mayest be feared." A human tribunal punishes in order to vindicate the majesty of the Law, but God maintains his reverence by mercy, he as it were coaxes man to virtue by generously overlooking vice, and by making the sinner realise that he has not erred beyond the range of pardon. For the father yearns for the return of his erring children : "Like as a father pitieth his children, so the Lord pitieth them that fear him" (Ps. ciii. 13), and as we have just seen, this fear is on its side won by the mercy which is the response to fear. He has no desire for the death of the sinner, but would have him return and live (Ezekiel xxxiii. 11).

"Neither the national and individual experiences recorded in the Old Testament, nor the words and general language used, seem to suggest any fundamental difference in the idea of forgiveness from that which we find in the New Testament....Indeed so far as the relation between the individual and God is concerned, there is nothing to indicate that the forgiveness granted by God in the experience of his people before the coming of Christ, was different in kind from that which Christ proclaimed" (Bethune-Baker, Hastings' *Dictionary*, II. 56).   This is clearly true, unless it be the fact that Jesus claimed the function of mediatorship between man and God in the matter of forgiveness.   The Old Testament—especially in the Psalter—assumes that man has direct access to the Father, and Pharisaism more than accepted—it confirmed and emphasised—this assumption.   The prophet—whether John the Baptist or another—might bring men to forgiveness; he did not bring forgiveness to men; it was not his to bring.   The mediatorial idea— suggested by the allegorising interpretation of scripture on the one hand and by the inroad of angelology and the doctrine of ancestral virtue with its mediatorial appeal on the other—was not altogether absent from later Rabbinic theology, but on the whole it is true to assert that the principle was left intact that God and God alone is the object of worship and the sole and immediate source of forgiveness.   A human potentate is reached through his ministers; but the presence of God is attainable without any such interpository etiquette.   (This, for instance, is the moral drawn in *Jer. Berachoth*, 13 a, from Joel ii. 32 : Whosoever shall call on the name of the Lord shall be delivered.   Cf. Schechter, *op. cit.* p. 45).

Important as this aspect of the relation between God and erring humanity may be theologically, it is not more important practically than another phase of the problem as to the direct and inalienable accessibility of the divine mercy.   Churches and Creeds do tend to raise barriers between man and God.   They ought to join; they too often seek to keep asunder.   They write their cheerless *Quicunque vult* over the threshold of heaven.   Israel, on his side, is the peculiar treasure of God, for whom the rest of the world is of lower concern; not entirely so (for see p. 149 below) but to a considerable extent.   On their side, of the rest of the world each group has its own key to the Presence, and the only route thither is marked on its especial and exclusive chart.   As a corrective to this natural dogmatism, there recurrently rises an equally natural but a far more gracious humanism. It cannot be that any quality of human nature can disqualify man from the father's love; be that quality inborn or acquired sinfulness or unbelief.   Inhumanity itself cannot rob its unhappy possessor of the rights of humanity.   "The Lord is gracious and merciful; slow to anger and of great loving-kindness.   The Lord is good to all; and his tender mercies are over all his works" (Ps. cxlv. 8, 9).   "He dealeth not with us after our sins, nor rewardeth us after our iniquities" (Ps. ciii. 10). But it is superfluous to multiply texts; the real, sufficing, ultimate text is inscribed on the tablets of every humane heart. As Philo says (*De opif. mund.* 61), "God exerts his providence for the benefit of the world. For it follows of necessity that the Creator must always care for that which he has created, just as parents do for their children."

Two reasons, however, produce some inevitable modifications of this amiable conception. In the first place, religion is disciplinary. It must, in the interests of morality, somehow take account of consequences in order to affect antecedents; it must make forgiveness in some measure dependent on desert. And, secondly, human nature, because it is imperfect, tends to find analogues to its own imperfections in the divine nature. In 1779 Erskine, defending Lieutenant Bourne for challenging to a duel his commanding officer Admiral Wallace, said : "There are some injuries which even Christianity does not call upon a man to forgive or to forget, because God, the author of Christianity, has not made our natures capable of forgiving or forgetting them." Men go further, and assimilating God to their own image, assert that there are injuries which God neither forgives nor forgets. To what extent have Judaism and Christianity followed a similar course in this curious limitation of God's mercy? "Out of the depths have I cried unto thee....O Israel, hope in the Lord ; for with the Lord there is mercy, and with him is plenteous redemption. And he shall redeem Israel from *all* his iniquities" (Ps. cxxx.). There is no limitation here. Or again : "But thou hast mercy on all men, because thou hast power to do all things, and thou overlookest the sins of men to the end that they may repent. For thou lovest all things that are, and abhorrest none of the things which thou didst make; for never wouldst thou have formed anything if thou didst hate it. And how would anything have endured, except thou hadst willed it ? Or that which was not called by thee, how would it have been preserved ? But thou sparest all things, because they are thine, O Sovereign Lord, thou Lover of men's souls" (Wisdom xi. 23—26). And similar ideas may be readily enough found also in the Gospels. "Knock, and it shall be opened unto you...and to him that knocketh it shall be opened" (Matthew vii. 7). " He maketh his sun to rise on the evil and the good, and sendeth rain on the just and the unjust" (Matthew v. 45). And though it be difficult for certain men to enter into the Kingdom of God, yet such things "are possible with God" (Luke xviii. 27). "I will

arise and go to my father," says the Prodigal Son, but "while he was
yet afar off, his father saw him, and was moved with compassion and
ran and fell on his neck and kissed him" (Luke xv. 18—20). In such
passages there is the fullest possible admission of the divine accessibility
to all men. Jesus indeed was animated by a strong, one may even
say a unique, sense of his own relation to and unbroken intercourse
with God. But this sense of nearness is weakened for all other men
when the intercourse with God is broken by the intrusion between
them and God of the person of Jesus. In this respect—of the
universality of access—the Pharisaic position varied, but it was in the
main,—as no doubt the Gospel position was—represented by such
thoughts as are enshrined in the following Parable :

> A King's son went out into evil courses, and the King sent his guardian
> ($\pi\alpha\iota\delta\alpha\gamma\omega\gamma\acute{o}s$) after him. "Return, my son," said he. But the son sent him back,
> saying to his father: "How can I return, I am ashamed." His father sent again
> saying: "My son, art thou indeed ashamed to return? *Is it not to thy father that
> thou returnest?*" (לא אצל אביך אתה חוזר). *Deut. Rabba* ii. § 24, in the name of
> R. Meir).

The Synoptists, not once or twice but often, dispute the general access
to God. The contrast of sheep and goats, of wheat and tares—the
gnashing of teeth and weeping of the iniquitous as they are cast into
the fire while the righteous bask in the sunshine of God—of narrow
and broad ways ; the declaration that those who refuse to receive
Jesus or his apostles are in a worse case than the men of Sodom and
Gomorrah ; the invariable intolerance and lack of sympathy when
addressing opponents, and the obvious expectation that they will be
excluded from the Kingdom—these things make it hard to accept
current judgments as to the universality of all the Gospel teaching in
reference to the divine forgiveness.

Under the stress partly of dogmatic controversy, partly of psychological experience, certain sinners were generally declared outside the pale
of pardon. Philo, whose doctrine on the divine relation to man is, on the
whole, so tenderly humane, holds that those who blaspheme against the
Divine, and ascribe to God rather than themselves the origin of their
evil, can obtain no pardon (*De prof.* 16, Mang. I. 558). This is parallel
to, though less emphatic than, Mark iii. 29 : "he that blasphemeth
against the Holy Spirit hath no forgiveness for ever." Similarly, there
are Rabbinic passages in which "the sin of the profanation of the
Name of God" is described as exempt from forgiveness (*Aboth de R.
Nathan*, 58 b). So, too, the man who causes many to sin *cannot* repent

(*Aboth*, v. 18). But the inability was not absolute—for, as some texts of *Yoma* 87 a read, it is only said to be *well-nigh* (כמעט) not entirely out of the power to repent. And in such cases "death atones" (*Mechilta*, 69 a, *Yoma*, 86 a. Comp. Schechter, *Aspects of Rabbinic Theology*, pp. 328 seq.). Yet it is true that certain sinners are "excluded from a portion in the world to come" (Mishnah, *Sanhedrin*, x. [xi.] 1), having "denied the root-truths of Judaism" and thus "gone out of the general body of Israel." (Comp. Maimonides on the Mishnah cited, and see *Jewish Quarterly Review*, xix. p. 57).

Such views, however, were theoretical metaphysics rather than practical religious teaching. In its dogmatic precisions religion may think of exclusions; in its humane practice it thinks of inclusions. "God holds no creature for unworthy, but opens the door to all at every hour: he who would enter can enter" (Midrash on Ps. cxx). This is the basic doctrine of all religion, including Pharisaism, and it is repeated again and again in various terms in Rabbinic literature. (For references see Montefiore in *Jewish Quarterly Review*, xvi. 229 seq.)

God owes it, as it were, to his own nature to forgive. "God, the father of the rational intellect, cares for all who have been endowed with reason, and takes thought even for those who live a culpable life, both giving them opportunity for amendment, and at the same time not transgressing his own merciful nature, which has goodness for its attendant, and such kindness towards man as is worthy to pervade the divinely ordered world" (Philo, *de prov.* Mangey, II. 634). But this view is not new to Philo; it underlies the whole Biblical and Rabbinic theory as to Providence (see E. G. Hirsch in *Jewish Encyclopedia*, x. 232—3). In the oldest liturgical prayer the "Eighteen" Benedictions—a prayer in essence pre-Maccabean in date, as all authorities are now practically agreed—God is the sustainer of the whole world in all its natural and human relations, and immediately after the expression of his omnipotence comes the appeal to him as the God who "delights in repentance," who "is gracious and doth abundantly forgive." This last phrase is from Isaiah lv., a chapter which is a most gracious comparison of God's fertilising energy in nature to his ever-ready love to the erring human soul. "Let the wicked forsake his way and the unrighteous man his thoughts; and let him return unto the Lord, and he will have mercy upon him; and to our God, for he will abundantly pardon." And this graciousness is based on the very greatness of God. "As the heavens are higher than the earth, so are my ways higher than your ways," and this power is correlatively shown in the divine interest in the affairs of men.   No passages in scripture are more often cited in the Rabbinic literature than this, unless it be Hosea's messages (ch. xiv), Ezekiel's (ch. xviii.), Isaiah's noble utterances in xliii. 25, xliv. 22, and Daniel's (ix. 9).   "To the Lord our God belong mercies and forgivenesses." Rabbinic exegesis had no doubt as to the *categorical* sense of Isaiah i. 18, "Though your sins be as scarlet, they shall be as white as snow," though the moderns mostly render this sentence interrogatively.

This last fact is of some importance.   To render : "*If* your sins be as scarlet, shall they be white as snow ?" may suit the context in Isaiah better, but it is doubtful grammar.   However, Rabbinic exegesis does often throw much light on the point we are considering.   Forgiveness was an inherent attribute of the divine nature, as Philo says and as the Rabbis also maintain.   But the texts on which the Rabbis base their conclusion as to the divine mercy are statements also of the divine retribution.   In particular is this the case with the greatest text of all, Exodus xxxiv. 6—7, "The Lord, the Lord, a God full of compassion and gracious, slow to anger and plenteous in mercy and truth ; keeping mercy for thousands, forgiving iniquity and transgression and sin : and that will by no means clear (the guilty); visiting the iniquity of the fathers upon the children, and upon the children's children upon the third and the fourth generation."   The difficulty might have been met by the application of the principle that Morality and the Law are the expression, not of God's mercy or any other quality, but simply of the divine will.   This idea is expressed in the passage (T. J. *Berachoth* v. 3) which denounces the ascription of such laws as that of the bird's nest to the mercy of God.   It is the divine will that bids man show kindness to the bird, and not the divine love.   This idea of Will did not, however, find much favour in Rabbinic theology, for it was directed against Gnosticism and had but a temporary value and vogue. That, on the contrary, the Law is an expression of Love was deeprooted and permanent in that theology.   Man's mercy to man was a reflection of God's mercy to man (see p. 166 below).   God is the "Merciful One," "the Loving One" (רחמנא), and the very same epithet is transferred to the Law itself, which is often cited as "The Merciful" (see dictionaries of Levy and Jastrow s.v.).   Hence, the retributive conclusion of the great pronouncement of God's mercy must be explained in terms of mercy.

This mercy is sometimes expressed in terms of *postponement*.   This

is not to be confounded with *limitation*. God's power and readiness
to forgive are absolute. But even in his attribute of judge he is not
harsh, and again and again postpones sentence. Philo's words (II. 634)
re-appear in the Midrash (*Tanḥuma* Buber, Numbers 12 b): "the
Merciful does not become the Tyrant (אין המוחל נעשה אכזרי)." But,
on his side, man must not behave as though God's patience is infinite.
God holds over thrice, but he strikes the fourth time (*Yoma* 86 a on
basis of Amos ii. 6). This is not literal, and the stress must be laid
on the *thrice* of the forgiveness, not on the *fourth* of the punishment.
Yet though there is no limitation to God's forgiveness, there must be
a limit to man's taking advantage of it. (*Aboth de R. Nathan* xxxix).
How does Pharisaism reconcile the contradiction?

This was done by calling into play the other note in the harmony
between God and man. If it be the nature of God to offer forgiveness,
it is the nature of man to need and to crave it. God's *métier* is pardon,
man's part is repentance. But though God's grace is in large measure
conditioned by man's desire for it, by his repentance, nevertheless God
makes repentance easy (*Pesiqta* xxv. 163 b). "He who sins and
regrets his act is at once forgiven" (*Ḥagiga* 5 a). God would have men
seek him in reverence, therefore he forgives. He is long-suffering, and
does not requite offence with penalty. He holds it over, giving the
sinner a long respite. He visits the sin of the fathers on the children
—if the children carry on the tradition of sin. He is merciful and so
he accepts the repentant. This is the meaning attached to the phrase
quoted above from Exodus. The Rabbis do not translate ונקה לא ינקה
(Exod. xxxiv. 7) "he will by no means clear the guilty," but stop at the
emphatic infinite (ונקה) "and he will altogether clear" the repentant,
though (לא ינקה) "he will not clear" the unrepentant, unless amendment follows at least in a subsequent generation (*Yoma* 86 a).

But this very idea of *postponement* is practically identical with the
idea that no man is ultimately obdurate. Even the worst type of
sinner—"he who makes others sin"—is not regarded as in a hopeless
case, even he may come to repent (*Yoma* 87 a). This thought underlies the liturgy. It will be noticed, e.g., that the Confession of Sins on
the Day of Atonement—a confession older according to Dr Rendel
Harris than the Didache—includes offences of the most varied kind,
including breaches of the Decalogue and also those sins ("profanation of
the name" and so forth) which in the theoretic theology were pronounced unpardonable. Yet after enumerating them the worshipper
adds: "For all these, O God of forgiveness, forgive us, pardon us, grant

us remission." Now, as Philo put it, God's mercies are uncircumscribed, but not so the faculties of the recipients " (Drummond, *Philo Judaeus*, II. 57). Because God is to man as a father, therefore he does not forgive without discipline. God judges while he pities. "He not only pities after he has judged, but he judges after he has pitied : for with him pity is older than judgment" (*Quod deus immut.* M. I. 284). Yet he also judges, in relation always to man's finitude. God works on human nature, a nature which though imperfect is not impotent for good. In a sense the Jewish doctrine is something like the *synergism* of Erasmus, which as his opponent saw was radically opposed to the Pauline theory of grace. Repentance and confession lead to grace, says Philo (*De excer.* 8, II. 435), and the Rabbis held the same view. Suppose there is no repentance, is there grace? The Rabbis would probably have answered that the supposition is a wild one, but that in any case there is grace. One by one they rescued from the category of the unforgivable the few individuals whom by name they had relegated to the category. For God cannot divest himself of his attribute of mercy. This is the meaning of God's prayer to himself that his grace may overcome his wrath (*Berachoth*, 7 a, *Moed Qaton*, 16 b). This is the meaning of Aqiba's saying (*Aboth*, iii. 20) that "the world is judged by grace (בטוב), yet all is according to the amount of the work." The antinomy is the ultimate doctrine of Pharisaism. Man's part in the divine scheme of mercy must be real. He must turn and live. But the world is nevertheless judged by grace. This does not mean that man can or ought to escape the consequences of sin. Man must pay : but God is a lenient creditor, and he himself provides the coin for the remission of the debt. Man recognizes, too, that God has the right to bring man back to himself by any means that he chooses. The main thing is that man must take his part *seriously*. Sometimes man cries to be turned back to God by mild means. There is a very human note in the prayer of Rabah (*Berachoth*, 17) : " O my God, before I was formed I was nothing worth, and now that I have been formed I am but as though I had not been formed. Dust am I in my life : how much more so in my death. Behold I am before thee like a vessel filled with shame and confusion. O may it be thy will, O Lord my God and God of my fathers, that I may sin no more, and as to the sins I have committed, purge them away in thine abounding compassion though not by means of affliction and sore diseases." As Maimon puts it in his Letter of Consolation (*Jewish Quarterly Review*, II. 68) : " When a child is rebellious against us, we punish him in a gentle way, giving him instruction, inflicting pain upon him, the effect of which, however, will not be permanent, with a thong which gives pain, but leaves no trace, and not with a whip which leaves a permanent mark, or with a rod, which would make a mark for the time, but cleaves not the flesh, as it is said, "If thou beatest him with a rod, he shall not die" (Prov. xxiii. 13). This idea readily passes over into the idea of "chastisements of love" (*Ber.* 5), which on the one hand are not the stripes for sin but the stigmata of service, a means of repentance. On the other hand, the prevalent idea is that God is the father, who corrects "as a father chastises his son" (Deut. viii. 5), who demands from his son genuine tokens of contrition and amendment, but whose love goes out to those who are weakest and least able to return. Philo on Genesis xxviii. 3 has a striking explanation of Isaac's selection of Esau for the blessing. He determines, in the first instance, to bless Esau not because he prefers him to Jacob, but because Esau is in greater need of the blessing. Jacob can "of himself do things well," but Esau is "impeded by his own character, and has no hope of salvation but in the prayer of the father." Thus, the father forgives just because the son does not deserve it. The Pharisaic position will never be understood by those who fail to realise that it tried to hold the balance between man's duty to *strive* to earn pardon, and his *inability* to attain it without God's gracious gift of it. Perhaps the point may be made clear by contrasting two Rabbinic parables. The first is from Deut. *Rabba* ch. iii.:

A King's bride brings two gems as her dowry, and her husband gives her two other gems. She loses her own gems, and the King takes back his two. When she again finds her two gems, he restores his two. So Israel brought into the covenant with God the gems of *justice and righteousness* (Gen. xviii. 19), inherited from Abraham. God added two other gems, *loving-kindness* (Deut. vii. 12) and *mercy* (xiii. 18). When Israel lost his gems (Amos vi. 12) God took away his (Jer. xvi. 15). When Israel again finds his lost gems (Isaiah i. 27), God restores his gift (Isaiah liv. 10) and the four jewels of *justice, righteousness, loving-kindness* and *mercy* together form a crown for Israel (Hosea ii. 21).

Here we have the idea that God's mercy is a gem the possession of which is conditioned by Israel's righteousness. It is surely noble teaching, but it is not the whole truth. The other half is told in another type of thought. If, in the famous saying of Antigonos of Socho (*Aboth* i. 3), Israel must serve without hope of reward, then on the other side God's gifts must be bestowable by him without condition. Israel must work without pay; God must pay without work. On the text: *I will be gracious to whom I will be gracious, and I will show mercy on whom I will show mercy* (Exodus xxxiii. 19) the Midrash has a remarkable passage.   It occurs on this text in the *Rabba* (ch. xlv. end), *Tanḥuma*, and *Yalquṭ* (§ 395).   It proclaims that though righteousness will receive its reward, God's grace extends in full measure to those who have not deserved it.   The idea is the same in all versions, except that in the *Yalquṭ* the point is missed that the last treasure was the *largest*.   (This point is brought out in the prose rendering of S. Singer in *Lectures and Addresses*, London 1908, p. 74.) The following verse translation was made from the *Yalquṭ* (Alice Lucas, *Talmudic Legends*, London 1908, p. 10):

> A legend tells, that when th' Almighty Lord
> Proclaimed to Moses his eternal word,
> He in a vision showed to him likewise
> The treasures that lie stored in Paradise.
> And at each one in turn the heavenly voice
> Spake: "This the treasure is, that shall rejoice
> His soul who freely giveth alms, and here
> His portion is who dries the orphan's tear."
> Thus one by one were all to him made known,
> Until unnamed remained but one alone.
> Then Moses said: "I pray thee, what is this?"
> And answer made the Lord most High: "It is
> The treasure of my mercy, freely given
> To those who else were treasureless in heaven."

This idea, that the Father gives undeservedly, is strongly brought out in the Philonean passage oft-alluded to, and now quoted as follows. (For another version see Eusebius, *Prep. Evangel.* viii. 14, Mangey II. 634, Aucher, *de Providentia* II. 53):

Quaestiones in Genesim

Δυοῖν ὄντων υἱῶν, τοῦ μὲν ἀγαθοῦ, τοῦ δὲ ὑπαιτίου, τὸν μὲν ὑπαίτιον εὐλογήσειν φησίν· οὐκ ἐπειδὴ τοῦ σπουδαίου προκρίνει τοῦτον, ἀλλ' ὅτι ἐκεῖνον οἶδε δι' αὑτοῦ κατορθοῦν δυνάμενον, τοῦτον δὲ τοῖς ἰδίοις τρόποις ἁλισκόμενον, μηδεμίαν δὲ ἔχοντα σωτηρίας ἐλπίδα, εἰ μὴ τὰς εὐχὰς τοῦ πατρός· ὧν εἰ μὴ τύχοι, πάντων ἂν εἴη κακοδαιμονέστατος.

(J. Rendel Harris, *Fragments of Philo Judaeus*, 1886, p. 43.)

Genesis xxvii. 3

§ 198. Quippe quod duo sunt filii: unus bonus, alter sub causa (sc. crimine, culpa). Istum itaque, qui sub causa est, benedicere ait, non quod plusquam bonum praeferat hunc, sed quia scit illum per se solum posse recte rem perficere; istum vero ut a suis moribus detentum impeditumque, spem salutis habere in sola patris oratione: quam si non assequatur, prae omnibus miser erit.

(Aucher's Latin translation from Armenian, p. 400.)

The Rabbis have another form of the same thought when they pronounce the penitent sinner superior to the righteous; the former has overcome a weakness to which the latter is not susceptible. The same thought underlies the Rabbinic discrimination between Jew and Gentile in regard to God. Often there is strong particularism in favour of Israel (*Jewish Quarterly Review*, XVI. 249 seq.), and Judaism did, under the stress of the Roman persecution, regard the obdurately unrepentant heathen as resting under the divine wrath, much as we find it in the Apocalypses, and in the particularist passages of the Synoptics. But the inherent universalism of Rabbinism reveals itself not only in the beautiful hope for the heathen contained in the liturgy (in the *Alenu* prayer), not only in such a saying as that the righteous of all nations have a share in the world to come—a saying which Maimonides raised to the dignity of a Jewish dogma—but the nations are actually represented as finding repentance easier than Israel finds it. (On the salvation of the heathen see M. Joseph, *Judaism as Creed and Life*, ch. x, ed. 2, 1910, p. 116.) And most striking of all is the use made of the story of Nineveh. The Book of Jonah is read on the Day of Atonement, and it was also in earlier times the subject of a discourse on fast days (Mishnah, *Ta'anith*, ii. 1). Thus the accepted repentance of a heathen nation was the model for the repentance of Israel. "The Lord is good unto all; and his tender mercies are over all his works." This is a verse in the 145th Psalm which was introduced thrice daily into the Rabbinic liturgy. Characteristically enough, too, it was the recitation of this particular Psalm which, it was held, opened the doors of paradise to men (*Berachoth* 4 b). And it is an absolutely universalistic Psalm.

Some other aspects of the questions treated in this note will be considered further in Note XX on "Man's forgiveness."

XX. MAN'S FORGIVENESS.

The Mishnaic tractate *Aboth* (Fathers) contains a collection of maxims by the Tannaim, the teachers of Pharisaism from the century before till the end of the second century after the beginning of the Christian era. Among these maxims occurs one which is of unusual character, for it consists merely of the citation of a passage of Scripture without addition or comment. The maxim referred to is found in ch. iv. (§ 19 or 26) of the tractate: "Samuel ha-Qatan was wont to say: Rejoice not when thine enemy falleth, and let not thine heart be glad when he stumbleth." This citation from Proverbs xxiv. 17 is remarkable. Samuel belonged to the end of the first century, and was associated in esteem with Hillel (T. J. Soṭah ix. § 12) as one "worthy of the Holy Spirit." The ingrained weakness of human nature, the desire for revenge against an enemy, is thus pointedly attacked by a great Pharisee, and in a manner as remarkable for its position as for its form.

In the Old Testament inculcation of kindliness to man Pharisaism found a firm basis for its own treatment of the subject. This doctrine does not consist of a few stray texts; it is of the essence of Old Testament religion. With regard to the special point before us, the repression of rancour and vindictiveness, the Hebrew Bible is permeated with example and admonition. No two nobler instances of forgiveness are to be found in literature than the records of Joseph's conduct to his brethren and of David's to Saul, culminating as the latter does in the Dirge of "magnanimous forgiveness" with which—to use Sir G. A. Smith's phrase—the second book of Samuel opens. And the admonition finds expression in every part of the Bible. It is found in the Law not in one but in many precepts. To the eternal glory of the Old Testament, the great texts "love thy neighbour as thyself," "hate not thy brother in thy heart," "avenge not," "bear no grudge," "love the stranger," are part of the Hebrew law of holiness.

There was little left for religion in subsequent ages except to draw out the full consequences of these and similar injunctions. Nothing that has been added can compare in sheer originality and power to the first formulation of these great principles. Theology, unhappily, has been engaged in belittling the Old Testament contribution to the gracious store, whittling away its words, or at best allowing to them grudgingly the least that the grammatical words compel! For instance, in the note on Leviticus xix. 18, in the *Cambridge Bible for Schools* (Leviticus Volume, 1914, p. 109), the editors are painfully anxious that the young student should not over-rate the text before him. And he is pointedly warned that the "stranger" of verse 34 is only the "stranger who worshipped Israel's God." Did Israel, then, worship Egypt's Gods? Yet the "stranger" is to be loved because the Israelites "were strangers in the land of Egypt." Must, then, the same word *gêr* mean two different things within the compass of the same Hebrew sentence? Whatever *gêr* means in other contexts, and in later ages, it is clear that in Leviticus xix. 34 it has a wide connotation. (On the whole question of the Rabbinic law on the stranger see D. Hoffmann, *Der Schulchan-Aruch und die Rabbinen über das Verhältniss der Juden zu Andersgläubigen*, Berlin, 1885.)

This, however, is a minor point. All honour to the great teachers of later times who set themselves to read as much into the law of brotherly love as they could. But the law is Hebraic. And it is not the Pentateuch alone which contains it. The prophetical teaching is saturated with the love of mercy. There is no need to quote. Zechariah sums up what he regards as the message of the older prophets: "Execute true judgment, and show mercy and compassion every man to his brother: and oppress not the widow, nor the fatherless, the stranger, nor the poor; and let none of you imagine evil against his brother in your heart" (Zech. vii. 9, 10; cf. viii. 16, 17 where there is added "love no false oath," with the glorious conclusion "for all these things are things that I hate, saith the Lord").

Similarly with the Wisdom literature of the Old Testament. Job, Proverbs, Ecclesiasticus, have splendid sayings on the subject of forgiveness. Again, there is no need to quote more than one passage. I select this passage, partly for its intrinsic merit, partly for its position in the Mishnah as already indicated, but mainly because it became a fundamental principle of Pharisaism.

> Rejoice not when thine enemy falleth,
> And let not thine heart be glad when he is overthrown:
> Lest the Lord see it, and it displease him,
> And he turn away his wrath from him. (PROV. xxiv. 17—18.)

What does this mean? Ibn Ezra among the older, and Dr Charles among the newer, commentators interpret the words to mean that malicious joy defeats its own end. This would not be a low standard, for many a bitter opponent has been restrained by the knowledge that to press revenge too relentlessly rouses for the victim a sympathy which would not otherwise be felt. But the great majority of interpreters, ancient and modern, read the sentence differently.

C. H. Toy's explanation in the Proverbs volume of the *International Critical Commentary* (p. 448) runs thus:

"The *turn his anger from him* (that is from the enemy) is not to be understood as affirming that God will cease punishing a wicked man, because another man is pleased at the punishment; the full force of the expression is 'turn from him to thee,' and the stress is to be laid on the 'to thee.' 'Thou,' says the sage, 'wilt then become the greater sinner, and Yahweh will be more concerned to punish thee than to punish him.'"

The same view is taken in the Kautzsch Bible, where Kamphausen (p. 808) renders the verses Proverbs xxiv. 17–18 thus: "Wenn dein Feind fällt, so freue dich nicht, und wenn er hinsinkt, frohlocke nicht dein Herz, dass nicht Jahwe es sehe und Missfallen empfinde und seinen Zorn von jenem hinweg [auf dich] wende." On this insertion, Wildeboer in Marti's *Kurzer Hand-Commentar* remarks: "Kamphausen rightly inserts the words *to thee*." In the "Century" Bible G. C. Martin takes the same view: "*from him*, i.e. 'lest the Lord turn His anger from the wicked man to you.'" As will be seen later, the Pharisaic theory consistently was that the unforgiving injured party became the *sinner* through his implacability.

That the moderns are, however, supported by older exegetes is clear. Thus, the most popular commentary on the Mishnah, that of Obadiah of Bertinoro, has this remark on the passage already cited (Aboth iv. 19 [26]): "והשיב עליו אפו: since it is not written ושב but והשיב, the meaning is: He will transfer his anger from thine enemy and will place it upon thee." The commentary on Aboth ascribed to Rashi interprets similarly. So does Gersonides, and so again does the popular Hebrew writer David Altschul in his commentary on Proverbs. Accepting this meaning it is a noble saying, just as in the very same chapter (Prov. xxiv. 29) is found that other noble verse: "Say not, I will do so to him as he hath done to me; I will render to the man according to his work." This is the highest possible expression of forgiveness as opposed to retaliation, unless the saying in Prov. xx. 22 be higher still: "Say not thou, I will recompense evil; wait on the

Lord and he shall save thee." Here, certainly, there is no reference at all to revenge ; God does not avenge, he saves.

The doctrine read in, or into, Proverbs xxiv. 18 by most commentators is confirmed by the opening of the great passage on forgiveness to be found in Ecclesiasticus xxvii., xxviii. The passage is quoted below ; here we are concerned with two introductory verses :

> Wrath and anger, these also are abominations ;
> And a sinful man shall possess them.
> He that taketh vengeance shall find vengeance from the Lord ;
> And He will surely make firm his sins. (ECCLUS. xxvii. 30, xxviii. 1.)

This seems to mean that God exacts vengeance from the vengeful, just as Prov. xxix. 18 teaches. At all events, the Pharisaic principle was just that. *The unforgiving man is the sinner* (see quotations below). And following on his elaboration of this principle, Maimonides (*Laws of Repentance* ii. 10) adds :

> It is prohibited for a man to be hard-hearted and refuse his forgiveness ; but he shall be "hard to provoke and easy to pacify" (Aboth v. 14). When the sinner seeks pardon, he must forgive with a perfect heart and a willing mind. Even though one has oppressed him and sinned against him greatly, he shall not be vengeful nor bear a grudge. For this is the way of the seed of Israel and those whose heart is right. But the heathen, of uncircumcised heart, are not so, for they retain their anger for ever. Therefore does the Scripture say of the Gibeonites (2 Samuel xxi. 2), in that they pardoned not and proved relentless, " They were not of the children of Israel."

No doubt it is a good thing for men to see themselves as others see them, and the Pharisees have enjoyed the privilege without stint ! Is it not well, too, for others sometimes to see men as they see themselves ? Let the Pharisees enjoy this privilege too !

It is important to observe the reference made by Maimonides to the incident of the Gibeonites' revenge. The claim of Maimonides that forgiveness was a characteristic of Israel is made in the Talmud also in reference to the Gibeonites (Yebamoth 79 a). Often it has been urged that the presence of vindictive passages in the Psalter must have weakened the appeal of the finer sentiments in other parts of the Psalms and of the Scriptures generally. But the argument is a fallacy. The New Testament teaching is not all on the same level as the Sermon on the Mount, there are passages which express a vindictive spirit. But Christians rightly treat such passages as negligible in presence of the nobler sayings, which dominate and colour the whole. So with the Jew and the Old Testament. He was impelled

invariably to interpret the lower in terms of the higher. The noblest
ideas dominated the rest. Never do we find in the Rabbinic literature
appeal made as precedents to those incidents at which the moral sense
boggled. What was disliked was explained away. "Eye for eye" was
never applied in practical Jewish law. Taken over theoretically from
the Code of Hammurabi, the lex talionis was not acted on in Israel.
No single instance of its application is on record. The unfavourable
reference to the law in Matthew v. 38 no more than the favourable
allusion to it in Philo (II. 329) implies that the law was extant as a
legal practice. The Talmud is emphatic that the retaliation was not
by mutilation of the offender but by the exactment of compensation by
fine. (*Baba Qama* 84 a, where only one authority argues for a literal
interpretation.) Perhaps the Dositheans were literalists in this respect,
but the phrase "eye for eye," with which so much play is made in
non-Jewish literature, was not familiar on Rabbinic lips. Some
writers do most erroneously confuse "eye for eye" (a principle of
human justice) with "measure for measure" (a theory of divine retribution). The one is a truculent policy, the other a not ungracious
philosophy. The Pharisees who like the Synoptists adopted the theory
of "measure for measure," like them also rejected the principle of
"eye for eye." In fact the very objection to the lex talionis as
literally conceived was used to support the need of traditional interpretation; the law as written cannot be understood without the
Pharisaic mitigations (see the quotations from Saadiah in Ibn Ezra's
elaborate note on Exodus xxi. 24). Similarly with the imprecatory
Psalms. These could not mean what they seem to say, and why not?
Because they do not consist with the forgiving spirit of other parts
of the Scriptures. Thus Psalm xli. 11 reads "Raise me up that I may
requite them." This contradicts the humaner spirit of Psalm xxxv. 13,
vii. 5, and so David must have meant: "Raise me up that I may
requite them *good for evil*" (see the quotation from Saadiah in Qimḥi's
note to Psalm xli.). This may be poor exegesis, but it is rich humanism.
There is another fact to remember. The imprecatory Psalms never
received a personal private interpretation.

Theologically we see the same phenomena. Anthropomorphisms are
brought into harmony with the developed spiritual conception of the
Godhead, by explaining them away, allegorising them. Economists
tell us that base coin drives out the genuine. But in Jewish history
we see the reverse process; the genuine drives out the base. This
tendency is shown in the Bible itself. Contrast 1 Chron. xxviii. 29

with 1 Kings ii. 1–12, whence it is seen that the author of the Book of Chronicles entirely omits the passage assailed, thus revealing that the feeling of the Chronicler was quite as tender and unvindictive as that of any modern moralist.   The example of Joseph so very deeply impressed Jewish thought, that it is set up as an exemplar for God himself! Here is an oft-repeated idea; it occurs in the Pesiqta Rabbathi ed. Friedmann, p. 138 a, also in the Pesiqta d. R. Cahana, in the Canticles Rabba on viii. 1, and elsewhere:

Comfort ye, comfort ye my people, saith your God (Isaiah xl. 1). This is what the Scripture hath: *O that Thou wert as my brother* (Cant. viii. 1). What kind of brother?...Such a brother as Joseph to his brethren. After all the evils they wrought unto him Joseph said, *Now therefore fear ye not: I will nourish you, and your little ones.   And he comforted them and spake to their heart* (Genesis i. 21)....Israel said unto God: Master of the World, come regard Joseph. After all the evils wrought by his brothers he comforted them and spake to their heart; and we, on our part, are conscious that we caused Thy house to be laid waste through our iniquities, we slew thy prophets, and transgressed all the precepts of the Law, yet, *O that Thou wert as a brother unto me!* Then the Lord answered: Verily, I will be unto you as Joseph. He comforted his people and spake to their heart. So, as for you, *Comfort ye, comfort ye my people.   Speak unto the heart of Jerusalem and say unto her that her warfare is accomplished, that her iniquity is pardoned.*

The ideal traits of the Biblical heroes and saints were set up for imitation, their faults never.

Like the Book of Proverbs, the Wisdom of Sirach (Ecclesiasticus) inculcates a lofty ideal on the subject of forgiveness. It is clear that the teaching is on the same line as that of the Synoptics: as is manifest from the passages set out in parallel columns:

Forgive thy neighbour the hurt that he hath done unto thee;	When ye stand praying, forgive, if ye have aught against any one;
So shall thy sins also be forgiven when thou prayest.	That your father also which is in heaven may forgive you your trespasses.
	MARK xi. 25; MATT. vi. 14; LUKE vi. 37.
One man cherisheth hatred against another,	Forgive us our debts, as we also have forgiven our debtors.
And doth he seek healing from the Lord?	For if ye forgive men their trespasses, your heavenly father will also forgive you.
He sheweth no mercy to a man like himself,	
And doth he make supplication for his own sins?	But if ye forgive not men their trespasses, neither will your father forgive your trespasses.
Being flesh himself he nourisheth wrath:	
Who shall atone for his sins?	
ECCLUS. xxviii. 3—5.	MATT. vi. 12, 14, 15.

Now this teaching of Jesus son of Sirach is absolutely identical with that of Jesus of Nazareth. Dr Charles, who holds that the Testaments of the Twelve Patriarchs belong to the second century B.C., cites from these Testaments a view on forgiveness which he characterises as "no less noble than that of the New Testament." I will repeat the quotation made by Dr Charles from Test. Gad vi. 1.

> 3. Love ye one another from the heart; and if a man sin against thee, cast forth the poison of hate and speak peaceably to him, and in thy soul hold not guile; and if he confess and repent, forgive him. 4. But if he deny it, do not get into a passion with him, lest catching the poison from thee, he take to swearing, and so thou sin doubly. 6. And though he deny it and yet have a sense of shame when reproved, give over reproving him. For he who denieth may repent so as not again to wrong thee: yea he may also honour and be at peace with thee. 7. But if he be shameless and persist in his wrongdoing, even so forgive him from the heart, and leave to God the avenging.

Thus the line of connected Jewish teaching is complete: Proverbs, Sirach, Twelve Patriarchs, Synoptics. Other links in the chain could be indicated. Philo, with much else as elevated, has these sayings (cited by C. G. Montefiore in his *Florilegium Philonis* in *J. Q. R.* VII. 543): "If you ask pardon for your sins, do you also forgive those who have trespassed against you? For remission is granted for remission" (Mang. II. 670). "Pardon is wont to beget repentance" (II. 672 συγγνώμη μετάνοιαν πέφυκε γεννᾶν). "Behave to your servants as you pray that God may behave to you. For as we hear them, so shall we be heard; and as we regard them, so shall we be regarded. Let us show pity for pity, so that we may receive back like for like" (*ibid.*).

The teaching of Judaism on the subject of forgiveness is in fact the brightest and strongest link in its golden chain. The doctrine was adopted by medieval moralists who insist on it with extraordinary frequency. And it was introduced into the authoritative Codes. As Maimonides puts it in his Code (*Laws of Repentance* II. 9, 10): "The man who does not pardon a wrong doing to him is the sinner; it is prohibited for a man to be vindictive (אכזרי, lit. *cruel, hard-hearted*) but he must forgive with a perfect heart and an eager soul." This is the spirit in which the Jew approaches God with his supplication for mercy on the great Day of Atonement. This is the teaching of Pharisaism. To attribute any other doctrine to it is unhistorical. There is no justification for representing as in a moral "backwater" the humanitarian religion of Hillel, Joḥanan ben Zakkai, Neḥunya ben Haqana, Meir, and the rest of a long, continuous line of teachers in

Jewry, who are organically connected with Sirach though they neither begin nor end with him.

That there are "imprecations" in the Psalter, that the Pharisaic literature shows some narrowness of sympathy where sectarians are concerned, and that through its whole course, until the rise of the liberal movement, Judaism has retained a "particularist" taint,—these facts must neither be ignored nor exaggerated. As to the Psalms, an admirable treatment of the question may be found in an anonymous little book (with Introduction by the Rev. Bernard Moultrie) entitled *The Use of the Psalms in the Christian Church with special reference to the Psalms of Imprecation* (St Leonards-on-Sea, 1908). The author shows how Paul, in warning Christians against revenge (Rom. xii. 19, 20), uses words borrowed from the Old Testament (Levit. xix. 18; Deut. xxxii. 35; Prov. xxv. 21, 22). Job in the course of his spirited protest, which contains the most perfect ideal of virtue ever formulated in literature, exclaims (xxxi. 29, 30)

> If I rejoiced at the destruction of him that hated me,
> Or lifted up myself when evil found him;
> (Yea, I suffered not my mouth to sin,
> By asking his life with a curse;)

As the author of the volume cited justly asserts (p. 63): "The opposition to revenge is so little peculiar to the New Testament, that the strongest and most numerous passages against it are to be found in the Old." The author goes on to show that, on the other hand, imprecations are found in the New Testament. (He cites: Rev. vi. 15—17; Matt. xiii. 56, xxiii. 33—36, xxiv. 50, 51, xxv. 41; Heb. x. 31, xii. 29; 2 Thess. i. 6—12.) But these, like the "imprecations" of the Psalter, are all based on the theory: "Do not I loathe them, O Lord, that hate thee: and am I not grieved with those that rise up against thee?" (Psalm cxxxix. 21). If this theory be no longer tenable in modern times, then those few whole Psalms, and single verses in other Psalms, which are based on like theory, should be expunged from public worship without casting a stone from the superior virtue heap at the former generations of Maccabean Zealots or English Puritans who saw in the theory nothing lowering or dangerous. The Synagogue has no need to eliminate Psalms lix. and cix. (the chief of the imprecating Psalms) because they are not used in regular Jewish public worship!

Of these two Psalms only this need be said. Of the imprecations in Ps. cix. (6—19) it is almost certain that the "Psalmist *quotes* the imprecations of his enemies in his complaint to God against them"

(W. Emery Barnes, *Lex in Corde*, 1910, p. 176). This view is disputed, but there is much in its favour. Of .Psalm lix. it is equally certain that the imprecations are not directed against a personal enemy. It may well be that the objects of animosity are the Samaritans, and that the Psalm belongs to Nehemiah's age.

Mr Montefiore's lament that Jesus displayed animosity against the Pharisees has been resented by critics of his volumes. His comment, it has been said, is due to psychological misunderstanding. If this be so, ought not the same principle to apply to the Pharisaic animosity —such as it was—against sectarians? If Jesus might with propriety assail the Pharisees with threats of dire retribution, the same measure must be meted out to them, when they are the assailants of those whom they thought wilfully blind to truth and open rebels against righteousness. In no age have the sects loved one another over much, and much as one may sigh at this display, among all creeds, of human nature red in tooth and claw, it is happily true that the consequences have not been entirely bad for the world. The prophet is almost necessarily a denunciator, and the sect must fight if it would maintain the cause. "The emulation of scholars increases wisdom" (B. Bathra, 21 a), and the same principle applies to sectarian differences. The Pharisees of the age of Jesus were no doubt good fighters against internal heresies, just as they were good fighters against the common enemy, Rome. But there was more of this a century before and a century after Jesus than in his actual age. For it is in fact found on examination that the Jewish ill-feeling against the "nations" is correlated to the ill-feeling of the "nations" against Israel. The Maccabean spirit of exclusiveness was roused by the Syrian plot against Judaism, just as the later Pharisaic exclusiveness was roused by the Roman assault on the religious life of Israel. And the same is true even of the apocalypses, with their tale of doom. All of them must be placed in their proper historical background if the picture is to be just. Undoubtedly, with the terrible experience of the Great War before our eyes, with the recollection of much said and written and done burnt into our minds, our world is better able to judge the past. And it is not necessary to appeal to our own immediate experience of the hour. One would not deduce the theory of brotherly love held by Dutch Christendom from the language of Boers regarding English during the South African War; one would not entirely gauge the condition of Elizabethan Anglicanism in relation to the forgiving spirit by its language or actions regarding Spanish Catholics. Nor would one be just to Puritanism if one read a complete theory of its attitude towards the persecutors of the Church into Milton's fiery sonnet on the massacre by the Piedmontese:

> Avenge, O Lord, thy slaughtered saints, whose bones
> Lie scattered on the Alpine mountains cold!

National, sectarian, animosities, even humanitarian indignations against the cruel and the unrighteous, do indeed stand on a different plane to personal vindictiveness, and men sometimes do well to be angry.

It is, however, not the case that the Pharisaic liturgy enshrines any vindictiveness against Christianity. This denial is obviously true of the first century, but it is also absolutely true of later centuries. As a Jewish heresy, early Christianity was the subject of antipathy, as an independent religion it was scarcely assailed at all. Paganism was another matter; against idolatry the Synagogue waged war, and sometimes idolaters came in for their share of the attack, and were, in moments of stress, regarded as outside the pale of the brotherhood of man. But even then, it was internal heresy that was more bitterly resented, and the deliberate sinner, the man of immoral and heretical life within the fold, was far more the object of recrimination than any one who stood outside. Here, again, we have a fact of human nature, not of Pharisaic nature only, and it is a pity that the Pharisees are made to bear the burden which should be put on the shoulders of mankind.

The Rabbinic sayings to the effect that it is permissible to "hate" the wicked within the fold, have no reference to personal wrongs. The offences which make "hatred" justifiable are invariably breaches of morality or of the law of God which should not be condoned until the offender had repented. The personal foe does not come into the category. The same page of the Talmud (*Pesaḥim* 113 b) which records the duty to show detestation of the adulterer records also that beloved of God is he who forgives wrongs personal to himself. "I believe it to be quite one of the crowning wickednesses of this age that we have starved and chilled our faculty of indignation" (Ruskin, *Lectures on Art*, 1870, p. 83; compare Sir J. Stephen, *History of the Criminal Law of England*, 1883, Vol. I. p. 478). In the category of those who were to be the object of this "indignation," were sometimes included the heretic and the disloyal (*Aboth de R. Nathan* xvi.). But almost always the offences were indeed detestable (e.g. *Ta'anith* 7 b). Beruriah, the wife of R. Meir, in an oft-quoted passage explained

Psalm civ. 35 as a prayer that sin not sinners should be made an end
of (*Berachoth* 10 a). It is not easy, in this tender fashion, to discriminate
between sin and sinners, but one ought never to lose sight of the
general Pharisaic repugnance against hatred. "Hatred of mankind"
(the term used is the widest possible שנאת הבריות) is one of the three
things (the other two are the "evil eye" and the "evil *yeṣer*"—envy
and lust) which "put a man out of the world" (Mishnah, *Aboth* ii. 11
[15]). So that we have in a late Midrash the splendid generalisation
that: Whoever hates any man is as one who hates Him who spake
and the world was (*Pesiq. Zuṭ.* on Numbers viii. seq.). This prohibition
applied to all men, even to Rome (see the strong rebuke in Eccles.
Rabba xi., on the text Deut. xxiii. 8). Even the command to remember
Amalek was explained by one Rabbi to mean: Remember your own
sins which led up to Amalek's assault:

> A King owned a vineyard, round which he built a fence. He placed inside the
> fence a savage dog. The King said: Should one come and break through the fence,
> the dog will bite him. The King's own son came, and broke down the fence. The
> dog bit him. Whenever the King wished to mention how his son had offended in
> the matter of the vineyard, he said to him: Remember what the dog did to you!
> So, whenever God wishes to recall Israel's sin at Rephidim (Exod. xvii. 8), he says
> unto them: Remember what Amalek did to you! (*Pesiqta K.*, iii. 27 a).

In passing, though the fact is of more than passing importance, let
note be taken of the quotation from the *Pesiqta Zuṭarta*. To hate man
is to hate God. We have the same thought underlying the preference
shown by Ben Azzai for Genesis ii. 4 as the "greatest commandment"
(cf. p. 20 above). R. Aqiba declared in favour of Leviticus xix. 18
"Love thy neighbour as thyself." But this is open to the objection
that if a man is himself in despicable state, he may despise his
neighbour (הואיל ונתבזיתי יתבזה חבירי). Hence, says Ben Azzai, greater
is the text: "These are the generations of the heaven and the earth
when they were created" (Gen. ii. 4). As R. Tanḥuma comments:
"If thou showest low regard for any man, remember whom thou art
despising: for the text says: In the image of God made he man."

Another aspect of the sectarian question is apt to be overlooked.
Sects, while their first inspiration is fresh and their numbers small,
have always been distinguished for the strength of brotherly love
within their own body. But when the membership transcends local
bounds, and the initial impulse is materialised into a systematised
organisation, that warmth of complete and unreserved fraternity is
necessarily apt to cool. It is superfluous to show how Christianity

was compelled by its own success to become less a brotherhood than a Church. Within Judaism we find at every epoch, from the period before the Christian era down to the present time, the continuous formation of new unions, which display intensity of brotherhood while young and small, and which progress in the normal way towards greater aloofness as the body grows older and bigger. Religion is kept fresh by the outbreak of sectarianisms; this is the great good accruing from the creation of new sects. For these recurrent outbreaks of sectarianism are also outbreaks of brotherliness within the new sect, they are the renewals of the religious stream, the openings up of new wells of the humane spirit which comes direct from God. And so we find Hippolytus saying of the Essene: "He will observe righteousness towards men and do injustice to none: he will not hate anyone who has done him injustice, but will pray for his enemies" (*Refutatio Omnium Haeresium*, IX. 18—28. Cf. Kohler, *Jewish Encyclopedia*, v. 239; Josephus, *War*, II. viii. 6—7). So, passing across many centuries, we have Luria (the mystic leader of Safed, 1534—1572) *opening the day* with the invocation: "Lo! I hold myself ready to fulfil the divine behest: Thou shalt love thy neighbour as thyself," and at night *closing the day* with the declaration: "Lo! I pardon everyone who has angered, or provoked me, or sinned against me, and I pray that no man whatsoever shall be punished because of me." (Cf. Steinthal, *Zu Bibel und Religionsphilosophie*, p. 161.)

And the same sensitiveness is observable at normal periods. There is, for instance, a whole series of more ancient personal prayers preserved in the Jerusalem Talmud (*Berachoth* iv. § 2). "May it be thy will, O Lord my God and God of my fathers, that hatred and envy of us enter not into the heart of man, nor hatred and envy of any man enter into our heart." On the same page may be seen the student's prayer. "May it be thy will, that I be not angered against my fellows, nor they against me." Yet another prayer occurs in the same context. "Bring us near to what thou lovest, keep us far from what thou hatest." These beautiful petitions may be paralleled by that of Mar Zutra, who every night on retiring to his couch said: "Forgiveness be to all who have troubled me" (שרי ליה לכל מאן דצערן *Megillah* 28 a).

Turning from the necessary distinction suggested above between public, national, humane enmities and private, individual, inhuman vindictiveness, we are arrested by an aspect of the subject which is an important element in the Pharisaic doctrine of forgiveness. The injured party must forgive, but what of the man who has done the wrong? Pharisaism did not reserve all its sympathy for the inflicter of the wrong; it had sympathy, too, with the sufferer of the wrong. It said to the injurer: You, too, pray for God's mercy, but you must not go to God red-handed. Before you ask God's forgiveness, seek the forgiveness of your injured fellow-man. Not even the Day of Atonement atones for wrongs done by man to man (Mishnah Yoma viii. 9). The man who brought a sin-offering and remembered at the very altar that he still held the stolen goods, was ordered to stop his sacrifice, make restitution, and then come back to his sacrifice (Tosefta, Baba Qama x. 18, p. 368. Cf. *Cambridge Biblical Essays*, 1909, p. 189; see also Philo *de opif.* chs. i and iv). And if the sin-offering prescribed in the Pentateuch was thus of no avail unless practical atonement had preceded, it is not surprising that we find the same declaration of the futility of prayer to God unless it had been preceded by an appeal to the injured neighbour. Undo the injury, beg your neighbour's forgiveness, realize the wickedness of wrong-doing, do not throw *all* the burden of reconciliation on the person wronged. *He* must forgive, but *you* must try to earn his forgiveness. It is not merely a piece of French wit: *Que messieurs les assassins commencent!* The criminal must not expect *all* the consideration, he must show some on his part to the rights of society. The Pharisees softened punishment by their theory that it was part, the main part of atonement: the prisoner came out, not crushed by disgrace, but ennobled if chastened by the sense that he had borne punishment to put himself right with the outraged moral law. It then became the duty of society to forgive on its part: to clean the slate, and forget the record. And so with regard to wrongs which do not fall within the scope of the law at all. Here, too, the perpetrator of the wrong must bear his share in the hard labour of atonement. It is almost pathetic to read in Jewish moral books how the offender must humble himself, must again and yet again present himself before his offended brother, seeking pardon, refusing to accept a rebuff. (Cf. Yoma 87 b.)

The Synoptics, on the whole, imply the same view. The Gospel exhortations to forgive take it for granted that, though the response must be prompt and complete, it is response rather than initiative that is contemplated. There are thus two elements: (a) approach by the offender, (b) pardon by the offended. Some theologians who, without foundation in fact, contrast the Pharisaic doctrine unfavourably with the Gospel teaching, in their just admiration of (b), which the Pharisees fully shared with the Synoptists, ignore (*a*), which the Synoptists fully shared with the Pharisees. The Gospel view is most clearly seen in the effective Parable of Matthew xviii. 23—35. The defaulting debtor is forgiven the debt after admitting it and praying for patience (v. 26—7). The debtor then refuses a similar prayer by *his* debtor (v. 29). In punishing this act—and the Parable of forgiveness a little loses its grace by making over vindictive the lord's resentment of unforgiveness—the lord says: "Thou wicked servant, I forgave thee all that debt, *because thou besoughtest me*" (v. 32). This be it remembered is the illustration of the injunction "until seventy times seven" (v. 22). Clearly the injured is expected to do his part in seeking pardon from the injured (cf. Hermas, *Mandate* iv. 8, 9).

And if the injured party be dead? Then at his grave must pardon be asked: the living appealing to the dead (Maim. Teshuba, ii. 11; Yoma 87 a). This terrible aspect of the case had great weight in completing the practical Pharisaic mechanism of forgiveness. For there are wrongs done by us over which we weep in vain. It is not that our friend *will* not always forgive; sometimes he *cannot*. The injury may have passed beyond him: it may have affected too many: you may fail to catch up with all its ramifying consequences. Or he may have died. It is the most heart-breaking experience, especially in family dissensions. You are hard, you will not bend: then you relent too late: the other side has hardened: or the other side has passed from earth, and heart cannot find the way back to heart this side of the grave.

It was this last consideration that impelled the Rabbis to pour all the vials of their indignation on the man who increases the inherent difficulty of reparation by his obduracy when asked to forgive. Such a one, Maimonides on the basis of the Mishnah (Baba Qama viii. 7 etc., Bam. Rabba § 19, Berachoth 12, Yalqut Samuel i. § 115) pronounces a sinner and a typical representative of the spirit of cruelty and hard nature. Here the theory of measure for measure was applied, the theory which finds so effective an expression in the Lord's prayer ("Forgive us our trespasses as we forgive them that trespass against us"). "If a man offends his neighbour and says: I have sinned, the neighbour is called sinner if he does not forgive" (see refs. just cited). "So long as thou art forgiving to thy fellow there is One to forgive thee; but if thou art not pitiful to thy fellow, there is none to have mercy on thee" (Buber Tanhuma Genesis, p. 104, cf. Sabbath, 151 b). The Midrash also argues that Job and Abraham received signal instances of God's beneficence *when they had prayed for the pardon of others*, and much more to the same effect. *The injured party must pray for the pardon of his injurer* (Tosefta B. Qama ix. 29 ed. Zuckermandel, p. 366 top), otherwise, he himself will suffer (Midrash Jonah, p. 102).

On the other side, of Neḥunya ben Haqana it was said (Megilla 28 a) that the curse of a comrade never went to bed with him. In response to R. Aqiba he said: "I never stood on my rights" (to exact revenge or even apology): and so Rava said (*loc. cit.*, and Rosh Hashana 17 a, Yoma 23 a): He who forgives (המעביר על מדותיו) received forgiveness, for in the Scripture (Micah vii. 18) the words "pardoneth iniquity" are followed by the words "passeth by transgression, i.e. God pardoneth the man who passes over wrongs." There is no self-righteousness here, no aggravating sense of superior virtue. Those, of whom the Rabbis speak, who humbled their spirit and heard their "reproach in silence," were, the same sentence (Pesiqta Rabbathi, p. 159 a) continues, also those who "attributed no virtues to themselves." To bear reproach and answer no word was an oft-praised virtue (Sabbath 88 b, Sanh. 48 b—49 a). This noblest of all applications of the principle of measure for measure which goes back to Psalm xviii. 25, 26 is found again and again in the Rabbinic writings. It is not "incidental" to them, it is permeative. "R. Judah says in the name of Rabban Gamliel: See, the Scripture saith, And He will show thee mercy and have compassion on thee and multiply thee; this token shall be in thy hand, Whilst thou art merciful, the Merciful will have mercy on thee" (Tosefta Baba Qama ix. 30).

The principle of "measure for measure" (see Matthew vi. 14—15) supplies the most efficient motive for forgiveness, but passing beyond that, the Rabbis make the duty of forgiveness absolute. The unforgiving man was the denier of God (Yalqut on Judges viii. 24); many private Rabbinic prayers breathe the most thorough feeling for a state of mutual good-will between men (e.g. Berachoth in both the Talmuds on iv. 2). In the future world there is to be no enmity (Berachoth 17 a), which is the Rabbinic mode of setting up the same ideal to be striven for on earth. The acme of the saintly disposition is slowness to be enraged and quickness to be reconciled (Aboth v. 11). And although we do not find in the Rabbinic literature a parallel to the striking paradox *Love your enemies*, we do find the fine saying (already quoted by Schöttgen): "Who is mightiest of the mighty? He who makes his enemy his friend" (מי שעושה שונאו אוהבו), Aboth de R. Nathan, xxiii). This ancient saying received more than lip-homage. Samuel ibn Nagrela was made Vizir of Habus, the Berber king of Granada in 1027. Near the palace of Habus, says Graetz (*History of the Jews*, E.T. III. viii.), there lived a Mussulman seller of spices, who no sooner beheld the Jewish minister in the company of the king, than he overwhelmed him with curses and reproaches. Habus, indignant at such conduct, commanded Samuel to punish this fanatic by cutting out his tongue. The Jewish Vizir however knew how to silence him who cursed. He treated him generously, and by his benefactions converted the curses into blessings. When Habus again noticed the seller of spices, he was astonished at the change, and questioned Samuel about it. The minister replied, "I have torn out his angry tongue, and given him instead a kind one." So, to return to the older period, the greatest crown of all was that won by Moses when he entreated God, not on his own behalf, but to forgive sinful Israel (Yalqut on Ps. xc. 1).

A Prayer of Moses (Psalm xc. 1). To what is the matter like? To three men, who came to seek the royal amnesty. The first came and made obeisance.—"What seekest thou?"—"Amnesty for my rebellion." His petition was granted. So with the second. Then came the third. "What seekest thou?"—"For myself, nothing. But such and such a Province is laid waste, and it is thine; command that it be rebuilt." Said the King, "That is a great crown—it is thine." So David and Habakkuk pray on their own behalf (Psalm xvii. 1, Habakkuk iii. 1). When Moses came, God asked him: "What seekest thou?"—"Forgive the iniquity of this people" (Numbers xiv. 19). God answered: "This is a great crown—it is thine, in that I change my will because of thee" (*Yalqut*, Psalms, § 841).

Very fine too is the following expression given to the desire to convert enemies into friends by the exhibition towards them of love:

> If thine enemy be hungry, give him bread to eat,
> And if he be thirsty, give him water to drink;
> For thou shalt heap coals of fire upon his head,
> And the Lord shall reward thee. (PROV. xxv. 21—22.)

R. Ḥama b. Ḥanina said: Even though he has risen up early to slay thee, and he come hungry and thirsty to thy house, give him food and drink. Why? *Because thou heapest coals of fire on his head and the Lord will make him at peace with thee* (v. 22). Read not *yeshalem*, will repay, but *yashlimenu*, will *make him at peace with thee* (Midrash *ad loc.* Cf. T. B. *Megillah* 15 b. See the passages as quoted in *Yalqut ha-Machiri*, Proverbs, p. 58 b).

As another Rabbi could claim, at the close of a long life (*Megillah* 28 a), "I never went to bed with the curse of my fellow" (לא עלתה קללת חברי על מטתי).

By a natural, and assuredly not dishonourable, stretch of moral chauvinism, this very quality of forgiveness, which is so rashly denied to the Pharisees, was by them treated as a special characteristic of Israel (cf. p. 153 above). "He who is merciful towards all men (הבריות) thereby shows himself of the seed of Abraham" (Beṣa 32 b. In all such passages the context shows that רחמן *merciful*, used indeed in the widest sense, is particularly employed in the meaning *forgiving*). Carrying to the extreme the maxim "Be of the persecuted not of the persecutors" (Baba Qama 93 b and elsewhere), the Rabbis even said "He who is not persecuted does not belong to Israel" (Ḥagiga 5 a). "Three gifts the Holy One bestowed on Israel: he made them forgiving, chaste, and charitable" (Bam. Rabba viii., Yebamoth 79 a). Or to sum up: "Ever shall a man bestow loving-kindness, even on one who does evil unto him; he shall not be vengeful nor bear a grudge. This is the way of Israel" (Midrash le'olam, ch. vii.).

And why? Because Israel is the child of God, and must strive to be like his Father. The great foundation of the forgiving spirit is not to be sought in the principle of measure for measure. Its basis is the *Imitatio Dei*, an idea which is very old, very frequent in the Pharisaic literature, and included by Maimonides as one of the precepts of the Pentateuch (Affirmative laws § 8). Portia, in her sublime praise of the quality of mercy, says:

> But mercy is above this sceptred sway,
> It is enthronèd in the hearts of Kings,
> It is an attribute to God himself;
> And earthly power doth then show likest God's,
> When mercy seasons Justice.

Her rebuke, cast at the Jew, almost reads like a quotation from the Jew's own books. "As God is merciful and gracious, so be thou merciful and gracious," is the Pharisaic commentary on "Ye shall be holy, for I the Lord am holy" (Sifra 86 b, and many other passages, Mechilta 37 a, Sabbath 133 b, and often. See Schechter, *Some Aspects of Rabbinic Theology*, ch. xiii.). "The profession of the Holy One, blessed be he, is charity and lovingkindness, and Abraham, who will command his children and his household after him 'that they shall keep the way of the Lord' (Gen. xviii. 19), is told by God: 'Thou hast chosen my profession, wherefore thou shalt also become like unto me, an ancient of days'" (Genesis Rabba, lviii. 9, Schechter, p. 202). Or to cite but one other passage (Sota, 14a), "Rabbi Ḥama b. R. Ḥanina said: What means the Biblical command: Walk ye after the Lord

your God? (Deut. xiii. 4).   Is it possible for a man to walk after the
Shechinah?   Is it not previously said : The Lord thy God is a con-
suming fire? (Deut. iv. 24).   But the meaning is : to walk after the
attributes of the Holy One.   As he clothed the naked—Adam and
Eve in the Garden (Genesis iii.)—so do thou clothe the naked ; as
the Holy One visited the sick (appearing unto Abraham when he
was ailing, Genesis xviii.), so do thou tend the sick ; as the Holy One
comforted the mourners (consoling Isaac after the demise of his
father, Genesis xxv.) so do thou comfort the mourners ; as the Holy
One buried the dead (interring Moses in the valley, Deut. xxxiv.),
so do thou bury the dead.   Observe the profundity, the ingenuity of
this Rabbinic exegesis : from first to last, from Adam's days in the
beginning to Moses' death in the end, from Genesis to Deuteronomy,
the law, according to the Rabbi, bids the Israelite *Imitate God*" (cf.
Jewish Addresses, 1904, pp. 41—51).   Most frequently this *Imitatio
Dei* interprets itself as an admonition to mercy.   God imparts of his
attribute of mercy to men that they may be merciful like himself
(Gen. R. xxxiii.).   That the connection of the law of holiness with
the *Imitatio Dei* goes back to the beginning of the Christian era is
shown from Philo's saying : "Holiness consists in imitating the deeds
of God," just as "earthly virtue is an imitation and representation of
the heavenly virtue" ($\mu\iota\mu\eta\mu\alpha$ is used several times in this context), a
"warder-off of the diseases of the soul" (*De alleg. legum*, I. 14, Mangey,
I. 52).   For God is the supreme archetype (see Drummond, *Philo-
Judæus* II. 81), and as all virtue is a reflection of his moral nature, so
man becomes moral when he strives to liken his character to the
heavenly exemplar.   So the "rewards of the virtuous, which fill the
soul with a transcendent joy" are, with Philo, the attainment to some
share in the nature of God (Drummond, II. 323).   This extension of
the idea is Pharisaic as well as Philonean (Pesiqta R. xi. end).   On
earth man is an appanage of God, cleaving to him in the desire to
imitate.   But hereafter man becomes self-existent in his resemblance
to God (הם הווים ודומים).

XXI. THE LIFE OF THE RESURRECTION.

The question as to the exact physical conditions of life after death has often divided Jewish opinion. Maimonides (Hilch. *Teshubah* viii. 2) unreservedly asserts: "In the world to come there are no bodies, but only the souls of the righteous, without bodies like angels." This view Maimonides based on Talmudic authority; but some of his critics protested against it and quoted such Rabbinic sayings as clearly inculcate the view that at the resurrection the dead arose with the same physical defects as in life (T.B. *Sanhedrin* 91 b), though these were forthwith healed, that the dead arose clothed (*Kethuboth* 114 a). So, in the Apocalypse of Baruch l. 2: "the earth will then assuredly restore the dead, making no change in their form," though (li.) the aspect of the resurrected saints would thereafter be transformed.

On the other hand, Maimonides rested his statement on the saying (*Berachoth* 17 a): "In the world to come there is neither eating nor drinking, no marital relations, no business affairs, no envy, hatred nor quarrelling; but the righteous sit with their garlands on their heads, enjoying the splendid light of the Divine Presence (Shechinah) as it is said: And they beheld God and they ate and drank (Exodus xxiv. 11)."

This saying (parallel to Mark xii. 25) is cited by the Talmud in the name of Abba Arika (Rab), who died in 247 A.D. But the main ideas involved in his sentence are all much older, and are not inconsistent with the belief in the bodily resurrection. In the first century the schools both of Hillel and Shammai believed in the restoration of the material form (*Genesis Rabba* xiv., ed. Theodor, p. 129; *Leviticus R.* xiv.). But it is certain that this bodily resurrection was only regarded as one stage in the process of attaining to immortality, and much ingenuity has been exercised (as by Nahmanides in *Shaar hagemul*) in reconciling with one another the various Rabbinic statements (including the famous parable of the lame and the blind, on which see p. 98 above).

The main metaphors in Rab's picture of the future life are (1) the banquet, (2) the light, (3) the crown. "The righteous sit with garlands on their heads, enjoying, etc." is a figure obviously derived from the banquet (Löw, *Gesammelte Schriften* iii. 417). It is a familiar figure which the evidence shows goes back in Rabbinic literature to the first century. In a famous passage of the Mishnah, Aqiba (*Aboth* iii. 16, last words) speaks of the future life as a banquet, which is prepared for all, wicked as well as righteous, for the sinner is to enjoy it when he has paid the penalty for his evil life (this universal interpretation is clearly derivable from the context, and the Bertinoro rightly so interprets). Aqiba held that the judgment on the wicked in Gehinnom lasted only twelve months (Mishnah, *Eduyott* ii. 10). The same figure is carried out in the Mishnaic saying of R. Jacob (*Aboth* iv. 16). He compares the earthly life to the πρόθυρον (vestibule or outer door) and the future world to the τρίκλινον (dining hall. The force of R. Jacob's comparison is well brought out by L. Löw, *Gesammelte Schriften* i. 127; cf. also iii. 417). An amplification of the figure, belonging, however, to an earlier date, is seen in the parable of the wise and foolish guests (T.B. *Sabbath* 153 a. This parable is ascribed to Johanan b. Zakkai by the Talmud, and to Judah the Patriarch in Eccles. Rabbah on ix. 8. The former ascription is adopted by Bacher, *Agada der Tannaiten*, ed. 2, vol. i. p. 36, and it is the more probable seeing that R. Meir knew it. The figure is frequently found in the Rabbinic literature of later centuries; cf. T.B. *Pesaḥim* 119 b; *Baba Bathra* 74 b, where the Leviathan appears as the main dish at the banquet).

Even older is the idea of the heavenly light which the righteous were to enjoy. In Daniel xii. 2 the resurrected saints are to shine as the brightness of the firmament, and in the Ethiopic Enoch (cviii. 12) they are to be clad in raiments of light. The term light played a great part in Jewish mystical terminology. The angels fed on the shining light of the Shechinah (*Numbers Rabba* xxi. 16) and the mystics made much play with the thought. The figure of the crown is also an old conception. Thus in *Wisdom* (v. 15 seq.) the righteous live for ever, and they shall receive the royal robe (βασίλειον) and the diadem of beauty (διάδημα τοῦ κάλλους) from the Lord's hand. It is not clear from the context whether this crowning of the righteous is regarded as part of the protection on earth or whether it is a feature of the life hereafter, but the two ideas lie near together. The crown may imply the notion of victory, or possibly the exact thought is of freedom. The phrase "with their crowns on their heads" occurs in the Sifra (*Behar* Perek ii., ed. Weiss, p. 106 d) in a context which leads Weiss to make this suggestion (foot of the page cited): the freed slaves "ate and drank and rejoiced *with their crowns on their heads*" between the first and tenth of Tishri in the Jubilee year.   In his book, *The Immanence of God in Rabbinical Literature* (p. 88), Dr Abelson has a fine passage in which he summarises the view of Nahmanides.   In Exodus xvi. 25 the text says of the Manna: "to-day ye shall not find it in the field," on which the Mechilta remarks: "Ye shall not find it in this life, but ye shall find it in the life to come." Dr Abelson thus reproduces Nahmanides' comment: "The worthy Israelite will find his manna, i.e. his source of continued vitality, even after death; he will find it in that blessed union with the Shechinah for which he has qualified himself in ascending stages of spiritual saintliness.   He will wear the crown upon his head.   Does not the prophet predict that 'in that day the Lord of Hosts shall be a Crown of glory' (Isaiah xxviii. 5)?   There will be a complete merging of the human life with the divine life."

INDEX I

Of Names and Subjects

INDEX II

Of New Testament Passages